SOLDIERS
to
GOVERNORS

SOLDIERS
to
GOVERNORS

PENNSYLVANIA'S CIVIL WAR VETERANS
WHO BECAME STATE LEADERS

RICHARD C. SAYLOR

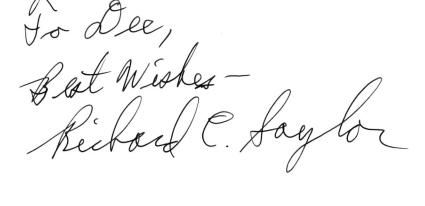

Pennsylvania Historical & Museum Commission

Pennsylvania Historical and Museum Commission
Harrisburg, Pennsylvania 17120-0024
www.phmc.state.pa.us

First edition 2010

Printed in the United States of America
10 9 8 7 6 5 4 3 2 1

All images appearing in this book are from the extensive collections of the
Pennsylvania State Archives and The State Museum of Pennsylvania.

ISBN-10: 0-89271-134-5 (cloth)
ISBN-13: 978-0-89271-134-5 (cloth)

Library of Congress Cataloging-in-Publication Data

Saylor, Richard C.
  Soldiers to governors: Pennsylvania's Civil War veterans who became state leaders / Richard C. Saylor.—1st ed.
     p. cm.
  Includes bibliographical references and index.
  ISBN-13: 978-0-89271-134-5 (cloth)
  ISBN-10: 0-89271-134-5 (cloth)
  1. Governors—Pennsylvania—Biography. 2. Pennsylvania—History—Civil War, 1861–1865—Veterans—Biography.
  3. Pennsylvania—Politics and government—1865–1950. I. Pennsylvania Historical and Museum Commission. II. Title.
  F154.S39 2010
  974.8'03—dc22
                                         2010003244

This book is dedicated to my parents
Jeanne and Richard for encouraging
and nurturing my childhood interest
in history, to my sisters Kathy and
Teresa who have always supported
me, and to my wife Anne and our
children Matthew and Allison
for their constant inspiration.

Richard C. Saylor joined the staff of the Pennsylvania Historical and Museum Commission (PHMC) in 1991 and has worked in PHMC's Bureau of Archives and History since 1999. He is a reference archivist for the Pennnsylvania State Archives, which is administered by PHMC. His previous PHMC duties have included serving as assistant curator of military, political, and industrial history at The State Museum of Pennsylvania, Harrisburg, and as the assistant registrar for the agency. Mr. Saylor is the author of a number of articles about Pennsylvania's military history, film censorship, and sports history. He is co-chair of Pennsylvania's Civil War Trails Interpretive Committee and serves as project archivist for the State Archives' Civil War Muster-Out Rolls Project. The author received a B.A. in history from Elizabethtown College and an M.A. in American Studies from the Pennsylvania State University.

The purpose of this book is to make the public more aware of the tremendous breadth and depth of the vast American Civil War collections held by PHMC. This book reveals images of artifacts and documents specifically in these collections. Objects, artifacts, documents, drawings, maps, and photographs illustrated in this book were drawn from two PHMC institutions, the Pennsylvania State Archives and The State Museum of Pennsylvania. While many Civil War materials are safeguarded and interpreted by PHMC's historic sites and museums, the collections related to the military and political careers of Governors John White Geary, John Frederick Hartranft, Henry Martyn Hoyt, James Addams Beaver, William Alexis Stone, and Samuel Whitaker Pennypacker reside in the Pennsylvania State Archives and The State Museum of Pennsylvania. Research information, anecdotal background material, and quotations, however, were gathered from a wide variety of resources both within and outside the agency, including published works and unpublished manuscripts.

Measurements of selected objects, artifacts, documents, and photographs are listed by height, width, and, if applicable, depth as shown in publication. A complete listing of the sources for these items appears on page 161 as "Illustration Credits."

Quoted material, such as correspondence, speeches, and official documents, has not been changed to correct mistakes in spelling, grammar, punctuation, and tense. In addition, the designation [sic] was not used in order to retain as much of the original character as possible. Words, such as military titles and names, were only added to improve readability and comprehension; these additions appear in brackets.

TABLE OF CONTENTS

Governor John White Geary, in office from 1867 to 1873

John White Geary (1819–1873) lived an action-packed life that included fighting in both the Mexican War and the American Civil War. During the Mexican War, he rose in command from captain to colonel of the Second Pennsylvania Regiment. During the Civil War, he ascended from colonel of the 28th Pennsylvania Volunteer Infantry to brevet major general of Volunteers. In civil pursuits, he was the first mayor of San Francisco, California, in 1849, and held the governorship of two different regions of the country—the Kansas Territory, from 1856 to 1857, and Pennsylvania for two consecutive terms, from 1867 to 1873. He died just two weeks after leaving the Pennsylvania governor's office, at the age of fifty-three.

Governor John Frederick Hartranft, in office from 1873 to 1879

John Frederick Hartranft (1830–1889) was a lawyer by training, a soldier by desire, and a politician because of fame. He entered the Civil War as colonel of the 4th Pennsylvania Volunteer Infantry in April 1861 and rose to the rank of brevet major general by the time the war ended in 1865. He was then charged with the duty of commanding the prison where the Lincoln assassination plot conspirators were held and the ultimate execution of four of them. Hartranft was the only governor of Pennsylvania to have earned the Medal of Honor, the highest award for valor in action while serving in the United States armed forces. He served in a number of state and federal government posts after the Civil War, including two terms as Pennsylvania's auditor general, from 1866 to 1872, two terms as governor, from 1873 to 1879, Philadelphia postmaster in 1879, and collector of the port of Philadelphia, from 1880 to 1885. He was also actively involved with the National Guard of Pennsylvania for nearly two decades, from 1870 to 1889, serving as its major general before and following his two terms as governor and commander-in-chief. Despite his many accolades and governmental posts, Hartranft died in difficult financial circumstances caused by business misfortunes suffered later in life.

Governor Henry Martyn Hoyt, in office from 1879 to 1883

Henry Martyn Hoyt (1830–1892) was a lawyer who volunteered for Civil War service in 1861 as lieutenant colonel of the 52nd Pennsylvania Volunteer Infantry. By the end of the conflict, he had risen in rank to brevet brigadier general. Elected governor of Pennsylvania in 1878, Hoyt served from 1879 to 1883, making him the third consecutive Civil War general to occupy the Commonwealth's highest elected office. Hoyt has the distinction of being only the second governor of Pennsylvania to have ever been a prisoner of war; he was captured by the Confederates at Charleston Harbor, in 1864. Following his term as governor, Hoyt returned to his law practice in Philadelphia.

James Addams Beaver (1837–1914) was a lawyer, a lionhearted officer, a politician, and a judge. He mustered into Civil War service as a first lieutenant in the 2nd Pennsylvania Volunteer Infantry in April 1861; by the end of the war he was a brevet brigadier general. He was wounded repeatedly during the war while leading his men in battle. His last wound cost him his right leg. Beaver has the distinction of being the only one-legged governor of the Commonwealth of Pennsylvania. Serving from 1887 to 1891, he was the fourth Civil War general elected governor of Pennsylvania. Beaver was active in the National Guard of Pennsylvania, serving as both a major general and a brigadier general from 1870, until his inauguration in January 1887. Beaver was a Superior Court judge in Pennsylvania for nearly two decades, from 1895 until his death in 1914.

William Alexis Stone (1846–1920) was only seventeen years old when he enlisted in the Union Army as a private in February 1864. He was promoted several times during his military service, reaching the rank of second lieutenant. He was a member of the military escort for President Abraham Lincoln's body while it was in Philadelphia, in April 1865. Following the war, Stone became a lawyer, a federal district attorney, a four-term U.S. Congressman, and governor of Pennsylvania from 1899 to 1903. He served for a time after the war as an assistant adjutant general in the National Guard of Pennsylvania. He returned to the practice of law after leaving the governor's office.

Samuel Whitaker Pennypacker (1843–1916) was twenty years old when he volunteered to join Pennsylvania's Emergency Militia during the Gettysburg Campaign in 1863. He was mustered into the 26th Pennsylvania Emergency Militia Regiment and saw brief action against the invading Confederate forces, west of Gettysburg, on June 26, 1863. Pennypacker was mustered out of the service at the end of July 1863. After his brief military service, he studied law, became a well-known Philadelphia lawyer and judge, and was elected governor of Pennsylvania in 1902, serving from 1903 to 1907. After his years as governor, Pennypacker returned to the practice of law in Philadelphia and authored more than fifty books.

INTRODUCTION

Six of Pennsylvania's first eight post-Civil War governors were veterans of the American Civil War. This streak spanned four decades, from the election of John White Geary in 1866 to Samuel W. Pennypacker's final day in office, in January 1907. Even though these individuals rose to great political height and power, they did not forget their combat memories or neglect their old military comrades. Their war experiences shaped their vision and beliefs, as they supported pensions for Union veterans, the establishment of a soldiers' and sailors' home, the creation and maintenance of orphan schools, and compensation for damages incurred by victims of the ravages of war along the Commonwealth's southern border. Several of these governors remained involved in the military after the war by serving in the National Guard of Pennsylvania. Most of them belonged to one or more veterans' organizations for extended periods of time. Through it all, they remained committed to the Republic they had helped preserve on the bloody battlefields of the Civil War.

The magnitude of the Civil War cannot be overstated—it exacted a horrific toll in human carnage and disease-induced deaths. Nearly 700,000 soldiers, North and South combined, lost their lives during the war, a total exceeding the number of American deaths in military conflicts from the Revolutionary War through the Vietnam War. Of that number, the Union Army lost 359,528 men to military service-related deaths out of the more than two million total soldiers who served in its forces during the war.[1] Of the

approximately 362,000 men the Commonwealth contributed to the Union effort, the Keystone State saw 33,183 of her sons lose their lives while in Civil War service. Made up of 178,975 African American soldiers, the United States Colored Troops, which played a crucial role in helping the Union win the war, suffered 36,847 deaths. Pennsylvania raised 8,612 African American soldiers for the United States Colored Troops, more than any other Northern state. Virtually every part of American society was affected by the pervasive nature of this great conflict and its staggering cost in terms of human life, suffering, and devastation.

Governor Robert Emory Pattison.

Governor Daniel Hartman Hastings.

The two post-Civil War governors in this era who did not serve during the war had good reasons. Democratic Governor Robert Emory Pattison (1850–1904) was too young to serve in the Civil War. He served two nonconsecutive terms as governor, between the administrations of Henry Martyn Hoyt and James Addams Beaver, from 1883 to 1887, and again between Beaver and Daniel Hartman Hastings, from 1891 to 1895. Republican Governor Daniel Hartman Hastings (1849–1903), in office from 1895 to 1899, attempted to enlist three times in the Union Army while underage, but each time his father stopped him and brought him back home.

Pennsylvania was not alone in electing Civil War veterans as governors in the post-war era. Between 1864 and 1910, many, but not all, Northern states elected numerous governors who were Union veterans. These individuals were predominantly Republicans, but scattered throughout the North during this period were also a number of Democratic governors who had served in the war. Prominent Pennsylvania veterans also played important roles on the national stage in the post-war Democratic Party, an example being Montgomery County native Major General Winfield Scott Hancock's nomination for the presidency of the United States, in 1880.

The Civil War generation of Pennsylvania occupied the gubernatorial seat of power, governing during turbulent and sometimes violent periods of the Commonwealth's late nineteenth- and early twentieth-century history. The Great Railroad Strike of 1877, repeated outbreaks of labor unrest and strikes in the coal industry, and the catastrophic Johnstown Flood of 1889 thrust the Keystone State into periods of turmoil, which these gubernatorial warriors met with a firm hand and by wielding the power of the National Guard of Pennsylvania. These individuals collectively shepherded Pennsylvanians through the economic depressions of 1873 and 1893. Technological advances and greater industrialization and prosperity in Pennsylvania—and throughout the nation—created what Mark Twain and Charles Dudley Warner dubbed the Gilded Age, while they held the mantle of Pennsylvania's chief executive. In the decades following the Civil War, the world changed rapidly. Modern inventions—and improvements to those inventions—altered the ways in which people had lived and worked for centuries. What did not change was Pennsylvania's propensity for electing Republican governors, who were Civil War veterans.

As a remnant of the war, their animosity toward their old enemy, the Confederate States of America and its soldiers, softened with the passing of time, running the gamut from Governor John W. Geary's desire to see former Confederate leaders hanging from tree limbs, to his successor, John F. Hartranft, inviting former Confederate Major General Fitzhugh Lee to visit the National Guard of Pennsylvania's encampment at Gettysburg in August 1884, and Governor James A. Beaver asking former Confederate General James Longstreet to take a role on his staff for the inaugural ceremonies of President Benjamin Harrison in 1889. One aspect that did not vary, however, was their reverence for their former comrades-in-arms as they supported the erection of monuments and memorials to Pennsylvania troops at battlefields, as well as in cemeteries, town squares, and government buildings and grounds throughout the state and nation.

The governors of Pennsylvania during the years between 1867 and 1907 possess fascinating stories that correspond with practically all significant Civil War military experiences. From the rank of private to major general. From suffering multiple wounds (and even an amputation) to passing through military service without a scratch. From entering service in the first month of the war and serving until its conclusion, to entering service as part of the Emergency Militia of 1863 and serving only six weeks. From having previous military experience in the Mexican War, to having no prior military training or experience whatsoever. From being too young to serve, to being too young to serve but attempting three times, albeit in vain, to enlist. From serving in the Army of the Potomac, to joining Major General William Tecumseh Sherman's March to the Sea. From fighting at the First Battle of Bull Run to fighting against the last offensive of the Army of Northern Virginia at Fort Stedman. From being present at General Robert E. Lee's surrender at Appomattox, Virginia, to witnessing the surrender of General Joseph E. Johnston near Raleigh, North Carolina. From serving honorably, and in one case earning the Medal of Honor, to paying for a substitute to fight in his stead after being drafted. Pennsylvania's governors fought at many significant battles, including Bull Run, Antietam, Chancellorsville, Gettysburg, Vicksburg, Lookout Mountain, The Wilderness, Petersburg, Cold Harbor, Atlanta, and many others. And these are their stories as they ascended to the Commonwealth's highest office.

Wherever possible, the governors speak for themselves through letters, reports, official communiqués, and diary entries. They shed light on critical military actions in which they took part, as well as on interesting episodes and incidents in their lives, particularly in the political arena. I have also endeavored to allow some of their contemporaries, famous and otherwise, to have their voices heard regarding these warrior-statesmen and their associations. These vignettes are by no means intended to be comprehensive biographies. Rather, they provide insight into the wartime experiences of these extraordinary individuals and their various military service, including—but not limited to—the National Guard of Pennsylvania, and gubernatorial events that were rooted in military matters or the mitigation of the costs of war. While not fail-safe, these types of first-person accounts of nineteenth-century events are generally considered to be quality historical evidence.

These are the stories of the six Pennsylvania Republican governors who, as veterans, were part of the American Civil War generation. In the aftermath of the war, they capitalized on their military service to capture the Commonwealth's highest elected office.

Richard C. Saylor
Reference Archivist
Pennsylvania State Archives

PREFACE

This impressive book, carrying fascinating stories and images on nearly every page, cuts across conventional boundaries to make sense of a broad expanse of American history. Encouraged by textbooks shaped to fit school calendars and bookstore shelves that divide history into predictable categories, the era of the American Civil War and the Gilded Age often seem only distantly related. It is almost as if one cast of characters, dressed in blue and gray, comes on stage in 1861 only to be replaced by another cast, with men in whiskers and women in shirtwaists, to occupy the stage through World War I. It has been easy to forget that the decades after 1865 were far more defined by the Civil War than were the decades before that conflict, despite the earlier period's convenient—if misleading—label of antebellum. A war that had cost nearly seven hundred thousand lives, freed four million people, saved the Union, and recast Americans' understanding of themselves could hardly be neatly contained by four years of battles.

Richard C. Saylor's book is a reminder of the difference the Civil War made. It reminds us that the war affected the North in powerful ways, even though all the notable battles but one took place below the Mason-Dixon Line. Few families in the North were untouched by a war that raged hundreds or even thousands of miles away. As the eloquent stories and documents in Saylor's book remind us, the war came hard and fast, overwhelming peaceful Pennsylvania communities and forever changing the lives of young men and their families. Those soldiers, whether seasoned veterans of the war with Mexico or mere schoolboys too young to enlist in 1861, saw their lives permanently altered by what they experienced on the battlefield.

Saylor's account makes clear what was lost in the war. The grieving letters of John White Geary after the death of his beloved son Edward on the battlefield can still evoke the pain a century and a half later. The stoic diary entries of James Addams Beaver after the amputation of his leg at the hip still inspire awe. But the proud letters home during the war also make clear what was won. All the men in this book craved an opportunity to win glory on the field and fumed when they were relegated to supporting roles; all of them sought not only fame but also the opportunity to give of themselves for their cause. They fought for the Union and against the spread of slavery. Even a jaded student of history cannot help but be impressed and inspired.

The post-Civil War decades emerge from this book as more interesting than most people imagine. The epic struggles over Reconstruction take on new weight when we understand how close those years were to the immense suffering of the war years. The apparently dull election contests of the years after Reconstruction, still marked by divisions begun during the Civil War, turn out to have been closely contested and bitterly personal. The decades of what is blandly called industrialization turn out to have been battlefields of their own and the veteran governors of Pennsylvania played lead roles in subduing striking railroad workers and miners.

The men in this book emerged from the war as committed Republicans, proud to have vanquished both the rebels of the South and the Democrats of the North. In large part, in fact, the governors of this book built their careers on keeping the Civil War and its issues alive, chastising the Democrats of Pennsylvania as the party of slavery, appeasement, disunion, and even disloyalty. These men became governor largely because they were part of a powerful engine, driven by memories of Civil War service and loyalty to the Republican Party.

Despite their proud identities as Republicans and as United States soldiers, however, these men, within a remarkably short time, set aside a major part of the Union cause—the rights of African Americans—so that they could better reconcile with their former enemies in the South. The Republicans fought for nearly a decade after the war to enact protections for former slaves in the South, but then acquiesced in the determination of white Southerners and white Northern Democrats to make the United States a white man's country once again.

Although the squares, parks, and cemeteries of Pennsylvania are today marked with monuments to individuals such as the governors in this book, the Union cause now seems to be taken for granted. Few of the heroes of our movies, novels, and paintings today played leading roles for the United States Army in the Civil War. Many Americans today, whatever their region, seem drawn to the underdogs, to Confederates such as Robert E. Lee and Thomas Jonathan "Stonewall" Jackson. The remarkable stories in this book remind us that the salvation of the Union and the destruction of slavery grew from enormous sacrifice and suffering; they did not simply happen because the time had inevitably come or because the North was industrializing or because the South was in decline. They happened because remarkable men such as John White Geary, John Frederick Hartranft, Henry Martyn Hoyt, James Addams Beaver, William Alexis Stone, and Samuel Whitaker Pennypacker made them happen. We should be grateful to them and grateful for this powerful account of their work.

Edward L. Ayers, Ph.D.
University of Richmond
Richmond, Virginia

ACKNOWLEDGMENTS

The creation of any book requires the assistance of many talented individuals. Fortunately, my colleagues at the Pennsylvania Historical and Museum Commission (PHMC) who helped me with this project are just that—talented! Moreover, I am indebted to Barbara Franco, PHMC executive director, for encouraging scholarship and publication by staff. John T. Zwierzyna, senior curator of military and industrial history, Curtis Miner, senior curator of political history and popular culture, and N. Lee Stevens, senior curator of fine arts, at The State Museum of Pennsylvania, Harrisburg, all generously opened up the treasure trove of objects and artifacts in their respective collections for me to explore, and shared with me their copious knowledge of the same. Mary Jane Miller, head of collections management for The State Museum, kindly allowed me to utilize the voluminous catalogue and vital information files that she ably oversees for PHMC. Christy Gauthier, former collections photographer for the museum, is responsible for the wonderful artifact photographs in this book and remained unruffled when I made "one last request" more than once. Robert D. Hill and Todd C. Galle, former State Museum assistant curators, helped me by locating a number of hard-to-find objects in The State Museum's collections. Museum photographer Don Giles expertly photographed oversized documents from the collections of the Pennsylvania State Archives. William A. Sisson, former chief curator of The State Museum, supported this project by permitting his staff to provide me with much needed assistance.

Fellow archivists at the Pennsylvania State Archives, Brett M. Reigh, Michael D. Sherbon, Stephen S. Noel, and Jerry Ellis, provided invaluable aid by scanning numerous images for this work. Cynthia Margolis assisted by determining which of the desired images had previously been scanned. Paula Heiman, PHMC librarian, tracked down a number of scarce volumes necessary for my research for this project. Linda A. Ries, head, Arrangement and Description Section, willingly shared her knowledge of nineteenth-century photography with me. Ted R. Walke, chief, Michael J. O'Malley III, editor, and Kimberly L. Stone, art director, of PHMC's Publications and Sales Division, made producing this book a genuine pleasure at every step of the process. Jeff Decker, formerly of the Publications and Sales Division, designed the handsome cover. Former conservation technicians Ruthanna M. Kulp, Brystal N. Gilliland, and Jennifer A. Bisht contributed by making countless muster-out rolls available for me to study.

Sincere thanks go to Pennsylvania State Archives management who collectively gave me the opportunity to undertake the necessary research and writing for this endeavor, and provided encouragement and associated staff time: State Archivist David A. Haury, director, Bureau of Archives and History; Cynthia Bendroth, chief, Division of Records Services; David W. Shoff, chief, State Archives Division; Harry F. Parker, former chief, State Archives Division; and Jonathan R. Stayer, head, Reference Section.

Several people outside of PHMC also provided me with assistance for this project including Carl Klase, assistant administrator of Pennypacker Mills, Montgomery County, who helped answer several significant questions about Samuel W. Pennypacker and made sure that I had a complete copy of Pennypacker's unpublished manuscript "Six Weeks in Uniform." A special thank you goes to Helen and Ronald Shireman who graciously gave us permission to use images donated from their family's wonderful collection of John F. Hartranft archival material.

I am also grateful to a number of my longtime PHMC colleagues who graciously agreed to read the manuscript version of this book and provide me with invaluable insight: Bruce S. Bazelon, former division chief, Bureau of Historic Sites and Museums; David A. Haury, director,

Bureau of Archives and History; Louis M. Waddell, former historian, Pennsylvania State Archives; Kenneth C. Wolensky, historian, Bureau for Historic Preservation; and John T. Zwierzyna, senior curator, The State Museum of Pennsylvania.

I would also like to thank four of my associates outside PHMC who reviewed the manuscript prior to publication. Wayne E. Motts, director of the Adams County Historical Society, willingly provided me with a perspective from Gettysburg; Charles B. Oellig, curator of the Pennsylvania National Guard Museum at Fort Indiantown Gap, kindly shared his extensive knowledge of the Pennsylvania National Guard; Dr. John S. Patterson, my M.A. thesis advisor at the Pennsylvania State University, courteously shared his academic perspective with me about the book's subject matter; and Dr. Richard J. Sommers, senior historian at the U.S. Army Military History Institute, Carlisle, who graciously provided an overall critique.

Finally, I thank Edward L. Ayers for generously writing the preface to this book. Dr. Ayers' work in making Civil War era primary source material readily available through his Web site, "The Valley of the Shadow," and his extensive writing about the post-Reconstruction period made him the ideal scholar to lead readers into this tome.

I genuinely appreciate the efforts of all involved in helping to bring forward the stories of these soldiers who became governors of Pennsylvania.

Richard C. Saylor

Governor
John White Geary
in office from 1867 to 1873

J ohn White Geary was a giant of a man, particularly by nineteenth-century standards, standing 6 feet 5½ inches tall and weighing 260 pounds. His lifetime accomplishments were nothing less than stellar. He became a Mexican War hero, first postmaster and mayor of San Francisco, California, governor of the Kansas Territory during the Bleeding Kansas period, American Civil War major general, and two-term governor of Pennsylvania. His was an amazing life packed into a brief fifty-three years.

One of four sons of an iron manufacturer living near Mount Pleasant, Westmoreland County, Geary was born on December 30, 1819. His father, Richard Geary, managed Mary Anne Furnace until it failed, leaving him bankrupt. Thereafter, he taught school until his death in 1834, still insolvent from his iron manufacturing debts. His mother, Margaret White Geary, originally from Washington County, Maryland, had inherited a number of slaves whom she educated and freed.

Geary attended Jefferson College in Canonsburg, Washington County, where he graduated in 1841. Following college, he worked as a clerk for a wholesale house in Pittsburgh. He discovered this type of business held little interest for him, so he continued his education by studying law and civil engineering, after which he worked for railroads in Kentucky and Pennsylvania. Upon returning to Pennsylvania from Kentucky, he satisfied his late father's outstanding debts and became assistant superintendent of the Allegheny Portage Railroad.

Circa 1865 carte de visite, or visiting card, of Brevet Major General John White Geary (1819–1873) by Henszey and Company, a Philadelphia photographic firm. The advent of the popular carte de visite made photography available to the masses in the second half of the nineteenth century. (4 x 2 ½ inches)

He married Margaret Ann Logan, of Unionville, Pennsylvania, in 1843. Together they had three sons, one of whom died in infancy. Margaret died on February 28, 1853. Geary later married the widowed Mary Church Henderson in November 1858, in Carlisle, Cumberland County, with whom he had two daughters. With his marriage to Henderson, Geary also acquired a stepson and stepdaughter.

His first military experience occured in 1835 when he joined a militia company as its lieutenant.[5] In December 1846, eight months after the Mexican War had broken out, Geary raised a company of Cambria County soldiers in Summit, the American Highlanders, which was incorporated into the 2nd Pennsylvania Volunteer Regiment as Company B. Geary was enrolled for service on December 21, at Summit. Captain Geary and his company were mustered into service on January 3, 1847, at Pittsburgh. Four days later, Geary was elected lieutenant colonel and served in the Mexican War with the 2nd Pennsylvania Volunteer Regiment. He and his men participated in

Captain Geary's American Highlanders militia coat and trousers, circa 1846. Historians believe that after the American Highlanders became part of the 2nd Pennsylvania Volunteer Regiment and were federalized during the Mexican War, their militia uniforms were left behind. It's likely that Geary and his men wore United States Army uniforms while fighting in Mexico.

General Winfield Scott's invasion of Mexico, linking up with Scott's army at Vera Cruz. Geary, like many other Civil War officers—both Union and Confederate—first saw combat while serving in the Mexican War.

On September 13, 1847, with Geary leading the regiment (since Colonel William B. Roberts was ill), the 2nd Pennsylvania Volunteers participated in the successful storming of Chapultepec Castle, which defended the western approach on Mexico City. Geary received his first battle-field wound, during this action, when hit in the groin by a spent canister ball. In his diary, he recounted the struggle for Chapultepec. "Early in the morning orders were given to prepare to storm the fortress, and about 7oclock all were ready and the storm began. I need not here pretend to give a description of the battle, for I would be totally inadequate to the task. Suffice it to say I was wounded about the middle of the action, but had an opportunity of witnessing the whole of the action. The fight was the most brilliant of the war, and the 2nd Pennsylvania Reg't came out 'A no.1.' In a few minutes of taking the fortress, we were again ordered forward in pursuit of the enemy, which I was able to lead, having nearly recovered from my contusion. The fire of the enemy was dreadful while we took the gates of San Cosme and Tacubaya, into the City of Mexico. After fighting all day and working nearly all night, we lay down for an hour or two, expecting to renew the conflict—more hotly than ever in the morning."[6]

Geary's belt, belt buckle, and saber chain from the period of his Mexican War service, circa 1847–1848. (31 x 1 3/4 inches)

A week later, on September 21, Geary wrote a letter to his brother Edward R. Geary from the National Palace of Mexico about the capture of Chapultepec Castle and his wound. "On the 12th the Castle of Chapultepec was bombarded, . . . my Regt. supported the batteries during the day, and so doing I had nine men wounded and myself slightly scratched on the hand with a musket ball.—On the 13th, Not withstanding all Santa Anna's preparations, they were of no avail. We stormed the [fort] and carried it at the point of the bayonet in less [than] one hour. And then driving them from fort to fort and gates of the city. We got possession of the 'Garitos' (gates) before night.—I will here state that the regt. I had the honor to command, immortalized itself by its great valor and prowess, and won a wreath of glory [for] the old 'Keystone State.' Your humble servant, was [wounded] smartly in the groin with a grape shot when leading his regt. with[in] 100 yards of the work. I was disabled for a few minutes, and cheered my boys on to the fort amidst a perfect storm of iron hail, under command of Major Brindle. —I soon regained my strength and over took my regt. (with the assistance of our, of my men) just [as] it was entering the Castle, and immediately assumed command. Which I continued during the day—though I was very lame. My wound or contusion is not dangerous.—The fight continued at the gates of the city until dark—when firing on both sides ceased. And we stretched our weary limbs upon the ground, (on the battle field, I should say, amid the dead and dying,) officers as well as soldiers without tents, blankets, or food; for my own part, although this was the third night we had bivouacked in the same manner, in succession, I could not sleep on account of my wounds.— . . . At the Garita I was struck with a spent ball in the head, which gave to my phrenological developments a new bump about the size of a walnut. —In these engagements my person was twice struck with balls and my clothes pierced in three other places. Making a total of five."[7]

Mexico City surrendered on September 14, and Geary served as its first United States commandant. His diary entry that day described the city's capitulation. "We were aroused early this morning and put in battle array expecting every moment to receive an iron hail storm from the enemy—but after waiting half and hour, judge our surprise to see a white flag approaching announcing the surrender of the citadel, the strongest military work in the city. This was of course

After the fall of Mexico City to United States forces, Geary wrote to his brother Edward on September 21, 1847, on official stationery taken from the National Palace of Mexico.

Private Samuel Roller of Company G, 2nd Pennsylvania Volunteer Regiment, captured this Mexican flag at the gates of Mexico City in September 1847. Lieutenant Colonel Geary was in command of the 2nd Pennsylvania Volunteers at the time. (34 x 49 inches)

Mexican Monument. Harrisburg, Pa.

equivalent to surrendering the city. So it proved. I was placed in command of the citadel with my regiment as a mark of dignity for good behavior the day previous."[8] In a letter to his brother Edward, Geary also described the surrender. "On the night of the 13th, Santa Anna and his Army shamefully fled from the city, leaving the inhabitants to the tender mercies of the '<u>Northern barbarians</u>' —On the 14th we took possession of the city, and the glorious old Stars and Stripes, which we have followed victoriously over so many bloody fields, at last was in triumph from their capital—the palace—the Halls of the Montezumas.— . . . My quarters are in the palace, in a hall hung with crimson velvet and gold, and furnished with lounges, sofas & chairs of the same kind of stuff. —the floor elegantly carpeted and the ceiling adorned with a beautiful chandelier.— . . . As a compliment to the gallantry of myself and regt. I was placed in command of the citadel, the strongest and most magnificent work of the city, and we remained there several days, when on my own request I was transferred to the palace.— . . . Our little army scarcely numbering 7000 effective men has fought its way through the bloody fields and forts of Contreras, San Antonio, Churubusco, Molino del Rey—Chapultepec, and the gates of San Cosme and Tucabaya, and thence into the capital of the Republic, against numbers and disadvantages sevenfold."[9]

On November 3, Geary succeeded Colonel William B. Roberts, who had succumbed to his illness, as colonel of the 2nd Pennsylvania Volunteers. Geary's advancement to colonel was not without controversy, however. A member of Company E in the 2nd Pennsylvania Volunteer Regiment, Private Richard Coulter, alleged that Geary manipulated the election to replace the regimental colonel in a way that practically guaranteed his own victory.[10] After the 2nd Regiment returned to Pennsylvania, Geary mustered out of service on July 21, 1848, at Pittsburgh.

In appreciation of his service during the Mexican War, President James K. Polk, in office from 1845 to 1849, appointed Geary the first postmaster of San Francisco, California, on January 22, 1849. Geary and his family traveled mainly by boat to the West Coast, passing through the Isthmus of Panama, and arriving in San Francisco on April 1. Their trip across Panama was not without incident, however. Geary described one such remarkable event that occurred while they were staying in the city of Panama, in a letter to his brother dated March 5, "Yesterday morning I had quite an adventure. A box of Ham and dried-beef which I had brought with me from New York had been standing on my porch, on a second story, for several days, was broken open and the meat stolen. Mrs. G. called my attention to the matter. And I immediately suspected a guard of 13 black soldiers (i.e. Black-guards.) as the <u>gentlemen of color</u> who had performed the wonderful feat. I immediately went to them and inquired who had been on guard during the latter part of the night, they said no one had kept watch, and that they had all slept. They wanted me to 'vamos' very badly. And brandishing their bayonets about me somewhat uncivilly, I knocked one down with my left hand, and another with my right, in the twinkling of an eye. This brought them to their senses, for they perceived I was something like a revolver, and not withstanding I had fired twice, was still ready. Their blankets was neatly folded up at the head of their beds, and one fellow to convince how well they had slept, lay down upon the blankets. I perceived this was a trick, and jabbing one of the blankets with my finger, I found there was something hard within. I ordered the fellow to rise, which he refused to do. I took him by the shoulder, & <u>gently</u> threw him against the opposite wall of the room. Upon unfolding the blanket I found a part of the meat, and after threatening the sergeant, I compelled him to hunt the remainder and carry the whole of my meat to my quarters and replace it where they got it. Thus by a couple of bold strokes '<u>I saved my bacon.</u>' I preferred charges against the whole guard, they have been tried, sentenced & whipt with 50 lashes each."[11]

San Francisco's citizens elected him their first alcade (the chief administrative and judicial officer of a community in a Spanish-speaking region) on August 1, 1849, and their first mayor on May 1, 1850. Geary played a significant role in forming the California Constitution, ensuring the addition of a Free State clause. Because his wife suffered poor health, Geary left San Francisco to return to Pennsylvania on February 1, 1852, where he began farming in Westmoreland County. In 1855, he was offered the governorship of the Utah Territory but declined to leave Pennsylvania.

Four years later, and two years after the death of Geary's first wife Margaret, President Franklin Pierce, in office from 1853 to 1857, appointed Geary, in July 1856, governor of the controversial and bloody Kansas Territory. His charges included restoring peace and bringing to justice those who violated the peace. "My name at this very minute burns in vital characters upon every telegraph throughout the length and breadth of the country," he wrote to his brother Edward. "Without any solicitation of myself or of my friends, the President has voluntarily sought me in my retirement and conferred upon me the difficult, dangerous and onerous appointment of Governor of the Territory of Kansas."[12]

By September 30, Geary was able to inform U.S. Secretary of State William L. Marcy, "Peace now reigns in Kansas. Confidence is being gradually restored. Citizens are resuming their ordinary pursuits. Settlers are returning to their claims, and general gladness pervades the community."[13] He attempted to govern Kansas in a nonpartisan fashion regarding the question of whether the territory should be a slave or free state, but served for little more than six months before resigning because of problems arising from his suspected anti-slavery beliefs. By early 1857, Geary was also experiencing problems with his lungs. He resigned on March 4, the day James Buchanan was inaugurated as the nation's fifteenth president. These two events were not unrelated.

Geary believed Buchanan harbored personal enmity against him, and Geary certainly had a sincere dislike of Buchanan. "I <u>know the man</u>," he wrote of the president, "and knowing him before I voluntarily resigned my position in Kansas, in which it was his settled determination to disgrace me if possible, I then determined to relieve him from any trouble in doing me injustice. . . . The old Buck little knows the foe he is grappleing

James Buchanan, the only native Pennsylvanian to serve as president, was in office from 1857 to 1861.

with, I have never in a single instance bowed the knee to mortal man, nor will I shrink from the discharge of any duty—however onerous or dangerous."[14]

Geary's experience in Kansas had given him an even greater distaste for slavery and slaveholders. His disdain for President Buchanan also continued to increase. In a November 23, 1857, letter to his brother, he made a dire forecast. "There will yet be trouble in Kansas," he predicted. "Mr. Buchanan will not sustain [Governor Robert J.] Walker, he will bow his neck to the yoke of the South like a craven, and will desert and if possible dishonor the land of his nativity. To avoid the 'Scilla' of the North, he will run into the 'Charybdis' of the South—and in either event the Democratic party will be disrupted. . . . He will foist slavery upon the fair plains of Oregon if within his power.

Civil War officer's forage, or Bummer's, cap worn by Geary while colonel of the 28th PVI, 1861–1862. The cap was made by Laing & Co., Philadelphia.

Civil War officer's boots, made by C. Benkert & Sons, Philadelphia, and worn by Brevet Major General Geary.

"Mr. Buchanan's Administration seems to be destined to be either a marked or doomed one."[15]

In 1860, shortly after the election of Abraham Lincoln as president, Geary wrote of the possibility of war to his brother Edward, "Of one thing, rest assured, should the Union be menaced, by any band of traitors, you may look for me in the front rank of those opposed to them, determined while life endures to lend my best exertions, and whatever strategic military skill I may possess, to preserve our liberties under the Constitution of the Union. . . ."[16] Interestingly, Geary was, at that time, an avowed Democrat and had not supported Lincoln for the presidency. Instead, he had supported United States Senator Stephen A. Douglas, of Illinois, in the 1860 election.[17]

After his experience in Kansas, Geary married Mary Church Henderson on November 2, 1858, returned to his farm near New Alexandria, in Westmoreland County, and practiced law, often in Philadelphia, until 1861. When the Civil War broke out in April 1861, the Gearys moved east, first to Philadelphia, then to New Cumberland and Carlisle, Cumberland County, but also kept their farm in Westmoreland County. Geary was mustered into military service on June 28 at the age of forty-one and appointed colonel of the 28th Pennsylvania Volunteer Infantry (PVI) Regiment, which he had organized and equipped at his own expense in Philadelphia. On July 27, ten companies of the 28th PVI left the Philadelphia area for the vicinity of Harpers Ferry. They encamped about twenty miles away at Camp DeKorponay at Point of Rocks, Maryland.

The first major engagement of the 28th PVI with the enemy occurred at Bolivar Heights, near Harpers Ferry, on October 16. Geary sustained a wound to his right knee in the engagement. His regiment was successful in the battle and earned commendation from the division commander, Major General Nathaniel P. Banks. The victory was one of the first for the Union after the disaster of First Bull Run. For his actions in this battle, Geary received the thanks of President Lincoln and Secretary of War Simon Cameron.

On April 25, 1862, Geary was promoted to brigadier general and given command of the 2nd Brigade in the 1st Division, Department of the Rappahannock. The 28th PVI held Geary in such esteem that it presented him with military accoutrements to celebrate his promotion.[18]

In August, Geary's brigade was re-designated as the 1st Brigade, 2nd Division, 2nd Corps, Army of Virginia. While leading his brigade in battle against Confederate forces led by Major General Thomas "Stonewall" Jackson at Cedar Mountain on August 9, Geary suffered wounds to his left foot and arm. The injuries were severe enough to require him to relinquish his command. He was

Native Philadelphian, Ralph Hamilton Humes (1902–1981) created a plaster sculpture entitled General Stonewall Jackson and Old Sorrel—Before the Battle of Manassas. *Humes was known for his sculptures of animals. The model of Thomas Jonathan Jackson (1824–1863)—who earned the sobriquet "Stonewall" for his actions at the First Battle of Manassas, also known as First Bull Run—was a gift of the artist's family to The State Museum of Pennsylvania in 1985. (21¹/₂ x 8 x 17 inches)*

ordered home for treatment and recuperation and missed the fighting at Second Bull Run and Antietam. Geary returned to action on September 25 and took command of the 2nd Division, the future White Star Division, of the 12th Corps, Army of the Potomac. He extolled his pride in fellow Pennsylvanians in a letter written from Hagerstown, Maryland, to his wife Mary that day. "Dear Old Pennsylvania I think still claims patriots sufficiently devoted to save the country, her tens of thousands are still in the field with stout hands and hearts ready to brave any danger. Many of her bravest and best sleep upon every battle field—and truly it may be said of them as the members of the 'Old Guard' used to speak of their Comrades. When the names of the dead were called, some of the rank and file would step forth, and say 'died upon the field of honor.'"[19]

He led his division at the Battle of Chancellorsville, Virginia, in May 1863, where he sustained a wound to his chest by a shell or cannon ball fragment. The division was one of the last to withdraw, and in good order, from the front after the Confederates routed most of the Union Army. Geary's son Edward, who was in Knap's Independent Battery E, Pennsylvania Light Artillery, wrote in exaggerating fashion on May 30, 1863, about his father's division and his wounding at Chancellorsville, "The rebels acknowledged the bravery of our division, as they said they never could move the White Stars—our division badge—with any force they threw against them. Gen. Jackson—now dead—fought our corps. One of his men who was captured, told Father, that he had given them orders to 'capture Geary dead or alive.' He was not obeyed.

American artist Peter Frederick Rothermel (1817–1895), born in Nescopeck, Luzerne County, painted Repulse of General Johnson's Division by General Geary's White Star Division, *circa 1872. Rothermel placed Geary in the far right of the painting, standing beneath the White Star Flag, and pointing toward the Confederate forces with his right hand. The painting depicts the valor of Geary's division at Culp's Hill on the third day of the Battle of Gettysburg. (36 x 67 ¹/₂ inches)*

"Father made a great many narrow escapes from death. A shell exploded so near to him, that the concussion knocked him down, and for some time deprived him of his speech. A piece of shell struck him on the knee, but did him no serious injury."[20]

During the early stages of the Gettysburg Campaign, in June 1863, Geary wrote to his wife from Leesburg, Virginia, about what might occur to their home in Carlisle. "I thank you much for the gallantry you have displayed by remaining at your post and home, and for making a proper distribution of the valuables," he wrote Mary. "If you leave your home it will be ransacked and destroyed, and if you remain you will not be injured or the house destroyed besides it seems so cowardly to run away. The rebels themselves will respect you more, and if you tell them you do not fear brave men, that cowards alone would injure a defenceless woman; I will wager their love of being reputed <u>brave</u> would cause them to protect you and your house. . . . Should that rebels burn your house, do not grieve about it, God will, I trust, give us a better one. 'Eternal in the heavens.'"[21]

In this letter, he also took note of his teenaged son William Logan Geary's desire to enlist in the Pennsylvania Emergency Militia of 1863. "I wish to compliment Willie G. for his patriotism, and the services he is ever ready to render to his country. Tell him not to expose himself to much, to take care of [his] health, but if it comes to a fight, to show his fellow-soldiers that he is of the right stock, and not to exhibit the 'white-feather,' and he must show that he is of true Geary blood."[22] Fourteen-year-old William L. Geary did enlist in Company D, 47th Pennsylvania Emergency

Prominent Pottsville businessman Joseph S. Patterson commissioned artist J. M. Boundy to create Portrait of General John White Geary at Gettysburg *during Geary's 1866 gubernatorial campaign. On at least one occasion, in 1866, the painting was carried in a campaign parade for Geary through the streets of the Schuylkill County seat of Pottsville. (70^1/$_2$ x 56 inches)*

Geary used a McClellan-style military saddle and saddle blanket during the Civil War. Philadelphia native and Civil War Major General George B. McClellan (1826–1885) developed the saddle which remained a standard cavalry issue for many years.

James Harris	"	18	New Cumberland Pa.	M.C.Brittain	July 5.1863
Charles Lee	"	19	Carbondale, Pa.	James Nicol	July 3.1863
William Walker	"	19	"	"	"
John Brady	"	39	New Cumberland Pa.	M.C.Brittain	July 2.1863
William Purdy	"	37	Carbondale, Pa.	James Nicol	July 3.1863
William L. Geary	Musician	16	New Cumberland Pa.	M.C.Brittain	July 5.1863
	Wagoner				
Brady, Hiram	Private	19	New Cumberland Pa.	M.C.Brittain	July 2.1863
Brady, William N.	"	19	"	"	"
Becker, Isaac	"	19	"	"	"
Burdick, Albert M.	"	22	Carbondale Pa.	James Nicol	July 3.1863
Baer, Henry	"	19	"	"	"
Burleigh Lafayette	"	29	"	"	"

Detail of Muster-Out Roll of Company D, 47th Pennsylvania Emergency Militia of 1863, lists Geary's son, William L. Geary, as a musician who enlisted at New Cumberland, Cumberland County, on July 1, 1863. He was mustered into service four days later in Harrisburg and was mustered out of service with his company on August 13, 1863, following the Pennsylvania Campaign. Although listed as being sixteen years old on this muster-out roll, it is believed that William L. Geary was only fourteen at the time of his service in 1863.

Militia, on July 1, at New Cumberland. He was mustered into service as a musician at Harrisburg. He was mustered out with his company on August 13, after the conclusion of the emergency. Before the Gettysburg Campaign, William was already a war veteran who had originally enrolled with his father's 28th PVI on July 17, 1861, as a twelve-year-old drummer boy, and was mustered out of his first period of service on September 9, 1862.

Lieutenant General Richard S. Ewell (1817–1872) whose Confederate corps fought against Geary's 2nd Division, 12th Corps, Army of the Potomac at the Battle of Gettysburg on July 3, 1863.

At the Battle of Gettysburg, Geary's White Star Division anchored the Union's extreme right flank on Culp's Hill on July 2. Geary was ordered that night to move part of his command to the left of the Union line. In his absence, Confederate forces attacked the remaining Union troops at Culp's Hill and overran Geary's former fortifications. Geary and his troops lost their way to their newly assigned position and, after a delay of several hours, returned near to their former location on Culp's Hill. In the early morning hours of July 3, the third and final day of the battle, Geary's division became engaged in a desperate fight. The Confederates viciously assaulted Geary's line repeatedly. For seven hours, his division repulsed attacks from Confederate Lieutenant General Richard S. Ewell's Corps and re-took their original works. During the struggle, Geary's fourteen hundred men withstood and rebuffed five thousand Confederate soldiers. Holding this position was critical to prevent the Confederates from gaining the rear of the Union position and capturing the Baltimore Pike.

"Yesterday I had the honor to defeat Gen Ewell's Corps (formerly Jackson's)," he wrote Mary on July 4 from Gettysburg. "They attacked my command at 3 oclock a.m. and we fought until 1/2 past 11—The result was I repulsed his command with a loss of about 1000 killed and

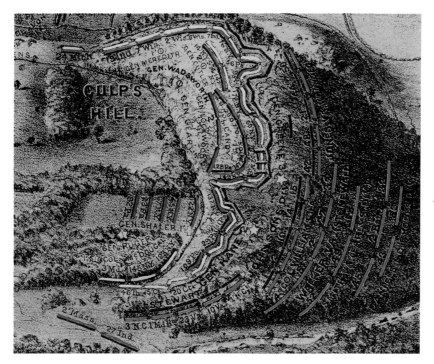

Detail of John B. Bachelder's 1863 lithograph entitled Gettysburg Battlefield *showing the alignment of Union and Confederate troops at Culp's Hill during the Battle of Gettysburg. Geary's White Star division, 2ⁿᵈ Division of the 12ᵗʰ Corps, is positioned at the far right of the Union's famous fishhook-shaped defensive position. Bachelder also noted the location of Geary's brigade commanders Brigadier Generals George S. Greene and Thomas L. Kane in the front line, with Colonel Charles Candy in reserve.*

3000 wounded we took also 500 prisoners—and about 5000 stand of arms—My loss is 110 killed 584 wounded—The whole fight was under my control, no one to interfere—<u>Thank God for so glorious a victory</u>. And that too, over the very troops who <u>broke</u> my <u>arm</u>, and whom we fought at Chancellorsville. Our prospects to drive out, speedily, the rebels is very good—and I think in another week there will not be a rebel in the state. . . .

"The country is already much devastated by the rebels, and of course it is not much improved by our presence. It is raining very hard today and there but little fighting being done. We are burying our own and the enemy's dead."[23] In a letter written to his wife the following day from Littlestown, Pennsylvania, Geary described the Union's pursuit of the retreating Army of Northern Virginia. He also mentioned his mounting weariness. "I have seen so much death and suffering this month that I am perfectly sick of the times. My very clothes smell of death. The stench of the battle fields was horrible and beyond description."[24]

On September 24, the 11ᵗʰ and 12ᵗʰ Corps were detached from the Army of the Potomac and dispatched to reinforce the Army of the Cumberland. Geary wrote to Mary from Bridgeport, Alabama, about the differences between the eastern army and the western troops, on October 25. "We find everything very different in the Army of the Cumberland from what we have been accustomed in the Army of the Potomac. Discipline the pride of that glorious body is unknown here. . . ."[25] In October and November, his division fought at the battles of Wauhatchie, Lookout Mountain, and Mission or Missionary Ridge, in Tennessee. This was a time of both

After the Battle of Gettysburg, this piece of a walnut tree embedded with a minie ball was collected from Culp's Hill in the vicinity where the 29ᵗʰ Pennsylvania Volunteer Infantry of Geary's 2ⁿᵈ Division had fought on July 3, 1863. Culp's Hill was one of the most popular locations for early battlefield visitors, who began arriving shortly after the conflict ended, due to the denuding and destruction of trees wrought by the bullets and shells fired there by both armies. Souvenirs of this type were actively sought by nineteenth-century sightseers.

professional triumph and personal tragedy for Geary. While his division was successful and commended for its actions in these battles, his eldest son Edward, eighteen years old and a lieutenant in Knap's Independent Battery E, Pennsylvania Light Artillery, was killed practically in Geary's presence at the Battle of Wauhatchie on October 29. The young Geary died after being shot through the head by a minie ball while sighting one of his cannon. "Poor dear boy, he is gone, cut down in the bud of his usefulness," Geary wrote to Mary on November 2 from a camp near Wauhatchie. "Oh my God, I feel this chastisement for the pride I took in him, his rapid development, and general character and ability. None knew him who did not love him. His praise was on every tongue. . . . My dear beloved boy is the sacrifice. Could I but recall him to life, the bubble of military fame might be absorbed by those who wish it."[26]

On November 6, 1863, Geary continued to pour out his grief to his wife. "An impenetrable gloom hangs over my mind in consequence of the death of my beloved Eddie. His rapid development in every particular, his high attainments and manly deportment, had filled to the brim the cup of paternal pride, and perhaps he was my idol; I feel now that I almost worshipped him, and dwelt more upon the creature than upon the Creator. My grief knows no bounds. . . ."[27] Geary unabashedly grieved for his son in letters to his wife through February 1864, and in correspondence to his brother Edward as late as October of that year.

Major General Joseph Hooker took particular note of Geary's valor in the Battle of Wauhatchie in his official report. "It was evident that a formidable adversary had gathered around him [Geary], and that he was battling him with all his might," he reported. "For almost three hours, without assistance, he repelled the repeated attacks of vastly superior numbers, and in the end drove them

Survivors of Knap's Independent Battery E, Pennsylvania Light Artillery, attended the dedication of their monument at Orchard Knob battlefield on November 15, 1897. Geary's son Edward served with the unit until he was killed in Tennessee during the Battle of Wauhatchie in late October 1863.

Founded in 1880, Kurz and Allison, a Chicago firm known for its colorful depictions of historical scenes, published a color lithograph entitled Battle of Chattanooga in 1888. The battle depicted took place November 23–25, 1863, in Tennessee. Topographical features such as Orchard Knob, Lookout Mountain, and Missionary Ridge played prominent roles in the fighting during the Chattanooga-Ringgold Campaign. Brigadier General John White Geary's White Star Division fought at all three locations. ($21^3/_4$ x $28^1/_4$ inches)

Brevet Major General Geary wore this general officer's coat during the Civil War. Officers of the 1st Battalion, 1st Michigan Cavalry, presented the gold bullion epaulettes to Geary while he was serving as a brigadier general.

Brigadier General Geary's White Star Identity Badge was presented to him on September 20, 1863, "From His Staff with Love and Esteem." The badge is engraved with the names of the battles in which the division had fought. Made predominantly of silver and trimmed with brass, the badge is inset with small rubies set in brass sockets. The obverse side of the badge is missing its originally present eagle motif within the silver star. The eagle's outline is still visible. Nearly one hundred years later, on June 6, 1963, the badge was found on the grounds of Fort Simcoe, a fortification established in southcentral Washington state in the 1850s by the U.S. Army to house soldiers to monitor the activities of the local Native Americans, and later given to the Pennsylvania Historical and Museum Commission. Historians theorize that John White Geary's estate sent the badge to his brother, Edward R. Geary, who lived in Oregon. ($2^{5}/_{8}$ x $2^{3}/_{16}$ x $^{3}/_{8}$ inches)

ingloriously from the field. At one time they had enveloped him on three sides, under circumstances that would have dismayed any officer except one endowed with an iron will and the most exalted courage. Such is the character of General Geary."[28]

During the Chattanooga-Ringgold Campaign, Geary led his division in a successful attack on Lookout Mountain, nicknamed the Battle Above the Clouds, on November 24, 1863, during which his men captured six enemy flags, two cannon, and several thousand prisoners. On the following day, he and his troops fought at the Battle of Missionary Ridge. Writing to Mary, on December 4 from Wauhatchie, Geary described the Battle of Lookout Mountain as helping to avenge Edward's death. "I am bereaved and transformed. Like the tiger robbed of his whelps, I have been like a destroying angel ever since, no height has been too bold no valley too deep, no fastness too strong, that I did not solicit to be permitted to storm. . . . I have been the instrument of Almighty God, of carrying <u>terror</u> and <u>terrible destruction</u> wherever it has pleased God to direct my footsteps. Under such impulses I stormed, what was considered the impassible and inaccessible heights of Lookout Mountain, I captured it—turned the right flank [of] Bragg's Army and drove him from his position. This feat will be celebrated until time shall be no more."[29] Geary actually turned Bragg's left flank.

Union Major General Joseph Hooker (1814–1879) received the nickname "Fighting Joe" during the Civil War.

Geary and his troops fought at Ringgold, Georgia, in late November, which he succinctly chronicled in a missive to his brother Edward. "On the 27th I fought at Ringgold Geo., and whipped the rebels at that place. My troops having been fired at from some of the houses, and

> **"I have been the instrument of Almighty God, of carrying <u>terror</u> and <u>terrible destruction</u> wherever it has pleased God to direct my footsteps."**

having lost some of my best and bravest soldiers, we were all greatly exasperated, and we burned the place, destroying among other things, three large tanneries—2 shoe shops. 7 mills—5 Bridges, Jail, Court-House, 5 depots on R.R. 6 miles of R.R., etc., etc., etc. It was a sweet revenge to sweep them like a hurricane. And to know I was avenging <u>Wauhatchie's bloody glen</u>."[30]

His division was made part of the 20th Corps, Army of the Cumberland, within Major General William Tecumseh Sherman's Military Division of the Mississippi, in April 1864. The 20th Corps took part in the Atlanta Campaign and Sherman's March to the Sea, beginning in May 1864. In writing, on July 9, to his brother Edward about the campaign to take Atlanta, Geary commented openly about his motivation and drive. "I continue to grieve deeply and continuously for the loss of my heroic and beloved son. I know it is wrong to do so, but it cannot be helped, Sometimes when the storm of battle wastes most fiercely I miss that noble boy wherever the strife was the thickest. And I cannot avoid invoking vengeance upon his murderers, —my hand and voice seem almost inspired. And regardless of danger, O, <u>how terribly he is avenged</u>. Do not blame me for if you had witnessed that terrible and unequal fight in Wauhatchie's bloody glen, you too, would have become a revengeful demon."[31]

Reporting on the end of the Atlanta Campaign—which lasted from May to September—after the occupation of the city on September 2, Geary compiled his official report. "Thus gloriously ended the campaign, unequalled for brilliant victories, over seemingly insurmountable difficulties, and unsurpassed in history—a campaign which will stand forever a monument of

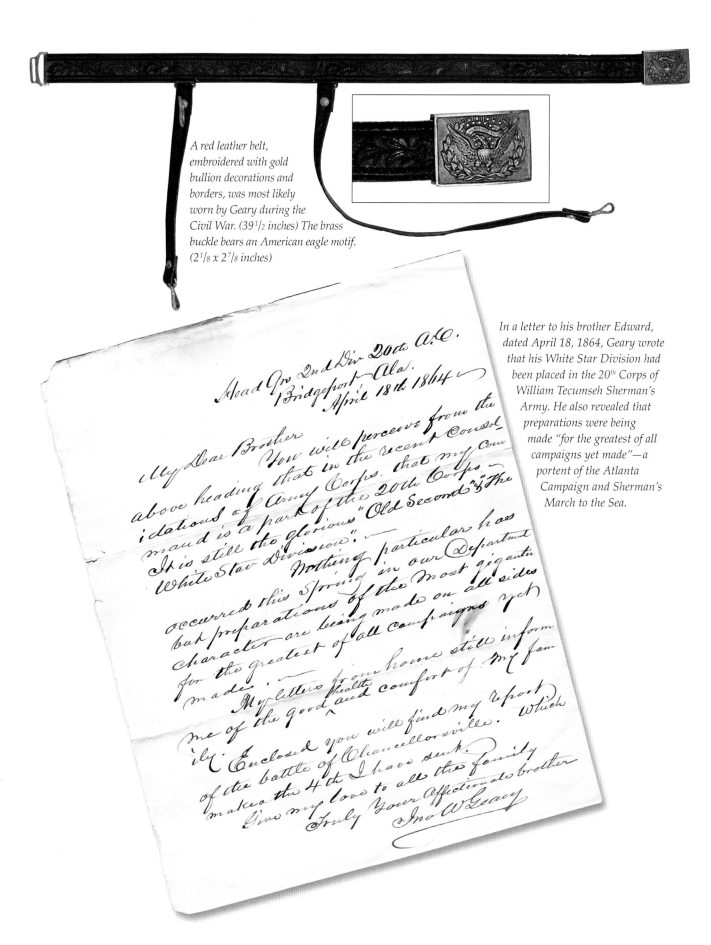

A red leather belt, embroidered with gold bullion decorations and borders, was most likely worn by Geary during the Civil War. (39$^{1}/_{2}$ inches) The brass buckle bears an American eagle motif. (2$^{1}/_{8}$ x 2$^{7}/_{8}$ inches)

In a letter to his brother Edward, dated April 18, 1864, Geary wrote that his White Star Division had been placed in the 20th Corps of William Tecumseh Sherman's Army. He also revealed that preparations were being made "for the greatest of all campaigns yet made"—a portent of the Atlanta Campaign and Sherman's March to the Sea.

the valor, endurance and patriotism of the American soldier; four months of hard, constant labor, under the hot sun of a southern summer, scarce a day which was passed out of the sound of the crash of musketry and roar of artillery; two hundred miles travelled through a country, in every mile of which nature and art seemed leagued for defence—mountains, rivers, lines of works—a campaign in which every march was a fight, in which battles followed in such rapid succession, and were so intimately connected by an unremitting series of skirmishes, that it may properly be regarded as one grand battle, which crowned with grander victory, attests the skill and patience of the hero who matured its plans and directed their execution."[32]

He described the taking of the city of Atlanta in a letter written in the captured city, to his wife Mary on September 3. "As stated in my telegram of the 2nd the city was occupied in the forenoon of that day: The 20th Corps being the 1st to enter. And the flags of the ever-a-head and glorious old White Star Division were the first to wave from the town Hall, and the battlements surrounding."[33] He and his division stayed in the vicinity of Atlanta until November 15, when Sherman commenced his famous March to the Sea. Geary's division led the advance on Savannah, accepting the city's surrender on December 21, 1864.

Geary served as military governor of Savannah from December 1864 until January 27, 1865, when he returned to the field. "My eventful career is still upon its everlasting whirl," he informed his wife from Savannah on December 23, 1864. "I am now the <u>Commandante</u> of the City, in honor of its capture by me, and of the surrender to me. My command was in the city five hours earlier than any other troops. We captured by ourselves alone about 75 Cannon with ammunition, 30,000 Bales of cotton, 400 prisoners. And liberated many of our own soldiers who had languished for months in the southern dungeons—Oh how pleasant it is to bid the captive go free, none but those who do it can taste its extatic pleasures."[34]

On January 23, 1865, the mayor and aldermen of Savannah adopted a resolution that in part stated, "that the thanks of the Mayor and Aldermen of the City of Savannah for themselves, and in behalf of the fellow citizens, be, and the same are hereby tendered to Brevet Major General John W. Geary for the uniform courtesy extended by him for all who came into official contact with him, and for his great judgment in the conduct of all his business transactions, and in that we will ever hold him in remembrance as the embodiment of the high toned gentlemen and chivalrous soldier."[35]

Geary was brevetted (a temporary promotion of a commissioned officer to a higher rank, usually without the pay of the higher rank) major general with a commission, dated January 12, 1865, for "fitness to command and promptness to execute." After leaving Savannah, his White Star Division fought from February through April 1865 in the Carolinas Campaign.

"Thus ended gloriously the campaign, unequalled for brilliant victories."

"We have just learned [of] the assassination of the President," he wrote from Raleigh, North Carolina, on April 19, "his untimely loss has created a profound sensation in the entire army, and if we have to fight anymore, woe be to Rebeldom! The cowardly assassins are only exhibiting the same <u>phases</u> which so greatly embittered me towards them ever since the Kansas affair, and no one understands better than I their nefarious designs."[36]

His troops were nearby at the surrender of Confederate forces by General Joseph E. Johnston near Raleigh, North Carolina, on April 26, 1865. Writing home three days later, he commented on the surrender. "Peace, Sweet Peace is made, and to-morrow we set out for Richmond and Washington City. On our way to home, sweet home. . . . Thus you see, I had the honor to participate in the last campaign of this ever memorable struggle."[37] His division took part in the Grand Review in Washington, D.C., on May 24 and remained in service until July 19, when mustered out. Geary suffered six wounds during the Civil War. Although he displayed bravery in combat, his tactical skills proved marginal. Keenly aware that his military service could help reap political dividends in the post-war years, Geary never failed to seek publicity for himself and his commands.

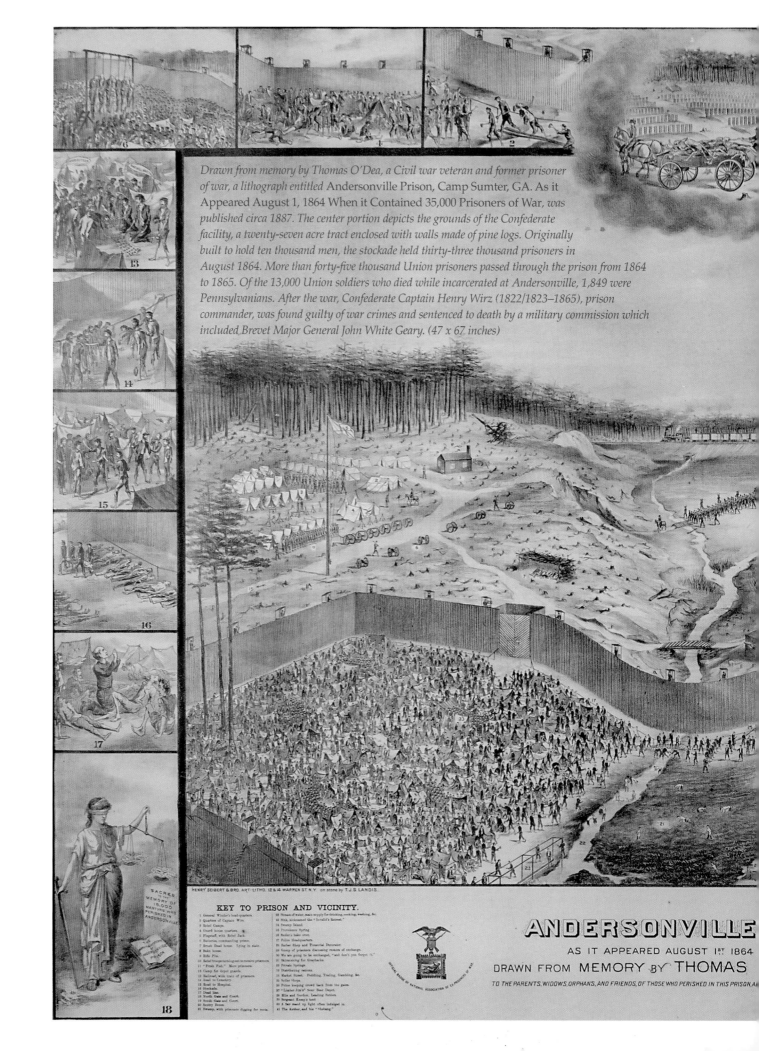

Drawn from memory by Thomas O'Dea, a Civil war veteran and former prisoner of war, a lithograph entitled Andersonville Prison, Camp Sumter, GA. As it Appeared August 1, 1864 When it Contained 35,000 Prisoners of War, was published circa 1887. The center portion depicts the grounds of the Confederate facility, a twenty-seven acre tract enclosed with walls made of pine logs. Originally built to hold ten thousand men, the stockade held thirty-three thousand prisoners in August 1864. More than forty-five thousand Union prisoners passed through the prison from 1864 to 1865. Of the 13,000 Union soldiers who died while incarcerated at Andersonville, 1,849 were Pennsylvanians. After the war, Confederate Captain Henry Wirz (1822/1823–1865), prison commander, was found guilty of war crimes and sentenced to death by a military commission which included Brevet Major General John White Geary. (47 x 67 inches)

HENRY SEIBERT & BRO. ART-LITHO. 12 & 14 WARREN ST N.Y.   on stone by T.J.S. LANDIS.

KEY TO PRISON AND VICINITY.

ANDERSONVILLE

AS IT APPEARED AUGUST 1ST 1864

DRAWN FROM MEMORY BY THOMAS

TO THE PARENTS, WIDOWS, ORPHANS, AND FRIENDS, OF THOSE WHO PERISHED IN THIS PRISON A

PRISON. ✦CAMP SUMTER, GA.✦

T CONTAINED 35,000 PRISONERS OF WAR.

A. LATE PRIVATE Cº E. 16TH REGT MAINE INFT VOLS

AINING SURVIVERS, IS THIS PICTURE RESPECTFULLY AND FRATERNALLY DEDICATED.

KEY TO MARGIN ILLUSTRATIONS.

John W. Geary's final Civil War-related military duty began on August 23, 1865. On that date, he was appointed as a member of a special military commission that convened in Washington, D.C., for the trial of Confederate Captain Henry Wirz. In 1864–1865, Wirz was the commandant of Andersonville Prison, a notorious Confederate prisoner of war camp in Georgia during the war.

The trial ended on October 24, 1865. The military commission found Wirz guilty of various war crimes committed against Union troops who were held as prisoners of war at Andersonville. His death sentence was handed down on November 3, and Wirz's plea for clemency was refused by President Andrew Johnson, in office from 1865 to 1869. He was executed by hanging on November 10 at the U.S. Arsenal Prison in Washington, D.C.—the same site where four Lincoln assassination conspirators had been executed four months earlier. Wirz's body was initially buried next to the remains of Lincoln conspirator George Atzerodt on the prison grounds.

The Wirz trial was the sole war crimes trial held that was related to the Civil War. The trial set a precedent for future war crimes trials held in the twentieth and twenty-first centuries. No longer was the excuse that a soldier was simply following orders a sufficient defense for wanton cruelty to the enemy during wartime.

Before and during the war, Geary was a staunch Democrat. Not long after the war ended, though, he joined the Republican Party. Pennsylvania's U.S. Representative John Covode, from Geary's home county of Westmoreland, and political power broker Simon Cameron recruited him to run as a Republican candidate for the governorship of Pennsylvania. U.S. Representative Thaddeus Stevens of Pennsylvania, a leader of the Radical Republicans, also supported Geary's campaign for governor.[38] During the campaign, in the summer of 1866, Geary made the statement, "The Democratic party has abandoned its old truths. You cannot get one of them to sign his name to any of its old cardinal doctrines. All the old Democratic doctrines and all the grand old principles of that party have come out and gone into the Republican party."[39] Geary's campaign for the governor's office, in 1866, had the full backing of Cameron's Republican machine. "My great desire now is to elect Geary," Simon Cameron wrote in August. "I care for that much more than for the Senatorship—for the one reason that in my opinion the safety of the country depends on the success of the Union party in Pennsylvania in October—and we will win."[40]

Thaddeus Stevens praised Geary during the 1866 gubernatorial campaign. "A purer patriot never breathed the air. . . . He risked all to save the country."[41] A Chicago Republican newspaper quoted General Ulysses S. Grant as saying, "to ask any soldier to vote for such a man [Hiester Clymer], of at one time known disloyalty, against another who had served four years in the Union army with credit to himself and benefit to his country, was a gross insult."[42]

Geary defeated Democrat Hiester Clymer (1827–1884), a rabid Copperhead (a reproachful name for Northerners who opposed the Civil War and wanted immediate peace with the Confederates), on October 9, by more than seventeen thousand votes. Clymer, a Pennsylvania state senator during the war years, came

Mid-nineteenth-century portrait of Simon Cameron (1799–1889) by John J. Libhart (1806-1883) of York County. Born in Maytown, Lancaster County, Cameron served as President Abraham Lincoln's secretary of war from 1861 to 1862. He established the Keystone State's Republican Party machine following the Civil War. Cameron served as a United States senator from 1845 to 1849, 1857 to 1861, and 1867 to 1877. (30 x 25 inches)

Cabinet card bearing an image of Thaddeus Stevens (1792–1868) by famous Civil War photographer Mathew B. Brady (1822–1896). Stevens served in the U.S. House of Representatives from 1848 to 1853 and again from 1859 to 1868 from Lancaster County. He was considered the most radical of Republicans in Congress during the Civil War and Reconstruction era.

from a distinguished family; his grandfather, George Clymer, had signed the Declaration of Independence. A campaign pamphlet circulated by his opponents attacked Clymer because he "never served in a military capacity, not even when the soil of his native state was invaded, and her towns devastated by hostile armies. . . ."[43] The pamphlet also noted that as a member of the state legislature, Clymer was "strenuous in his opposition to every measure calculated to suppress rebellion."[44] He had been quoted in the resolutions from a meeting in Reading, Berks County, on April 21, 1863, "We do not approve of this war as at present conducted. We never did approve of it itself."[45] Clymer was known for opposing Lincoln's war policies, Black rights—particularly the right to vote—and for his anti-Freedman's Bureau rhetoric. He campaigned as the "white man's candidate."

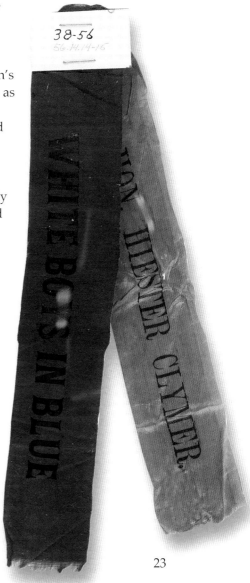

Following the Civil War, Northern Democrats fought vigorously against supporting voting rights for African Americans. They trumpeted the Democratic Party ticket in elections as the "White Man's ticket." They organized their own overtly racist veterans' clubs, such as the White Boys in Blue, and paraded with signs reading "White Supremacy" and "No [Black] Voting." This group strongly supported Clymer in the 1866 gubernatorial campaign, which focused on Reconstruction in the United States. Historian Erwin Stanley Bradley asserted that Republican supporters countered with the contention, "The fruits of victory . . . could be realized only by supporting the party which had made victory possible. To vote for the Democracy, reasoned the Radicals, was equivalent to a shameless repudiation of the heroic deed and an insult to the living veteran."[46]

Geary peppered his inaugural address, delivered on January 15, 1867, with praise for the North and condemnation of the South. "The object of the South was avowedly the dissolution of the Union and the establishment of a confederacy based upon 'the corner stone of human slavery.' To have submitted to this on our part, and to have shrunk from a manly resistance under such circumstances, would have been deeply and lastingly degrading, and would have destroyed the value of the priceless legacy bequeathed to us by our fathers, and which we are obligated to transmit unimpaired to future generations. The patriotic and Union-loving people felt that the alternative was that of life or death to the Union; and under the

Democrat Hiester Clymer battled Geary in 1866 for Pennsylvania's governor's office. One of the organizations that supported Clymer was the White Boys in Blue, an overtly racist group of Union veterans who protested granting voting rights to African Americans.

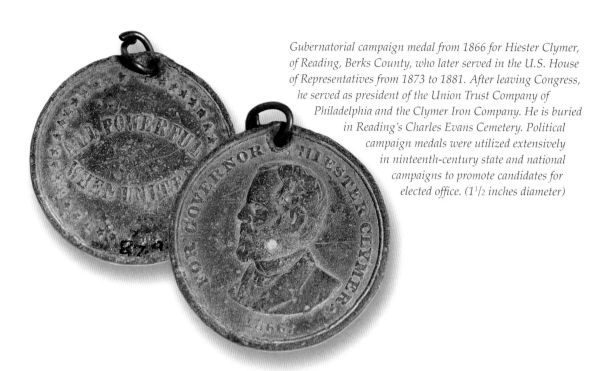

Gubernatorial campaign medal from 1866 for Hiester Clymer, of Reading, Berks County, who later served in the U.S. House of Representatives from 1873 to 1881. After leaving Congress, he served as president of the Union Trust Company of Philadelphia and the Clymer Iron Company. He is buried in Reading's Charles Evans Cemetery. Political campaign medals were utilized extensively in nineteenth-century state and national campaigns to promote candidates for elected office. (1¹/₂ inches diameter)

An 1866 anti-Freedman's Bureau and anti-Geary poster announced that Republican "Geary is for the Freedman's Bureau." and his Democratic opponent "Clymer is Opposed to it." The poster capitalized on labor's discontent with unemployment and high taxes following the war and blamed the problems on the Freedman's Bureau and its assistance to freed slaves. (18³/₄ x 23³/₄ inches)

Kurze Beschreibung der Jugendjahre
sowie der Militair- und Civil-Dienste des

General-Majors John White Geary,
Candidat der National-Union-Partei
für Gouverneur von Pennsylvanien.
1866.

An 1866 gubernatorial campaign booklet for Geary is written entirely in German, in deference to the large numbers of German-speaking residents of Pennsylvania in the mid-nineteenth century. The cover translates to A Short Description of the Years of his Youth as well as the Military and Civil Services of Major General John White Geary, Candidate of the National Union Party for Governor of Pennsylvania.

auspicious guidance of Abraham Lincoln, that virtuous and patriotic Chief Magistrate, with the blessing of Him who directs the destinies of nations, after open action and arbitrary violence on the part of the South, the appeal to arms was made. We had a just cause, and our citizens approving it with a degree of unanimity heretofore unknown in this or any other country, left their various employments, their homes and all that was dear to them, and hastened with enthusiasm to the scenes where duty and danger called, and as the surest pledge of the unswerving love and fidelity to the Union, they unhesitatingly offered their lives for its preservation."[47]

Geary remarked on the Keystone State's role in the Civil War in this address, pronouncing, "In every phase of this terrible conflict, Pennsylvania bore an honorable and conspicuous part. She contributed three hundred and sixty-six thousand three hundred and twenty-six volunteer soldiers to the rescue of the nation; and nearly every battlefield has been moistened with the blood, and whitened with the bones, of her heroes. To them we owe our victories, unsurpassed in brilliancy and importance of their consequences. To the dead—the thrice honored dead—we are deeply indebted, for without their services it is possible that our cause might not have been successful.

"The generosity of the people of Pennsylvania to the Union soldiers has been imitated, but not equaled, by other States. There is something peculiar in the loyalty of Pennsylvania. She seemed to feel, from the first, as if upon her devolved the setting of a superior example. The fact that she carried upon her standard the brightest jewel of the Republic; that in her bosom was conceived and from her commercial capital was issued the Declaration of Independence, gave to her contributions, in men and money, and her unparalleled charitable organizations, all the dignity and force of a model for others to copy. The rebel foe seemed to feel that if he could strike a fatal blow at Pennsylvania, he would recover all of his losses, and establish a resistless prestige in the old world. But thanks to Divine Providence, and to the enduring bravery of our citizen soldiers, the invasion of our beloved State sealed her more closely to the cause of freedom.

"The result of the battle of Gettysburg broke the power of the rebellion, and although the final issue was delayed, it was inevitable from the date of that great event. That battle rescued all the other free States; and when the arch of victory was completed by Sherman's successful advance from the sea, so that the two conquerors could shake hands over the two fields that closed the war, the soldiers of Pennsylvania were equal sharers in this glorious consummation."[48]

An early photograph of Culp's Hill at Gettysburg along unpaved North Slocum Avenue shows the monument to the 78th and 102nd New York Volunteers (right foreground) and a monument to the 28th Pennsylvania Volunteers (left background). These three regiments were part of Geary's 2nd Division of 12th Corps. In the center background is the monument to the 150th New York Volunteers, part of the 1st Division, 12th Corps.

Geary articulated his disdain for leaders of the Confederacy and his desire to see them punished: "And here I cannot refrain from an expression of regret that the General Government has not taken any steps to inflict the proper penalties of the Constitution and laws upon the leaders of those who rudely and ferociously invaded the ever sacred soil of our State.

"It is certainly a morbid clemency and censurable forbearance, which fail to punish the greatest crimes 'known to the laws of civilized nations;' and may not the hope be reasonably indulged, that the Federal authorities will cease to extend unmerited mercy to those who inaugurated the rebellion and controlled the movements of its armies? If this be done, treason will be 'rendered odious,' and it will be distinctly proclaimed, on the pages of our future history, that no attempt can be made with impunity to destroy our Republican form of government."[49]

He went on to suggest that former Confederates should not be welcomed back to the restored federal government, "The violators of the most solemn obligations, the perpetrators of the most atrocious crimes in the annals of time, the murderers of our heroic soldiers on fields of battle, and in loathsome dungeons and barbarous prisons, they must not, shall not, re-appear in the council chambers of the nation, to aid in its legislation, or control

Carte de visite of Ulysses S. Grant, who Governor Geary fervently supported as a candidate for the presidency of the United States in 1868.

unless it shall be on conditions which will preserve our institutions from their baleful purposes and influence, and secure republican forms of government, in their purity and vigor, in every section of the country."[50]

Geary's 1866 campaign and his 1869 reelection campaign were among the first in Pennsylvania to use the political tactic known as "Waving the Bloody Shirt." This approach reminded voters that many Union soldiers had lost their lives during the war, and that they should vote as they had fought—with the Republican Party. Many of their candidates for governor, among them Geary, and for president, including Ulysses S. Grant, were military heroes responsible for preserving the Union. In a letter to his brother Edward on December 5, 1868, Governor Geary expressed his approval of President-elect Grant. "Peace seems already to be spreading her beneficent wings over the country—the mere election of Grant and [Vice President Schuyler] Colfax is a panacea for many of our evils, and I have no doubt but that tranquility and prosperity will soon resume their fullest sway as in the days of yore."[51]

Image of John White Geary as governor, from 1867 to 1873.

During his first term, Geary freed himself of Pennsylvania's Republican Party machine control. In 1869, without Cameron's support, Governor Geary won reelection over Democratic candidate Asa Packer, founder of the Lehigh Valley Railroad, by 4,596 votes. Geary, who served two consecutive terms as governor, from 1867 to 1873, was the first of six Civil War veterans to become chief executive of the Commonwealth of Pennsylvania. He continued to support the enfranchisement of African Americans. His most common gubernatorial campaign slogan, "I Vote as I Fight," aimed to curry favor among veterans. In a letter dated January 7, 1870, he remarked on his reelection as governor using many military terms. "It was a victory,—a grand victory, the 'Lookout Mountain' of my political life," he wrote. "The most decided victory of them all. I had to contend with the Curtin, and Cameron factions combined at my nomination in the Philadelphia Convention in June last, and in that I distanced them both. . . . and in it I took positive ground against faction, and as I expected I had to meet all the miserable thieving rascals and 'stay-at-homes' of the Republican party combined with the common enemy for my defeat. They were headed by Asa Packer with $20,000,000. He spent about $1,000,000 to accomplish his object. And used every denunciation in his power, I fought squarely and uncovered under the muzzles of the enemy's guns, and made him and his allies wince at every turn. . . . The whole storm of the battle was received upon my devoted head. . . . I am stronger in the state to-day than I ever

"I Vote as I Fight," emblazoned on a political campaign medal produced for Geary's reelection to the governor's office in 1869. Bearing the 12th Corps star, the medal evidenced his desire to capitalize on the veterans' vote by reminding them of his military service and valor during the Civil War. (1 1/4 inches diameter)

was before, and my influence is not only acknowledged by all, but deeply feared when they come in competition with it."[52]

Governor Geary vigorously attacked the state debt, reducing it by more than ten million dollars. He also advocated political reforms that necessitated the 1872–1873 state constitutional convention that produced the 1874 Constitution of the Commonwealth of Pennsylvania. Geary did not forget Union veterans while in office and pushed for the establishment of a veterans' home and the expansion of the orphans' home system for children of veterans. In his 1867 inaugural address, he stated, "Among our most solemn obligations is the maintenance of the indigent widows, and the support and education of the orphan children, of these noble men who fell in defence of the Union. To affirm that we owe a debt of gratitude to those who have been rendered homeless and fatherless, by their parents' patriotic devotion to the country, is a truth

The Democratic Party chose wealthy industrialist Asa Packer as its 1869 gubernatorial candidate. Due to the Commonwealth's large German-speaking population, this campaign poster was written in German. Packer lost the office to Geary by 4,596 votes, one of the closest gubernatorial elections in Pennsylvania's history. (46 1/4 x 31 3/4 inches)

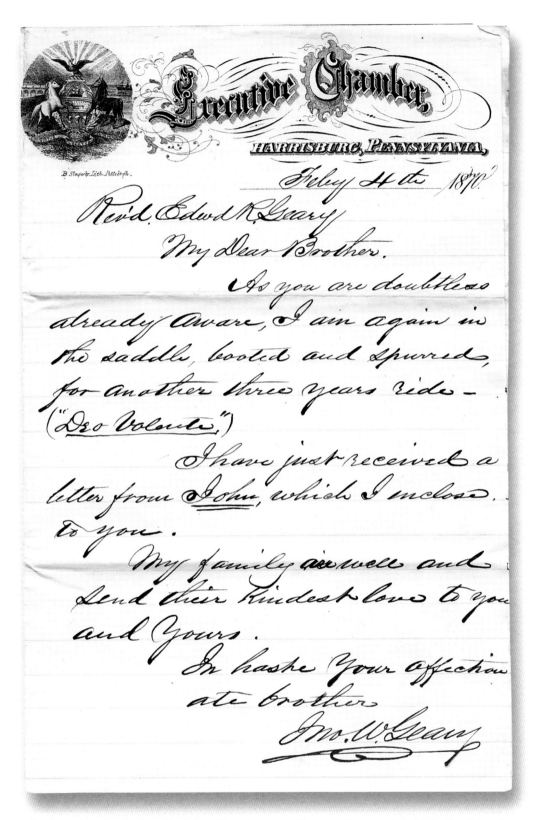

On Executive Chamber letterhead, in military language, Governor Geary wrote to his brother Edward about beginning his second term: "As you are doubtless already aware, I am again in the saddle, booted and spurred, for another three years ride."

A circa 1893 photograph of the Boys Battalion at the Harford Soldiers' Orphan School, located on the grounds of the Franklin Academy in Harford, Susquehanna County. Orphan schools not only offered students an academic curriculum and training in trades but also calisthenics and military-style drills.

to which all mankind will yield a ready assent; and though we cannot call the dead to life, it is a privilege, as well as duty, to take the orphan by the hand, and be to him a protector and a father."[53]

On January 6, 1869, Geary reported to the general assembly on the status of the Soldiers' Orphan School system created in 1864 by Governor Andrew Gregg Curtin. "The schools are all in good condition and improving, and their usefulness is daily becoming more manifest. They are among the most philanthropic institutions of the age, and reflect high honor on the patriotism of the Legislature by which they have been so liberally endowed and upon our people by whom they are sustained. The children who are the recipients of their benefits are the offspring of brave men who voluntarily endangered their lives in the cause of their country in the most trying hour of its existence, and who, glowing with patriotic ardor, fought as bravely and as heroically as the noblest men in the world's history. Thousands of them who left their homes in the bloom of health and with the brightest hopes of manhood, now sleep in death, leaving their widows and little ones to the care of the country in whose service they fell, and which promised them its protection. Their children are the wards of this great Commonwealth; and too much praise cannot be awarded its people for the munificent and tender manner in which they have thus far, through their representatives, discharged the sacred and delicate trust."[54]

In his 1870 annual message to the general assembly, he spoke out for the need of establishing a home for disabled soldiers. "This is a home for the soldiers who have 'borne the battle' in defence of the honor, integrity and perpetuity of the American Union," he explained. "No men living have as powerful claims upon the generosity and nurturing care of the Commonwealth of Pennsylvania, as those who, upon the battle-field, fought to protect it against threatened devastation and destruction, and who in this patriotic service, endangered their lives, sacrificed their health, lost their limbs, and became enfeebled and disabled for life. And yet we daily see these men (and who does not blush to see them?) to whom we owe the preservation of our government, the homes we enjoy, and almost everything we possess, hobbling about streets on crutches, with missing limbs, and otherwise so enfeebled as to be entirely unfitted for any remunerative employment, begging their bread from door to door, or sitting upon the corners of the streets turning an organ for the few pennies the charitable passerby may feel disposed to bestow. Every one of these helpless men, whose patriotic devotion to his country has brought him to this deplorable condition, is a burning reproach to the State for whose welfare he has met the most serious and lamentable of all misfortunes. All of them appeal, by their wounds and destitution, to the people of the Commonwealth for that care which, in such contingencies, was promised the soldier of the Union, his widow, and his orphan children. It is time that all such promises should be redeemed. The wounded and helpless soldiers have a claim upon the State which should not, and cannot be ignored. And I do earnestly recommend in their name, and in their behalf, that measures be taken by your honorable body, to establish for them a home where they shall be amply provided with the necessary comforts of life, and no longer be compelled to be pensioners upon the scanty charity of the world. This is a debt the State absolutely owes, and no time should be lost in its honorable liquidation."[55]

> "No men living have as powerful claims upon the . . . care of the Commonwealth of Pennsylvania, as those who . . . fought to protect it against threatened devastation . . . and who . . . endangered their lives, sacrificed their health, lost their limbs, and became . . . disabled for life."

During Geary's administration, a system was established to handle damage claims from citizens who lost property during Confederate incursions into Pennsylvania. In 1866, the Commonwealth of Pennsylvania paid prorated sums only to damage claimants of the burning of Chambersburg. In his message to the general assembly on May 28, 1871, Geary recommended that the legislature establish a system for adjudicating additional damage claims and seeking further settlement from the federal government. "The claims of a large portion of the citizens of the border counties of the State, for extraordinary losses arising from the late war, demand the dispassionate and serious consideration of the Legislature; and it is but just to a people who have been called upon to bear unequal burdens in our national deliverance, that they should have the fullest exercise of the sovereign power of the Commonwealth to secure just restitution from the general government.

"Most of these losses were suffered because the State, in discharging the full measure of her duty in maintaining free government, patriotically and promptly transferred her own defensive troops to strengthen the shattered federal armies, and our citizens thereby suffered for the general welfare. Leaving all abstract principles out of view, justice and fair dealing demand that proper restitution be

made to our citizens by the general government; and it is due to the claimants that the Legislature take such action in the matter as will secure a most careful adjudication of the losses, and clothe the officers of the State with the amplest power and authority to enforce their payment.

"While justice should be secured for all our citizens, the people of Chambersburg have been almost utterly crushed in their business operations, and their conditions should hasten the generous action of the Legislature. The blow struck at Chambersburg was a wound inflicted upon the Commonwealth, and it should be the pride, as well as the pleasure of every patriotic citizen, to sanction such action as will secure reasonable restitution to the citizens of that ill-fated town, as well as others who suffered."[56]

In Geary's last known letter to his brother Edward, dated February 1, 1873, he reflected briefly on his administration, "On the 21st ultimo, after having performed the duties of Gov of our native State for <u>six years and six days</u>, I have become again a private citizen. I have truly

A panoramic photographic image, "View of the Ruins of Chambersburg," with two smaller detailed photographs, made by Charles L. Lockman, Carlisle, Cumberland County, shortly after Confederate Brigadier General John McCausland's forces devastated the Franklin County community by burning it, on July 30, 1864. (15$^{1}/_{2}$ x 36$^{1}/_{2}$ inches)

endeavored to perform my whole duty, and I believe have succeeded about as well as I could have expected, in conducting the ship of State through the troubled waters that followed upon the close of the War. 'All's well that ends well.'"[57]

Upon leaving office, Geary remained in Harrisburg while making plans for various business ventures and a possible run at the presidency. It was not to be. He died suddenly of a heart attack while at his family's breakfast table at the age fifty-three on February 8, only two weeks after leaving office. His body lay in state in the Pennsylvania House of Representatives chamber on February 12. John White Geary was buried in Harrisburg Cemetery the following day.

Chambersburg resident Benjamin F. Nead filed an application seeking reimbursement in the amount of $7,582.95 for real estate and personal property he lost during the July 30, 1864, Confederate attack on the community.

In 1866, Nead was awarded a prorated settlement (below) of $2,358.81 for his property losses after Confederate troops burned Chambersburg. Unfortunately for many Keystone State residents in counties bordering the Pennsylvania-Maryland boundary line, only the claims of Chambersburg residents were paid by the Commonwealth or the federal government.

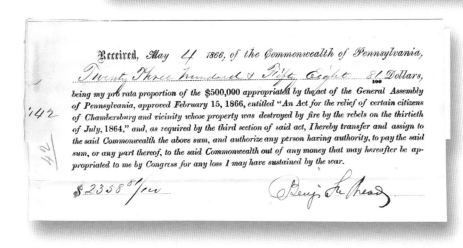

1864		Amount Brought up		2665.70
July	30	2 Paddles	@ 12.50	25.00
"	"	3 Meat Vessels	@ 3.00	9.00
"	"	1 Kraut Stand	@	2.00
"	"	6 Beds & Bedding	@	150.00
"	"	13 Quilts	@ 2.50	32.50
"	"	6 Quilts	@ 5.00	30.00
"	"	4 Pair Blankets	@ 10.00	40.00
"	"	3 Pair Blankets	@ 6.00	18.00
"	"	2 Coverlets	@ 5.00	10.00
"	"	3 tons of Hay	@ 10.00	30.00
"	"	1 Cutting Box	@	30.00
"	"	Stable Fixtures	@	5.00
"	"	2 Doz of Bags	@ 50	12.00
"	"	2½ tons of Coal	@ 10	25.00
"	"	1½ Cords of Hickory Wood	@	8.00
"	"	Axes Wedges & Saw	@	3.50
"	"	Ink Stands Sand Boxes & Roulers	@	2.00
"	"	2 Reams of Writing Paper	@ 4.00	8.00
"	"	¼ Ream of Bill Paper	@ 6.00	1.50
"	"	½ Box of Envelopes	@ 2.50	1.25
"	"	Large Lot of School & Classical Books	@	50.00
"	"	2 Vol Sheet Music Bound	@ 5.00	10.00
"	"	3 Spinning Wheels	@ 3.00	9.00
"	"	1 New Platers Hammer	@	3.00
"	"	1 Large Chest	@	5.00
"	"	1 Chest	@	2.50
"	"			3187.95
"	"	Real Estate as Valued by Committee of Citizens		5000.00
"	"	North Side of East Market St		$8187.95
		Deduct from Person Prop. (1 Diploma)		5.00
				$8,182.95

The reverse of Nead's Chambersburg War Damage Claim Application contains a partial list of the property he lost in the burning of Chambersburg. Among the items he listed were writing paper, chests, blankets, coverlets, quilts, hay, coal, beds, and a "Large Lot of School & Classical Books." (12 11/16 x 7 13/16 inches)

Governor
John Frederick Hartranft
in office from 1873 to 1879

John Frederick Hartranft was born in New Hanover Township, Montgomery County, on December 16, 1830, the only child of Samuel Engle and Lydia Bucher Hartranft. His ancestors, who belonged to the Schwenkfelder faith (a Protestant church that followed the sixteenth-century teachings of Caspar Schwenkfeld von Ossig of Silesia, and migrated to Pennsylvania to escape religious persecution from 1731 to 1737), had immigrated to America, in 1734, as religious refugees from Europe's Germanic states and settled in what is now popularly called Pennsylvania Dutch Country. During his childhood, his parents owned several inns, the first of which was located near Gilbertsville. Later, they owned an inn in Boyertown and finally one in Norristown, in 1844.

Hartranft graduated from Union College in Schenectady, New York, in 1853, where he studied civil engineering. He worked on several surveying jobs immediately after college, including work for a railroad in Easton, eventually settling in Norristown. In 1854, he was appointed deputy sheriff of Montgomery County and served two terms. While serving as deputy sheriff, he began studying law and was admitted to the bar in 1860. On January 26, 1854, Hartranft married Sallie Douglas Sebring of Easton, daughter of a judge, and together they had seven children.

Photograph of John Frederick Hartranft (1830–1889) in the uniform coat of a Union brigadier general but with the shoulder straps of a major general.

In 1857, he joined a local militia company, the Norris City Rifles, as a private. He earned the ranks of 2nd lieutenant and 1st lieutenant with the Rifles, eventually being elected as its captain. He also became a member of a local fire company, becoming its president in 1858. The following year he was elected lieutenant colonel of the 1st Regiment Pennsylvania Militia from Montgomery County and later became its colonel.

After the outbreak of the American Civil War on April 12, 1861, President Lincoln issued his first call for seventy-five thousand troops. Hartranft offered his services and that of his militia regiment to Governor Andrew Gregg Curtin on April 17. His militia regiment became the backbone of the companies that made up the 4th Pennsylvania Volunteer Infantry (PVI) Regiment. On April 20, Colonel Hartranft was given command of the regiment comprised largely of men from Montgomery County. The 4th PVI was mustered into service for a term of three months, on April 20, at Harrisburg. The regiment was immediately sent to help guard the railroad lines

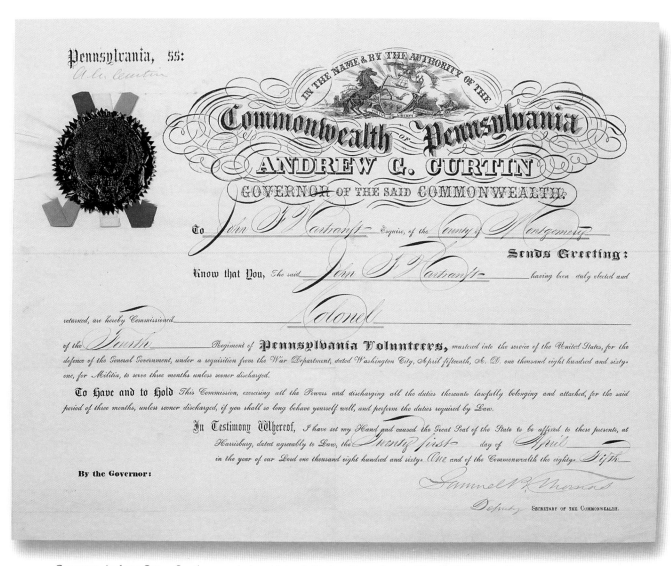

Governor Andrew Gregg Curtin commissioned John F. Hartranft as colonel of the 4th PVI on April 21, 1861. The document, along with thirty-seven other items, was donated to the Pennsylvania State Archives in 1965 by Hartranft's grandson, Hartranft Stockham (1902–1983). (13³/4 x 17 inches)

between Perryville, Maryland, and Washington, D.C. Not long afterward, these troops were moved to Washington. Military life agreed with Hartranft from the very beginning. "I never had any thing to do in my life that pleased me so well as my present occupation," he wrote on June 17 to his wife Sallie, "and I do sincerely regret that I never had a military education. . . . I cannot think for one moment of returning home from the field until this war is ended—I have my heart and soul in it and <u>will</u> keep the 4th Regt. in the field though many stay at home."[58]

By June 24, 1861, the 4th PVI was ordered forward to Alexandria, Virginia. Nearby, the regiment first came under fire with a brief skirmish with the enemy on June 30. This minor engagement, which ended with two members of the 4th wounded, one mortally, and one Confederate killed and several wounded, was the first clash of arms experienced by Pennsylvania troops in the Civil War.

On July 20, the day before the First Battle of Bull Run, the 4th PVI's enlistment expired, and the soldiers, except for four men, refused to stay longer than their enlistments required, despite Hartranft's pleas. They were authorized to leave the front by Brigadier General Irvin McDowell, although he also tried to persuade them to remain and fight. Nevertheless, they headed back toward Harrisburg and were discharged on the morning of July 21. Terribly embarrassed by his

Twenty-six-year-old Hartranft (seated, far left) was a member of William Maffet's Survey Corps in 1856.

regiment's decision to leave the front, Hartranft resolved to remain and fight. He offered his services to Brigadier General McDowell and was quickly assigned to Colonel William B. Franklin's staff. He distinguished himself at the First Battle of Bull Run by rallying confused and disorganized Union troops for a rear guard stand, while most of the Army of Northeastern Virginia was in full retreat back toward Washington, D.C., Colonel Franklin later wrote about Hartranft's actions that day, "Colonel Hartranft, of the Fourth Pennsylvania Regiment, whose regiment refused to march forward that morning, accompanied me to the field as aide-de-camp. His services were exceedingly valuable to me, and he distinguished himself in his attempts to rally the regiments which had been thrown into confusion."[59] The 4th PVI's refusal to fight followed Hartranft throughout his military career, slowing his advancement at times along the way, such as when Major General Ambrose E. Burnside recommended him for promotion to brigadier general, on at least three separate occasions between September 25, 1862, and June 16, 1863, without success. His personal gallantry in action, however, was recognized on August 26, 1886, when he received the Medal of Honor for his actions at the First Battle of Bull Run. He is Pennsylvania's only governor to ever earn the nation's highest military award.

Hartranft was mustered out of service as colonel of the 4th PVI on July 27, 1861. He organized a new volunteer regiment, the 51st Pennsylvania Volunteer Infantry (PVI) Regiment, from July 27 until mid-November. He received his commission as colonel of the 51st on November 16, to be effective from July 27. The majority of companies in this regiment were from Montgomery County and a number of the men from the former 4th PVI. Hartranft and the 51st PVI left Camp Curtin on November 18, for Annapolis, Maryland.

Hartranft concentrated on drilling the regiment into an effective fighting force throughout its first months of service. In February 1862, the 51st PVI and Hartranft were part of Burnside's campaign along the coast of North Carolina. Fighting in nineteen major battles as part of the 2nd

Hartranft, photographed in 1863 as colonel of the 51st PVI with a U.S. Model 1850 staff and field officers' sword presented to him in August 1861 by the citizens of his hometown of Norristown, Montgomery County, in appreciation of his military service.

Brigade, 2nd Division of the 9th Corps of the Army of the Potomac, the 51st won battle honors at Antietam and South Mountain, Maryland; New Bern and Roanoke Island, North Carolina; Campbell's Station, Tennessee; and Chantilly, Second Bull Run, Fredericksburg, and Spotsylvania, Virginia. One of Hartranft's most dramatic military moments came when he and his 51st PVI stormed across Burnside Bridge at the Battle of Antietam on September 17, 1862. Their successful taking of the bridge allowed the rest of the 9th Corps to move forward. The 51st lost nearly 25 percent of its men as casualties in the battle. Major General Ambrose Burnside recommended Hartranft for promotion to brigadier general on September 25, shortly after his heroics at Antietam. However, he would have to wait nearly twenty months until he received his first star.

Frustrated after the Battle of Fredericksburg, Hartranft wrote to his wife Sallie on December 16, 1862, "We have again passed through one of the severest fighting battles of the campaign. . . . What the army may do now is rather doubtful, I think the winter campaign is pretty well settled. Our loss in killed is 1500, wounded 6500 without gaining a point and the moral affect of a defeat to overcome. Not that I consider a defeat was actually sustained by us because we held every inch of ground we took, and our brigade with 900 men held theirs all day on Monday, But our army could not advance upon the Batteries beyond the line we occupied without losing almost all, and our Generals decided to withdraw for the present. . . . We may then go into winter quarters, as I think that to take Richmond now by this route is doubtful."[60]

On March 26, 1863, the 9th Corps was sent to Kentucky to help protect the state from guerilla raids. On June 3, the 9th Corps was ordered to Vicksburg, Mississippi, to support Major General Ulysses S. Grant's siege. Hartranft was temporarily commanding a brigade at this juncture. However, he fell ill during the Vicksburg Campaign and was incapacitated, from July through October, and sent home on leave of absence. After the fall of Vicksburg on July 4, the 9th Corps assisted in capturing Jackson, Mississippi, and the 51st PVI was the first Union unit to enter the city. On August 6, the 51st PVI was sent back to Kentucky. In the autumn of 1863, the 9th Corps moved into Tennessee, and Hartranft and his men were instrumental to the Union cause at the Battle of Campbell's Station, Tennessee, on November 16.

Although Major General Ambrose E. Burnside (1824–1881) recommended that Hartranft be promoted to brigadier general for his heroism at the Battle of Antietam, the distinction eluded him for nearly twenty months.

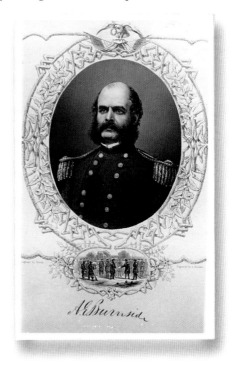

Map entitled Battle-Field of Fredericksburg, Va., *printed by B. Singerley of Harrisburg, illustrates the battlefield's topographical features as well as troop placement during the battle on December 13, 1862. (6 5/8 x 10 7/8 inches)*

A print entitled Fredericksburg *depicts Union troops attempting to cross Virginia's Rappahannock River by boats and pontoon bridges on December 11, 1862. The Battle of Fredericksburg, which lasted from December 11 through December 15, pitted General Robert E. Lee's Army of Northern Virginia against Major General Ambrose E. Burnside's Army of the Potomac.*

41

John F. Hartranft (standing, third from right) attended a reunion of the 51st Pennsylvania Volunteer Infantry and visited the regiment's monument at Burnside Bridge on the Antietam Battlefield. Two monuments honor the 51st at the Maryland battlefield, where the bloodiest one-day engagement of the Civil War resulted in twenty-three thousand casualties.

In the spring of 1864, the 9th Corps rejoined the Army of the Potomac and fought in the first two battles of Grant's Overland Campaign in May, at The Wilderness and at Spotsylvania, Virginia. At The Wilderness on May 5, Hartranft, leading the 1st Brigade of the 3rd Division of the 9th Corps, quickly discovered the difficulty and cost of maneuvering troops into position in the thick undergrowth of the area. Hartranft was promoted to brigadier general of volunteers, dating from the day he successfully led his brigade in an assault on Confederate lines at the Battle of Spotsylvania, on May 12. His brigade played an active role in the rest of the Overland Campaign, including Cold Harbor, that culminated with the start of the siege of Petersburg, Virginia.

The 9th Corps arrived on June 17 at Petersburg, where Hartranft's brigade was ordered to attack the Confederate lines. The attack failed, costing numerous Union casualties. Hartranft received his only wound of the war during this assault on Petersburg, when a minie ball clipped his wrist. Later that month, Hartranft's brigade was assigned to protect the anthracite miners of the 48th Pennsylvania Volunteers, also of the 9th Corps, who dug the tunnel and created the explosion at the Battle of the

A circa 1864 photograph of the 51st Pennsylvania Volunteer Infantry's tattered first state color evidences the many battles in which the regiment had fought in 1862–1863.

Crater, on July 30, 1864. His brigade also participated in the assault on the Confederate lines immediately after the detonation. Hartranft was stuck amid the chaos of the Union troops in the Crater after the explosion. On August 1, he wrote home to his wife about his experiences in the battle. "We lost the best opportunity of a Grand Victory on the 30th I have ever seen. . . . The Army of the Potomac stood on the hills and cooly looked upon the struggle, but not a man would they send to reinforce or secure a victory. I was in the crater when the color[ed] troops were repulsed by the enemy. All the ground then gained was lost besides many prisoners of white troops as well as blacks—my troops were then in part of the fort not blown up, where I used two brass guns against the enemy as they continued to advance, with the guns and infantry we killed and wounded nearly their entire force coming against us [about 500] we soon afterwards received the order to retire from this part of the rebel line to our original line—But before we were ready to do so they again attacked us and I gave the order to retire—But I know that we could have repulsed them again, if we had not been ordered to retire—I had two of my orderlies killed by my side in the crater—a morter shell exploded within six feet of me but not a scratch did I receive—I did not expose myself unnecessarily but I think I did my duty to the best of my understanding."[61]

On December 1, Hartranft was given command of the newly formed 3rd Division of the 9th Corps, consisting of regiments exclusively raised in the Keystone State. Despite his reputation for showing good judgment in many battles, Hartranft was not promoted to major general until after his forces crushed the last significant attack by the Confederate Army of Northern Virginia on March 25, 1865. As commander of the 3rd Division, 9th Corps, his troops recaptured Fort Stedman near Petersburg. In describing the results of this action, Hartranft reported, "at least fifteen hundred of the prisoners and all the battle flags captured, were taken by and or passed to the rear through the lines of my division. . . ."[62] He was brevetted as a major general for "conspicuous gallantry in repulsing and driving back the enemy from the lodgment on our lines at Fort Stedman, Virginia."[63] Fort Stedman is considered by most historians to be the Confederate Army of Northern Virginia's final offensive thrust of the war. Hartranft dispatched a congratulatory order to his division that day: "With feelings of pride and satisfaction the Brigadier-General Commanding tenders his congratulations to the officers and men of his command for their gallant and heroic conduct in the brilliant and triumphant achievement of today, which resulted in the recapture of Fort Stedman and the entire line together with battle flags and a large number of prisoners and small arms.

> *"—a morter shell exploded within six feet of me but not a scratch did I receive—"*

President Abraham Lincoln and Secretary of War Edwin M. Stanton signed, on May 14, 1864, the commission appointing Hartranft as Brigadier General of Volunteers. (19 3/8 x 15 5/8 inches)

Capture of the Works at Petersburg, *is a circa 1868 lithograph published by Johnson, Fry and Company, New York, after a 1864 painting by Thomas Nast (1840–1902), an illustrator whose works appeared in popular periodicals of the day. (8 1/2 x 11 inches)*

"You have won a name and reputation of which veterans might feel proud, and have proved yourselves worthy of being associates of the brave soldiers of the old Ninth Army Corps; and the General Commanding hopes that this, your first engagement and signal victory, will nerve and stimulate you for the performances of future deeds of gallantry."[64]

Hartranft and his division helped attack the Confederate lines at Petersburg on April 2, but at a heavy cost. His troops were some of the first to enter the city after the Confederates withdrew, and helped pursue General Robert E. Lee and his forces on their final retreat towards Appomattox Court House. They did not again, however, exchange fire with the enemy. The 9th was one of the first corps to return to Washington, D.C., following Lee's surrender and President Lincoln's assassination, and helped to provide security in the nation's capital during the hunt for the conspirators. The 9th Corps later marched in the Grand Review, also in Washington, D.C.

Hartranft was next assigned to the U.S. Arsenal Prison in the nation's capital and detailed to take charge of the Lincoln assassination plot conspirators. Serving as special provost marshal and military governor of the U.S. Arsenal Prison in Washington, D.C., beginning on April 29, 1865, he oversaw the imprisonment, treatment, and execution of the conspirators.

Photograph of monument commemorating Hartranft's 3rd Division, 9th Corps, at Fort Stedman, Virginia. The Commonwealth of Pennsylvania erected two monuments on the battlefield of Petersburg, Virginia, commemorating the heroism of Brigadier General Hartranft's 3rd Division, 9th Corps, at Fort Stedman and the 48th PVI at Petersburg. President William Howard Taft dedicated the monuments on May 19, 1909.

Not long after he was promoted to brevet major general, John F. Hartranft and his staff sat for a portrait in 1865 by Alexander Gardner (1821–1882), a Washington, D.C., photographer best known for his photographs of the Civil War and President Abraham Lincoln. (From left) Captain F. B. Moore, Brevet Lieutenant Colonel John D. Bertolette, Hartranft, Captain Richard A. Watts, Surgeon A. F. Whelen, and Brevet Major George Shorkley.

Major General Winfield Scott Hancock, commander of the Middle Military Division, sent a letter to Hartranft on April 29, containing twenty-eight separate rules of the prison. The first rule was Hartranft's appointment: "Bvt. Maj. Gen. J.F. Hartranft, U.S. Vols. Is hereby appointed Military Governor of the Military Prison at the U.S. Arsenal, Washington, D.C., and Commander of the troops assembled for its defense. He will select two field officers to assist him in his duties and will report their names to these Headquarters."[65] The remaining twenty-seven points consisted of various rules regarding the duties and conduct of the soldiers detailed to provide security both inside and outside of the prison, prohibitions in the prison, medical inspections, and provisions which could be supplied to the prisoners.

On April 30, Hartranft received an order from the secretary of war, Edwin M. Stanton: "You will receive from Colonel [Lafayette C.] Baker, Mrs. Mary E. Suratt, a prisoner implicated in the murder of the late President Mr. Lincoln and keep her safely in the Military prison now under your command, to abide further orders from this department."[66] On May 1, Hartranft began reporting at least daily to his superior officer, Major General Hancock, regarding the state of the prisoners, the food they were served, their visitors, their accommodations, the logistics of their presence at their trial, and the execution of their respective sentences.[67]

Hancock, also a native Pennsylvanian, from Montgomery County, serving as commander of the Middle Military Division (including Washington, D.C.), sent Hartranft the order to execute

Carte de visite of Major General Winfield Scott Hancock (1824–1886). Born in Montgomery Square, just northwest of Philadelphia, Hancock, as commander of the Middle Military Division, including Washington, D.C., supervised Hartranft's handling of the Lincoln assassination conspirators.

On April 30, 1865, just two weeks after President Lincoln was assassinated, Brigadier General James A. Hardie, by order of Secretary of War Edwin M. Stanton, instructed (top) Hartranft to take responsibility for Mary E. Surratt, one of the assassination plot conspirators. Stanton (left) signed a pass (above) on June 18, 1865, allowing Dr. John Purdue Gray (1825–1886), one of the foremost forensic psychiatrists of the latter half of the nineteenth century, to examine all the prisoners implicated in the conspiracy. Dr. Gray's renown stemmed from his involvement in murder cases, where the mental stability of the defendants was disputed.

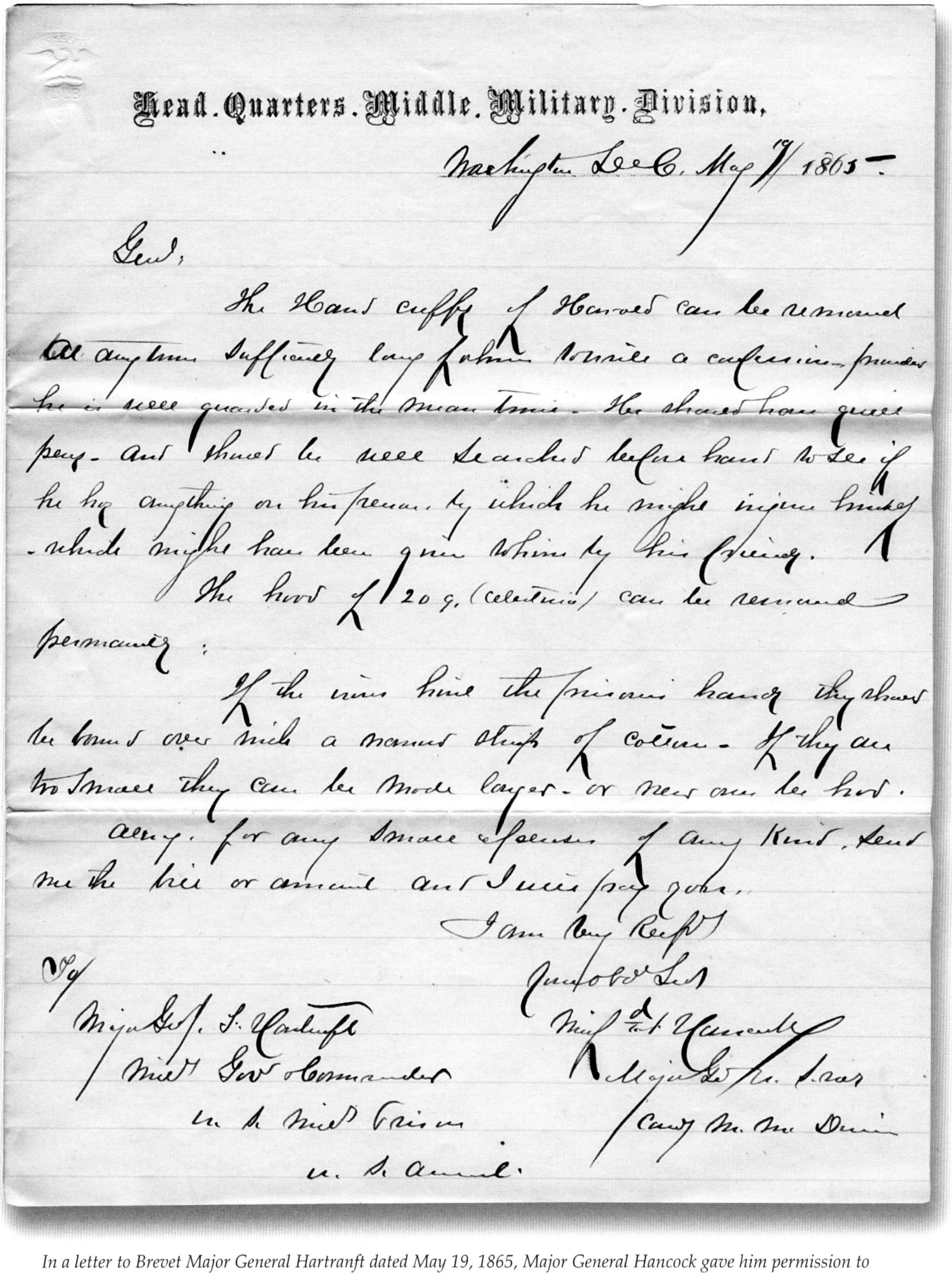

𝕳𝖊𝖆𝖉.𝕼𝖚𝖆𝖗𝖙𝖊𝖗𝖘.𝕸𝖎𝖉𝖉𝖑𝖊.𝕸𝖎𝖑𝖎𝖙𝖆𝖗𝖞.𝕯𝖎𝖛𝖎𝖘𝖎𝖔𝖓,

Washington D.C. May 19/ 1865 —

Genl,

The Hand cuffs of Harold can be removed at anytime sufficiently long for him to make a confession — provided he is well guarded in the mean time. He should have a steel pen — and should be well searched before hand to see if he has anything on his person, by which he might injure himself — which might have been given to him by his friends.

The hood of [No. 20 g. (celestine) can be removed permanently.

If the irons hurt the prisoner's hands they should be bound over with a narrow strip of cotton. If they are too small they can be made larger — or new ones be had.

Any. for any small expenses of any kind, send me the bill or amount and I will pay you.

I am very Respt
your obdt Svt
Winfield S. Hancock
Major Genl U.S.A.
Comdg M. M. Divn

Oy

Major Genl J. F. Hartranft
Milit Govr & Commander
in the Milit Prison
U. S. Arsenal.

In a letter to Brevet Major General Hartranft dated May 19, 1865, Major General Hancock gave him permission to remove David E. Herold's handcuffs long enough for him to write a confession. Hancock also advised Hartranft that the hood of one prisoner could be removed, and that the prisoners' iron handcuffs could be replaced with larger pairs if they were too small and inflicting pain.

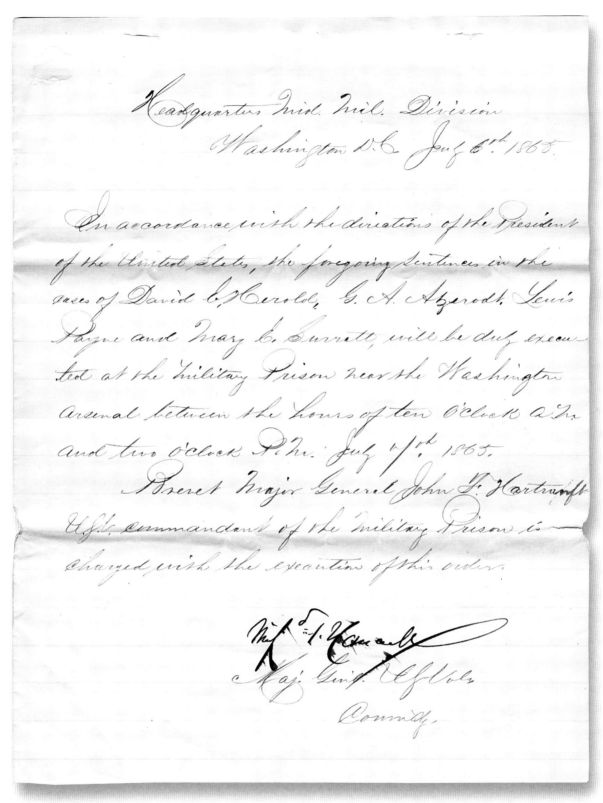

The order issued by Major General Winfield Scott Hancock, dated July 6, 1865, instructing Brevet Major General Hartranft to execute four of the prisoners who had been found guilty by a military commission of conspiring to assassinate President Lincoln. Hartranft oversaw the hanging of Mary E. Surratt, Lewis Powell (also known as Lewis Payne), David E. Herold, and George A. Atzerodt in Washington, D.C., on July 7, 1865. Surratt was the first woman in American history to be executed by the federal government.

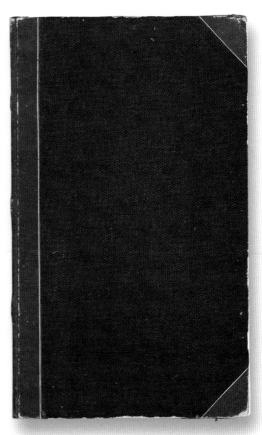

Washington, D.C., photographer Alexander Gardner recorded for posterity the hanging of the Lincoln conspirators (above) with a series of images. The accused were seated in chairs on the platform of the gallows while Brevet Major General Hartranft read their death warrant.

Brevet Major General John Frederick Hartranft's letter book (right) which contains record copies of letters sent from his headquarters at the military prison at the U.S. Arsenal, Washington, D.C., dated April 30 to July 19, 1865. (13 ⁵/₈ x 8 ¹/₂ x ¹¹/₁₆ inches)

For the hanging of (from left) Mary E. Surratt, Lewis Powell (Lewis Payne), David E. Herold, and George A. Atzerodt, on July 7, 1865, at 1:30 p.m., a large number of soldiers guarded the courtyard of the U.S. Arsenal Prison for fear that former Confederates or Southern sympathizers would attempt to rescue the condemned prisoners. (6 ⁷/₈ x 8 ⁷/₈ inches)

Alexander Gardner's photograph, "Major General Hartranft and Staff in Charge of the Conspirators," dated July 1865, was taken at the U.S. Arsenal Prison in Washington, D.C. Standing (from left): Lieutenant Colonel George W. Frederick, Second Lieutenant David H. Geissinger, and Surgeon George L. Porter; seated (from left): Captain Richard A. Watts, Lieutenant Colonel William H. H. McCall, Brevet Major General John F. Hartranft, Colonel Levi A. Dodd, and Captain Christian Rath. The four seated officers flanking Hartranft are posed in chairs used by the prisoners on the scaffold just before their execution.

four of the conspirators, "In accordance with the directions of the President of the United States, the foregoing sentences, in the cases of David E. Herold, G.A. Atzerodt, Lewis Payne, and Mary E. Surratt, will be duly executed at the Military Prison near the Washington Arsenal, between the hours of 10 o'clock A.M. and two o'clock P.M. July 7, 1865. Brevet Major General John F. Hartranft, USV. Commandant of the Military Prison is charged with the execution of this order."[68]

Hartranft read the charges, verdicts, and death orders to the condemned prisoners from the gallows platform before their hanging on July 7. His report to Hancock following the execution included revealing passages, such as "on July 6, 1865 between the hours of 11 A.M. and 12 M, read the 'Findings & sentences' of Lewis Payne, G.A. Atzerott, David E. Herold and Mary E. Surratt to each of them and also delivered a copy of the same to each. . . . The scaffold was erected by workmen furnished by Major Benton under the direction of Capt. C. Rath one of my staff officers, who also took charge of the details during the execution. . . . Every thing being in readiness at 1 P.M. 7th inst., the prisoners were conducted to the scaffold in the following order 1st Mary E. Surratt her guard and Father's Walter & Niger—2nd G.A. Atzerodt his guard and Rev. Mr. Busler—3rd David E. Herold his guard and Rev. Mr. Olds—4th Lewis Payne his guard and Rev. Dr. Gillette, each of the prisoners was seated in a chair on the platform while the ministers in attendance offered a prayer in their behalf. The prisoners were made to stand and everything in readiness the drop fell at 1:30 P.M. Life was pronounced by the board of surgeons appointed for that purpose to be extinct in each of the bodies at 1:50 P.M. The report of this board is forwarded herewith.

"About 9 o'clock A.M. Brig. Gen'l. C.H. Morgan reported with a brigade of infantry for duty during the execution. Gen'l Morgan was very efficient in the disposition of troops and maintained perfect order at all points."[69] The troops selected for guard duty on the day of the execution were supplied with forty rounds of cartridges. There was genuine concern on the part of the authorities that an escape or rescue attempt might be made for the condemned prisoners by Confederate sympathizers or former Confederate soldiers. After the execution, the gallows ropes were cut into souvenirs and Hartranft received four pieces.

Pennsylvania, ss:

Jno. W. Geary

IN THE NAME AND BY THE AUTHORITY OF THE

Commonwealth of Pennsylvania

JOHN W. GEARY,

GOVERNOR OF THE SAID COMMONWEALTH.

To all to whom these Presents shall Come,

SENDS GREETING:

Know Ye, That *John F Hartranft*

of the *County of Montgomery* having been duly appointed by me, the said JOHN W. GEARY,

by and with the advice and consent of the Senate of Pennsylvania,

MAJOR GENERAL

of the National Guard of Pennsylvania, in the *Second* Division, composed of the Uniformed Militia

of the Counties of *Bucks Montgomery and Delaware*

I do Commission Him to Rank as such from the *Second* day of *September* Anno Domini

one thousand eight hundred and *Seventy*

He is, Therefore, Carefully and diligently to discharge the duty of **Major General** of the *Second* Division,

by doing and performing all manner of things thereunto properly belonging. **This Commission** to continue in force for the term of five years, unless

the same shall be otherwise lawfully determined and annulled.

Given under my Hand and the Great Seal of the State, at Harrisburg, this *Twenty-fourth* day of *March*

in the year of our Lord one thousand eight hundred and *Seventy-one* and of the Commonwealth the *Ninety-fifth*

By the Governor:

F. Jordan

Secretary of the Commonwealth.

Governor John White Geary signed the commission appointing John F. Hartranft Major General of the 2ⁿᵈ Division of the National Guard of Pennsylvania. Geary, like Hartranft, was a staunch post-war Republican and had served as a brevet major general during the Civil War. The 2ⁿᵈ Division was made up of the uniformed militia of Bucks, Montgomery, and Delaware counties. Although Hartranft was appointed Major General of the 2ⁿᵈ Division on September 2, 1870, Geary did not sign the official commission for this appointment until March 24, 1871. (16 ³/₄ x 16 inches)

A circa 1872 paper campaign advertisement (left) reminded voters that Major General Hartranft possessed experience as a high-ranking military officer during one of the most turbulent eras in the history of the United States.

Campaign medal, circa 1872 or 1875, for one of Hartranft's gubernatorial campaigns touts him as "The Hero of Fort Steadman" for his leadership in defeating the Army of Northern Virginia's last offensive thrust of the war at Petersburg, Virginia, on March 25, 1865. Civil War veterans seeking political offices relied on capturing the votes of former soldiers.

After discharging this responsibility, Hartranft was relieved of the duty as commander of Washington's U.S. Arsenal Prison twelve days later, on July 19, 1865. Shortly thereafter, he was ordered to Kentucky to serve on a military commission to try Confederate guerrillas. He was given the opportunity to stay on in the regular army with the rank of colonel, on August 29, but declined and returned home to his wife and children. On January 15, 1866, Hartranft was mustered out of military service in Philadelphia.

Following the Civil War, Hartranft returned to Pennsylvania, changed his political party affiliation from Democrat to Republican, and served two terms, from 1866 to 1872, as the Commonwealth's auditor general. He was also an officer in the 2nd Division of the Pennsylvania Militia. He was appointed by Governor John White Geary to be major general of the 2nd Division of the National Guard of Pennsylvania on September 2, 1870.

After six years as state auditor general, Hartranft sought the governorship in 1872. With the support of Simon Cameron, he succeeded Geary as governor, defeating Democrat Charles B. Buckalew by 35,627 out of 672,416 votes cast.

In his 1873 inaugural address, Hartranft addressed several issues directly stemming from the war which were dear to his heart—and none more so than providing for orphaned children. "No part of our system of education has secured so universal commendation as that which is embraced in the circle of instruction of those who were made orphans by the casualties of war. The helpless condition of these little ones touchingly appealed to the hearts of our people, and the response was the establishment of the orphans' schools that are now the pride of our State. But in rescuing these children from destitution, and providing for their education until they have attained the age of sixteen years, have we filled the measure of our duty to them?

"Thrown out into the world to do battle with life's trials at an age peculiarly dangerous to youth, does not common humanity require that the State should maintain its guardianship of these children until their habits are somewhat settled, and they have acquired the ability to earn their own livelihood?"[70] He also called for the creation of industrial schools and a stronger state militia system emphasizing, "It is highly important that in times of insurrection and riot there should be at command a good and efficient force of militia to assist the civil power to protect property and maintain its authority."[71]

In his annual message to the General Assembly of Pennsylvania on January 6, 1875, Hartranft again addressed the issue of soldiers' orphan schools. "No object should make a more successful appeal to our consideration, than the condition of these unfortunate children, whose future will be shaped and usefulness largely determined by the instruction they receive from the State. A number of these orphans, distinguished by good conduct and mental

Republican John Frederick Hartranft served two consecutive three-year terms as governor of Pennsylvania, from 1873 to 1879. He was the Keystone State's only governor to be awarded the Medal of Honor, for actions during the Civil War.

qualities that adapted them to the calling of teachers, have been transferred upon expiration of their terms, from Orphan to Normal schools of the State, where they are being fitted for that useful occupation. What the State should do to obtain employment or a means of livelihood for the residue of these children who are in need of assistance, is a matter, I feel assured, you will not think unworthy of attention."[72]

Hartranft won reelection in 1875 to a second term as governor by a narrow margin of twelve thousand votes, over Democrat Cyrus L. Pershing. While seeking reelection, he was also the National Commander of the Grand Army of the Republic (GAR), from 1875 to 1876. He was the fifth national commander of that Civil War veterans' organization and the first from Pennsylvania. He was active in a number of other veterans' groups following the war, including the Society of the Army of the Potomac, the Military Order of the Loyal Legion of the United States, and the Veterans' Club of Philadelphia.

With the country mired in a deep financial depression from the Panic of 1873, which lasted until 1879, Hartranft's administration was marred by labor strikes and violence. Beginning in the spring of 1874, he dispatched National Guard of Pennsylvania troops to various counties to quell riots and strikes wracking railroads and mining. In his 1875 annual message to the general assembly, he spoke out about lawlessness and the proper use of the National Guard. "The people of free governments are always unwilling to contribute largely to the maintenance of armies, and are ever jealous of military power, but experience has likewise demonstrated how impolitic and unsafe it is for a State to have no disciplined or efficient force strong enough to compel obedience to its authority, when the law and its officers are condemned and opposed with violence by large bodies of men. Pennsylvania has, at times, been constrained to the painful necessity of employing troops to enforce compliance with law and wisdom of providing like contingencies can no longer be doubted. Men smarting under a sense of wrong, or corporations in pursuit of what they conceive to be their rights sometimes seek their remedy through violence and in disregard for the law and its process. No government can tolerate this mode of redress and exist. The supremacy of the law must be unquestioned and justice obtained through the proper and established channels in the manner prescribed by the people themselves. Bodies of men or corporations have no more constitutional rights than individuals, and they cannot be permitted to use their aggregate strength to procure what is denied to the individual, and what through weakness he could not obtain. All alike must resort to the law and abide by its decrees, and if there are any who refuse and seek to accomplish their ends in an illegal way, the Executive power must enforce obedience to authority without fear or favor, and for this purpose the Constitution wisely provides a body of citizen soldiery. But if there are grave emergencies when it becomes necessary to use troops to secure peace and respect for law, it certainly never was intended that the National Guard should constitute a State police force to perform the duties imposed upon the local civil authorities, and that upon every breach of order its aid could be invoked to suppress the affray.

"In no event and under no circumstances should a military force be used until the power of the civil authorities is exhausted and the outbreak assumes proportions of such magnitude that these officers would be powerless to overcome it."[73]

Miners struck in northeastern Pennsylvania's anthracite region and nearly two dozen Molly Maguires, an alleged secret society of Irish mine workers, were hanged for their crimes, including leader John "Black Jack" Kehoe. Kehoe, tried in 1877 for the murder of Frank W. Langdon, was found guilty and sentenced to death. Kehoe appealed to Hartranft for a pardon, but the Board of Pardons did not convene, and on December 18, 1878, he was hanged at Pottsville, Schuylkill County. The executions signalled an end to the Molly Maguires.

Molly Maguire (circa 2005–2006), a plaster cast sculpture by Philadelphia-based artist Zenos Frudakis (1951–). The subject is a bound and hooded man awaiting execution by hanging and represents the twenty anthracite miners found guilty of acts of violence and hanged in Pottsville, Schuylkill County, and Mauch Chunk (now Jim Thorpe), Carbon County, between 1877 and 1879. The men were believed to be members of the Molly Maguires, an alleged secret society that terrorized mine officials. A bronze version of the sculpture has been installed in the Molly Maguire Historical Park in Mahanoy City, Schuylkill County. (80 x 30 x 27 inches)

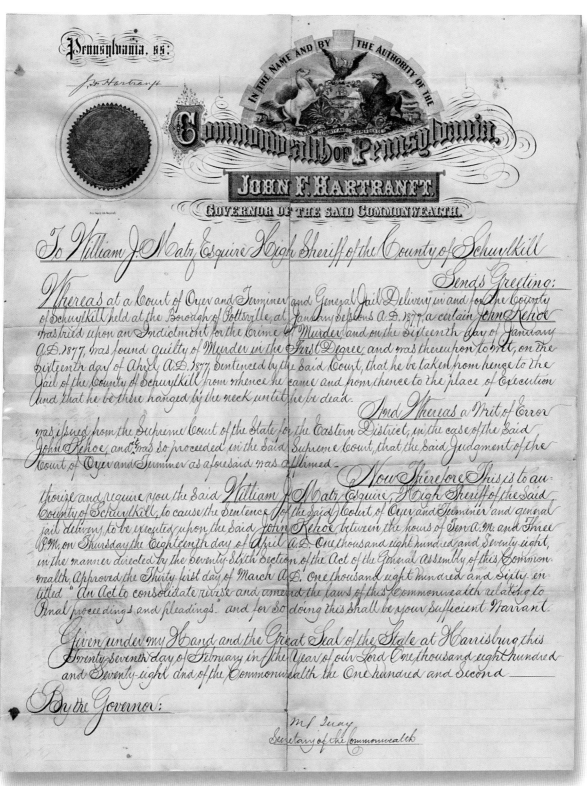

On February 27, 1878, Governor Hartranft and Secretary of the Commonwealth Matthew S. Quay signed a death warrant for John "Black Jack" Kehoe, of Girardville, Schuylkill County. Kehoe, reputedly a leader of the Molly Maguires, an alleged secret society of Irish coal miners in northeastern Pennsylvania, was found guilty of the murder of mine foreman Frank W. Langdon. Kehoe appealed the verdict and asked for clemency. The Board of Pardons refused to convene to consider the appeal, and Hartranft had no choice but to set the date for the execution. Kehoe was hanged on December 18, 1878, in the Schuylkill County seat of Pottsville. (23 x 17 ⁷/₈ inches)

Governor Hartranft (fourth from left), in civilian clothes, with officers at an encampment circa 1873–1879, took great pride in his military career.

At the Republican National Convention in Cincinnati in June 1876, Hartranft was nominated as a "favorite son" candidate for president. His candidacy was promoted by Simon Cameron in an effort to thwart President Grant from gaining support for a third term, and to stop Cameron's hated rival, Senator James G. Blaine of Maine, also a Pennsylvania native, from gaining the nomination. Cameron's plan succeeded and delegates compromised on an independent Republican and former Civil War brevet major general, Governor Rutherford B. Hayes of Ohio, who won the nomination. Hartranft was not enthused about being promoted as a presidential candidate and did little to secure the selection, although his name had been floated as a candidate in several newspapers as early as February of that year. One of his early supporters for the presidential nomination was Henry Martyn Hoyt, who later served as governor of Pennsylvania. It had been widely reported before the convention that Cameron had negotiated with U.S. Senator Roscoe Conkling to transfer all of Pennsylvania's fifty-eight delegates to Conkling after the first vote at the convention. However, that did not transpire. Through seven ballots, Conkling never received a single delegate vote from Pennsylvania. Hartranft hit his high point of delegates on the fourth ballot, with seventy-one votes, but never seriously challenged for ultimate victory.[74] Hayes won the nomination on the seventh ballot.

During the Railroad Strike of 1877, rioting in Pittsburgh erupted on July 19 and resulted in numerous deaths and millions of dollars in property damage. Governor Hartranft responded by calling out the National Guard of Pennsylvania in addition to requesting federal forces. At the outbreak of the riots, which also occurred to lesser extents in Harrisburg, Philadelphia, Scranton, and Reading, Hartranft was on a train bound for the Pacific Coast. On July 21, Secretary of the Commonwealth Matthew S. Quay sent him a troubling missive. "A collision has occurred here between the strikers and the troops. Number of persons have been killed and wounded. Intense excitement prevails in city [Pittsburgh] and there are indications of further bloodshed and that the trouble will be widespread and protracted. I suggest that you return allowing your party to go forward."[75]

On the following day, as reports indicated that mobs had taken over railroad yards in Harrisburg and Philadelphia, Hartranft changed his travel plans and hurriedly returned to Pennsylvania. He arrived in the Commonwealth on July 24 and issued an order from Pittsburgh: "All other means of quelling riots and restoring order having first been exhausted, the officer commanding the troops shall notify the rioters that they will be fired upon unless they promptly disperse. The order to fire will then be deliberately given, and every soldier will be expected to fire with effect. The firing will continue until the mob disappears."[76] This order came after the firing by troops into the mob at Pittsburgh on July 20 and into an unarmed crowd in Reading on July 23, 1877.

Hartranft traveled on to Philadelphia and gathered four thousand militiamen and six hundred regular army troops from Major General Winfield Scott Hancock's command. He had them board a heavily guarded train that set off for Pittsburgh on July 26. Under Hartranft's personal command, the force restored order and once again made the railroad operable. The strike and the resulting riots caused the destruction of more property than all of the losses that the Commonwealth suffered during three Confederate invasions of the state during the Civil War.[77] The entire affair made Hartranft painfully aware of the inadequacies of the Commonwealth's militia system. That year, he began petitioning the state legislature to overhaul its structure. On June 12, the legislature passed an act that reorganized the militia system into the National Guard of Pennsylvania, with only one division comprised of five brigades.

Because of the changes made to the Pennsylvania Constitution of 1874, Hartranft was the last governor eligible to serve two consecutive three-year terms. The revised constitution increased the term of the office from three to four years and prohibited an incumbent governor from being eligible to seek a succeeding term. This did not affect Hartranft's ability to seek a second term, however, nor did it change the length of his second term. Succeeding oneself as governor of Pennsylvania was prohibited after Hartranft's second term, and it remained law until Pennsylvania's Constitution of 1968 took effect. The 1968 Constitution permits governors to serve two consecutive four-year terms.

After completing his second term, Hartranft was appointed by Governor Henry Martyn Hoyt as major general and division commander of the National Guard of Pennsylvania. As the first commander of the reorganized National Guard, appointed on January 23, 1879, he was sworn in on March 3. Because of his role in restructuring it, Hartranft is widely considered to be the father of the modern Pennsylvania National Guard. Even as governor, he devoted much time to it, frequently visiting armories and encampments.

Hartranft led the National Guard of Pennsylvania at the inaugural processions of Presidents James Garfield in 1881, Grover Cleveland in 1885, and Benjamin Harrison in 1889. Commanding General of the United States Army William Tecumseh Sherman was grand marshal of the 1881 inaugural parade and wrote to compliment Hartranft shortly after the event, "I beg to add my own professional admiration of the bearing and soldierly behavior of your entire command on Inauguration day—for I watched them closely as they passed in Review—on Massachusetts Avenue and I have no hesitation in saying that a finer body of men was never seen by me."[78] Appointed first by fellow Republican and friend Governor Hoyt, Hartranft was so well respected for his role in the National Guard that Democratic Governor Robert E. Pattison re-appointed him major general in October 1883.

As major general of the National Guard of Pennsylvania, Hartranft had the pleasure of inviting and welcoming Lieutenant General Philip H. Sheridan to the guard's annual encampment twice, once in August 1884 and the second time on August 12, 1887. The 1887 invitation involved two other individuals who served as Pennsylvania's chief executive: Governor James Addams Beaver and General Daniel Hartman Hastings, then adjutant general of Pennsylvania. Over the years, Hartranft also invited several former Confederate officers to visit National Guard encampments. One invitee was former Confederate Major General Fitzhugh Lee, a nephew of Robert E. Lee, whom Hartranft invited to camp in Gettysburg, in August 1884. Lee, who had led a brigade of Confederate cavalry at the Battle of Gettysburg, replied facetiously to Hartranft. "Twenty one years ago I went on horseback, at the invitation of an uncle of mine & to be frank I did not enjoy myself," Lee wrote. "Indeed there was so much mire and confusion that a man's life was really not safe. I did not stay long. The weather was very hot and so was the reception by Gen Meade & others whom we had tried to entertain in Virginia. My first and last visit to Gettysburg produced an impression. I spend my 4th of Julys now in Virginia. All of that happened so many years ago, however. A noticeable improvement in the surroundings has probably taken place since. I would like to see Gettysburg without its war paint."[79] Two previous commitments prevented him from accepting Hartranft's invitation, however.

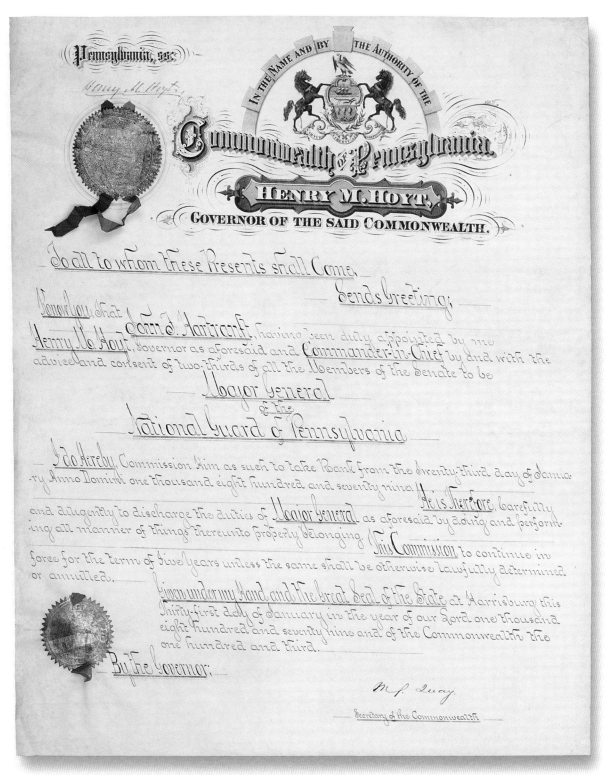

Hartranft's commission as Major General of the National Guard of Pennsylvania was signed on January 31, 1879, by Governor Henry Martyn Hoyt and Secretary of the Commonwealth Matthew S. Quay. The commission, which made Hartranft the commanding officer of the National Guard, was given to him shortly after his second term as governor had expired. Like Hartranft, Governor Hoyt was a Civil War veteran and a fellow Republican. (22³/₈ x 18³/₈ inches)

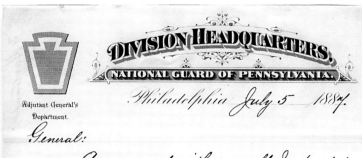

DIVISION HEADQUARTERS,
NATIONAL GUARD OF PENNSYLVANIA.

Adjutant General's
Department.

Philadelphia July 5 1887

General:

As arranged with yourself, I extended to Lt. Gen. P.H. Sheridan an invitation to review the division of the National Guard of Pennsylvania during the coming annual Encampment. The enclosed copies of his answers will convey to you the gratifying information of his acceptance.

The day fixed upon is Friday, Aug 12ᵗʰ.

I have to request that you will make the necessary arrangements for the transportation of the General and his party from Washington City to the Encampment.

Yours Very Respectfully

J.F. Hartranft

To Brig Gen D.H. Hastings,
Adj. Gen. of Pa.
2 Enclosures
Harrisburg, Pa.

In his letter of July 5, 1887, to Adjutant General of Pennsylvania Daniel Hartman Hastings, Hartranft expressed his satisfaction that Lieutenant General Philip H. Sheridan (1831–1888) had accepted an invitation to visit the National Guard of Pennsylvania's annual encampment on August 12. Not only was Sheridan a Civil War hero, but he was also the Commanding General of the United States Army at the time of the invitation.

that to the best of my ... will support and defend the Constitution of the United States and of the Commonwealth of Pennsylvania against all enemies, foreign and domestic; and that I will well and faithfully discharge the duties of the office on which I am about to enter. **So Help Me God.**

Sworn and subscribed this *Third* day of *March* A. D. 1879 before me.

J.F. Hartranft

James W. Latta.
Adjt. Genl. Of Pa.

Hartranft's Oath of Allegiance for service in the National Guard of Pennsylvania, signed and dated March 3, 1879.

Major General John F. Hartranft (seated) and staff at a National Guard of Pennsylvania encampment in Philadelphia's expansive Fairmount Park, circa 1879.

Major General of the National Guard of Pennsylvania John F. Hartranft (front row, center) and Lieutenant General Commanding the United States Army Philip H. Sheridan (front row, right) attended the National Guard's encampment at Gettysburg, August 2–9, 1884. Sheridan also visited the National Guard's encampment at Mount Gretna, Lebanon County, on August 12, 1887.

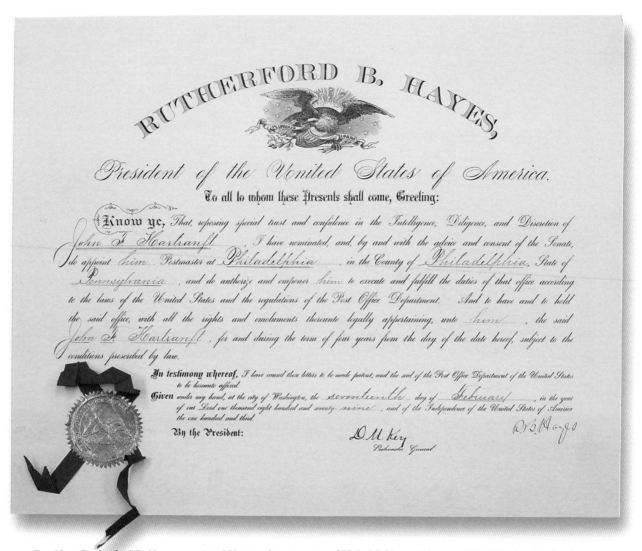

President Rutherford B. Hayes appointed Hartranft postmaster of Philadelphia on February 17, 1879, shortly after he finished his second term as governor. President Hayes, like Hartranft, was a Republican and former Civil War officer. (13 3/4 x 16 3/4 inches)

After his second term as governor ended, Hartranft moved to Philadelphia. He was appointed postmaster of Philadelphia on February 17, 1879, and later collector of the Philadelphia port from June 17, 1880, to July 30, 1885. He was also for a time the president of the board of trustees of the University of Pennsylvania. He received the Medal of Honor on August 26, 1886, for his actions at the First Battle of Bull Run. In 1888, he was appointed manager of the National Home for Disabled Volunteer Soldiers. He was so popular in post-war Pennsylvania that the Bank of Montgomery County, headquartered in Norristown, pictured him on its currency (along with three other Union officers, including Major General Winfield Scott Hancock), and a Harrisburg cigar manufacturer, C. E. Bair and Sons, named a cigar after him and adorned the box with his portrait.

Hartranft entered into a number of business ventures in his post-gubernatorial years, including serving as president of the Commercial Mutual Accident Insurance Company, the Pennsylvania Boiler Insurance Company, the Lynchburg Manufacturing and Mining Company, and the Quinnimont Coal and Iron Company. None of these companies made Hartranft much money and in the case of the Lynchburg company, he lost money when the firm declared bankruptcy.[80]

Major General Hartranft in full uniform with sash and five medals, including the Medal of Honor, circa 1886–1887. Hartranft received the Medal of Honor for his bravery during the First Battle of Bull Run, July 21, 1861, where he voluntarily served as an aide after his term of service had expired and rallied several Union regiments that had been thrown into confusion.

One of his many activities with veterans' organizations came in support of creating homes for poor Confederate soldiers. "The movement to establish homes in the South for destitute and disabled Confederate veterans meet[s] my hearty approval," he announced in March 1889. "After every battlefield in the war, the gallant and generous foemen, vied with each other in relieving the suffering and the wounded. There are no longer foes but fellow countrymen. I do not see that the lapse of 25 years makes any difference in the principles or the obligation. I shall rejoice to do all in my power to aide the southern people in binding up their wounds and moving from the land every cause for a single bitter recollection of the contest which, will not have left us 'a more perfect union.'"[81]

On October 17, 1889, at the age of fifty-eight, Hartranft died of Bright's Disease, a form of kidney disease he had suffered since at least 1873, while still in command of the National Guard of Pennsylvania.[82] Governor James Addams Beaver commented on Hartranft's health in a letter dated January 20, 1890, stating, "his health was broken, and his very death hastened by chronic diarrhea which he contracted in the service, and which troubled him more or less during his subsequent life. . . ."[83] Governor Beaver also issued the following proclamation in part, "The calm courage, the quiet devotion, the intrepid zeal and the lofty patriotism which characterized his military service and won for him the success which crowned his efforts are known and appreciated by all who have given heed to the history of the stirring times during which his service was rendered."[84] Even in death, it was more important to many people that Hartranft be remembered as a general rather than as a governor.

The soldiers of the National Guard of Pennsylvania contributed to a fund for an obelisk at Hartranft's grave site in Norristown's Montgomery Cemetery, which they dedicated on June 6, 1891.[85] Pennsylvania honored Hartranft by installing an equestrian statue of him in front of the State Capitol. The Commonwealth commissioned New York sculptor F. W. Ruckstuhl to create the statue, costing eighteen thousand dollars. Unveiled on May 12, 1899, it had been placed in front of the building in November 1898, but the outbreak of the Spanish-American War delayed its unveiling. Hartranft is the only governor to be so honored at the State Capitol.

Circa 1889 memorial, or mourning, ribbon for Hartranft, who was remembered more as a general than anything else, including being a two-term governor.

IN MEMORIAM

MAJOR GENERAL
JOHN F. HARTRANFT

BORN
December 16, 1830.

DIED
October 17th, 1889.

A photograph entitled "Gen. John F. Hartranft—Members of his Staff During The War—At the Reunion, April 2d, 1888," records an event that was important to Civil War officers and enlisted men through the first third of the twentieth century. Hartranft (front row, center) was joined by fourteen members of his 3rd Division, 9th Corps, staff for the reunion.

The twenty-fifth anniversary of the Battle of Fort Stedman was celebrated by the 3rd Division, 9th Corps, in Harrisburg on March 25, 1890. Even though Hartranft died in October 1889, he was fondly remembered by his troops on this broadside. Dignitaries who attended the reunion included President Benjamin Harrison, Governor James Addams Beaver, as well as a former governor, Andrew Gregg Curtin, and a future governor, Daniel Hartman Hastings. This clearly demonstrates the political power wielded by veterans' groups in the late nineteenth century. (25 1/2 x 19 1/4 inches)

RE-UNION.

Maj. Gen. John F. Hartranft's
DIVISION, 9th ARMY CORPS.

MARCH 25TH, HARRISBURG, PA.

A Reunion of the Third Division, Ninth Army Corps, will meet to celebrate the 25th Anniversary of the Battle of Ft. Stedman. Come on Boys, we will tell again the Story of our Valor.

President Harrison, Gen. Parke, Gov. James A. Beaver, Gen. J. P. S. Gobin, Ex-Gov. A. G. Curtin, Col. C. W. Hazzard, Hon. Thos. J. Stewart, Capt. Geo. W. Skinner, and D. H. Hastings, Adjt. Gen. of Penn'a, will be with us.

Come, Boys, and make it the largest gathering of our old Division that will ever be held on this side of the river. Come, and bring your comrades. Our invited guest, Maj. Hodgkins, of Boston, Mass., will tell again the story of our valor.

The Legislature of Pa. has granted us the use of the Capitol for our Business meeting. A Grand Old Camp-Fire will be held in the Opera House at night.

Excursion Rates have been made with all railroads to Harrisburg. Hotel rates have been reduced and ample arrangements and accommodations made for all.

By order of Committee of Arrangements   For further information, address

Col. George W. Frederick, Pres. of Div., Philadelpha, Pa.; M. A. Embick, Sec'y, Boiling Springs, Cumberland co., Pa.; E. M. Bishop, Treas., Harrisburg, Pa.; V. H. Moore, Chairman Ex. Committee, Harrisburg.

Even before the statue's delivery, the site of its installation had become a point of contention, however, "As for the change of site I trust you will do all in your power to prevent any change," Ruckstuhl wrote to Governor Daniel H. Hastings on April 26, 1898. "The statue was made for that place—I contracted for that place—and my indifference to the low price to be paid was largely due to the fact that the statue was to occupy that place. The architect can, and ought to be made to so design his building front and approaches that they will harmonize with the monument when in place. I shall never consent to recommend a change of site."[86]

Governor William A. Stone, three thousand Union veterans, and a number of Hartranft's relatives attended the unveiling ceremony. One of the speakers was Confederate officer Henry Kyd Douglas, leader of the first brigade of General Gordon's corps at the struggle for Fort Stedman, the last offensive thrust of the Army of Northern Virginia which Hartranft had stopped and successfully counterattacked. Douglas cited Hartranft's humane treatment of the Lincoln assassination conspirators while he served as their jailor. He also noted that Hartranft had helped him secure funds to remove Confederate dead that fell on Pennsylvania soil during the Gettysburg Campaign. He described Hartranft as "a man of sound judgment and of the most uncompromising honesty; modest, retiring, diffident, and reticent. He knew his own counsel and kept it. He was true to his friends and to his word of honor. He was never known to desert a friend for any purpose on earth, in adversity or in trouble. He was silent, heroic and manly. At a time when it would have been easy for him as for others to enrich himself from the public treasury, his hands remained pure and clean."[87]

Hartranft's gravesite and memorial obelisk in Norristown's Montgomery Cemetery. The photograph most likely dates to Decoration Day, now popularly known as Memorial Day, in 1891.

The large bronze equestrian statue of Brevet Major General Hartranft (above) on the grounds of the State Capitol in Harrisburg, draped by flags and bunting, was dedicated on May 12, 1899. Surviving members of the 3rd Division, 9th Corps, and the 51st Pennsylvania Volunteers took part in a parade in coordination with the dedication.

A medallion commemorating the event (right) pays tribute to Hartranft's military service instead of his political prowess.

The United States Flag was removed to unveil the Hartranft equestrian statue (above) at the State Capitol, during the 1899 dedication ceremonies.

A circa 1906 postcard (left) shows the Hartranft statue. The monument was originally placed on the main steps in front of the State Capitol, but it was moved to a location south of the building's central entrance in 1927.

Governor
Henry Martyn Hoyt
in office from 1879 to 1883

enry Martyn Hoyt was born June 8, 1830, in Kingston, Luzerne County, to Ziba and Nancy Herbert Hoyt, who were originally from Connecticut. He graduated from Williams College in Massachusetts in 1849. Initially a school teacher, Hoyt taught in Pennsylvania, Tennessee, and Wyoming. Residing in Wilkes-Barre, he began studying law and was admitted to the bar in 1853. On September 25, 1855, he married Mary Elizabeth Loveland, with whom he had a son and two daughters.

When the American Civil War broke out, he helped organize the 52nd Pennsylvania Volunteer Infantry (PVI) Regiment of which he was commissioned lieutenant colonel. Hoyt was enrolled for service at the age of thirty-one on August 14, 1861, at the Luzerne County seat of Wilkes-Barre. He mustered into service on November 5 at Harrisburg. The regiment as a whole was organized at Camp Curtin, just north of Harrisburg's city limits, and left on November 8 for the nation's capital.

During the Peninsula Campaign, beginning in the spring of 1862, the 52nd PVI took part in the Battle of Fair Oaks (Battle of Seven Pines) and the Seven Days' Battles. Lieutenant Colonel Hoyt wrote to Governor

Portrait of Governor Henry Martyn Hoyt (1830–1892), circa 1879–1883, who helped organize the 52nd Pennsylvania Volunteers in 1861 after the outbreak of the Civil War, and later served as Republican governor of Pennsylvania from 1879 to 1883.

Andrew Curtin on June 1, from "Camp Before Richmond," pleading for justice for the reputation of his regiment. Reports were circulating that the 52nd had not done its duty during the Battle of Fair Oaks. Hoyt wrote that on May 24, the 52nd PVI, along with the 104th PVI and Gregg's Cavalry, "were then under a thorough fire of musketry & cannon & not a man broke. . . . We went a full half mile nearer Richmond than any regt. on the left & to this day no one is encamped beyond our old camp. Here for ten days then we were in the front, without half rations, wet, no change of clothes, no sleep, for every musket was in line of battle night and day—the men slept with their belts & cartridge boxes on & our horses were never unsaddled. . . . On the left, the attack was too sudden for the 52nd to rejoin the balance of the Brigade—they were taken into the action by Gen. [Henry M.] Naglee's aid & not a man ever turned his back. . . . The official reports will show how the 52nd performed that day. Nobody here is ashamed of it. Of the 248 taken in 21 were killed & 93 wounded!! Are these Pennsylvanians cowardly? God forbid . . . . Gov. Curtin, we desire you to believe the 52nd has not brought discredit on our Commth. —it has not & will not. . . . I wish you, too, to look after us, inquire into our conduct & you will find that no one regt. has earned more of the ground to Richmond than our own little 52nd. In any possible continuation of Penn regts. See that we are protected. Can we be filled up? I have written you freely & frankly, Governor. I have a stake here, more precious than life, the honor of our corps & old Commth. & it is not lightly to be blasted. . . . tonight the Grand Army of the Potomac holds the lines we gained and have not yet advanced them one foot. . . . Our Division never was a splendid one, but it never disgraced itself. The whole stream of correspondence is against [Major General George B.] McClelland's [McClellan's] version & it's too much to expect us to sit down quietly & have the balance of the Army glorified at our expense. I had rather lose a thousand commissions than stand it. Now that the worst is done, at least, our own immediate friends shall know the facts & shall not be involved in disgrace."[88]

In 1863, Hoyt's 52nd PVI took part in the siege of Fort Wagner, South Carolina. He described the famous siege waged in Charleston Harbor which lasted from mid-July until September 7. "It is difficult to give any adequate notion of the energies and activity displayed by the besieging forces. . . . Works of great strength were built, provided with magazines, depots, and bomb-proofs. It became of course the focus of the fire from all their lurid circumference. It was found that Fort Sumter must first be reduced or silenced, as it threw plunging shot into our works over the heads of the garrison of Wagner.

"On the 18th of August these [Union] batteries opened. . . . Every puff of smoke from these ungainly piles of sand, over which these Parrotts loomed long and black, was followed by a little cloud from Sumter. These great bolts went hissing quietly, but unerringly into the sides of this old fort, across the miles of intervening swamp and water. At the end of the first day Sumter had the appearance of a bad case of small pox. The next day gaps began to appear in her parapet, and by the 25th it was a shapeless pile of brick-dust, and as a Fort was demolished; but remained a garrison for infantry for more than a year.

"I have a stake here, more precious than life, the honor of our corps & old Commth. & it is not lightly to be blasted."

"All arms of the service were engaged in this work. By turns each was engineer, artillerist, and infantry. Operations were suspended during the day, for now, everybody was under the musketry of fire of Wagner, at will. At dusk . . . the process involved great vigilance, and more dodging than always comported with dignity. The guards once fairly posted, became quiet, and the busy workers behind them took up their chorus of industry. Here . . . was a squad of busy men with shovels— here a party filling sand bags . . . repairing yesterday's damage, . . . there was the telegraph operator with his instrument well in advance, and Professor Grant pouring his powerful calcium light on the ragged eminences of Fort Wagner.

"This kind of duty continued for forty days. . . . At last the fifth parallel is pushed to within a hundred yards of Wagner. Early on the morning of September 5th the work is done, and everything is ready for a final test of the effect of shell on a sand fort. A hundred guns open with their great throats on Wagner, from sea and land. For forty hours its sand boils as a great cauldron; its sand-bags, guns, carriages, and splinters are thrown high in air. All this while no man can live in its parapet, and its garrison lies smothering in its bomb-proofs."[89]

The Confederate forces at Fort Wagner withdrew under cover of night on September 7, ending the siege and eliminating one of the major obstacles to taking Charleston. The 52nd PVI subsequently settled down to garrison Morris Island.

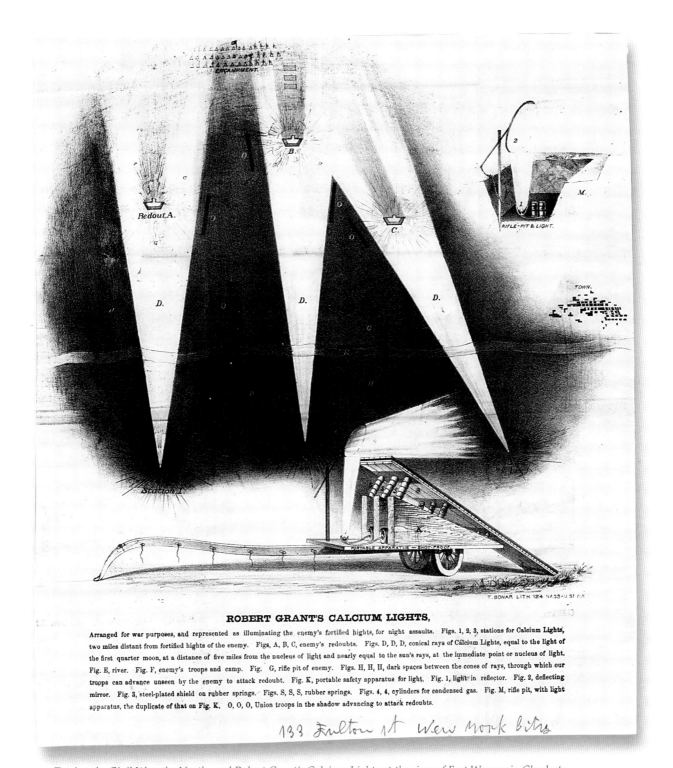

ROBERT GRANT'S CALCIUM LIGHTS,

Arranged for war purposes, and represented as illuminating the enemy's fortified hights, for night assaults. Figs. 1, 2, 3, stations for Calcium Lights, two miles distant from fortified hights of the enemy. Figs. A, B, C, enemy's redoubts. Figs. D, D, D, conical rays of Calcium Lights, equal to the light of the first quarter moon, at a distance of five miles from the nucleus of light and nearly equal to the sun's rays, at the immediate point or nucleus of light. Fig. E, river. Fig. F, enemy's troops and camp. Fig. G, rifle pit of enemy. Figs. H, H, H, dark spaces between the cones of rays, through which our troops can advance unseen by the enemy to attack redoubt. Fig. K, portable safety apparatus for light. Fig. 1, light in reflector. Fig. 2, deflecting mirror. Fig. 3, steel-plated shield on rubber springs. Figs. S, S, S, rubber springs. Figs. 4, 4, cylinders for condensed gas. Fig. M, rifle pit, with light apparatus, the duplicate of that on Fig. K. O, O, O, Union troops in the shadow advancing to attack redoubts.

During the Civil War, the North used Robert Grant's Calcium Lights at the siege of Fort Wagner in Charleston Harbor to partially blind Confederate forces so they could not effectively return fire. The device also helped prevent the Confederates from repairing the fortification at night, because they could be easily seen and targeted by the Union troops. Calcium lights, like those developed by Robert Grant, gave rise to the word limelight, or light produced by calcium oxide burning in a flame of gases. Lieutenant Colonel Hoyt wrote about this system of lighting in his report describing the actions of the 52nd PVI during the fifty-day siege. (12 3/4 x 11 3/8 inches)

A number of men in the 52ⁿᵈ PVI regiment re-enlisted in December 1863. This was a time when bounties were being offered on a wide scale in the North. Hoyt was promoted to full colonel on January 9, 1864, and on February 29, he wrote while on leave in Wilkes-Barre to Governor Curtin about bounty problems his regiment was facing while they were home on furlough. "Such portion of the 52ⁿᵈ PA Vols. as have re-enlisted as 'veterans' are now in Penna. On furlough from Morris Island. When they re-enlisted they did so upon the bounty & c offered by the U.S. & without reference to local bounties. At the time, they were credited to the different Cong. Districts—most of them to this. As a citizen of Penna. I am ashamed to say not one dollar of local bounty has been offered in this District. Any access to Hon. Mr. Denison our M.C. seems difficult & I feel unwilling

> **"My officers are, as a body, an unusually skilled & conscientious roster of good soldiers & gentlemen."**

to make so vicious a Copperhead the medium of any application. What I desire to put earnestly to you is this, permission on the part of these 'veterans' to select the district to which they may [be] credited. Their muster in rolls of course show them on the record from somewhere. They should be allowed to change a selection made in ignorance of material facts. For my part, I think it an outrage that this community should have the benefits of their re-enlistment & pay nothing; while other Districts are offering handsome bounties. This is a Copperhead Community & I trust these gallant boys of the 52 P.V. may not unjustly be made to count of their quota. & thus save a large number of them from the coming draft. The whole subject may be beyond your control, but all difficulty will be over come if the veterans, at this time may be allowed to choose their own district—the rolls at the Adjt. Genl. Office can be made to conform."⁹⁰

Bored for some time while garrisoning Morris Island, Colonel Hoyt wrote two letters to Governor Curtin on March 18, 1864, requesting that his regiment be placed in a different corps. The second letter alluded to the first, "I enclosed today a memorial touching the transfer of our regt. to some other place. You can do no act for us, which will be hailed with such joy, as to make it successful. It has become a point of honor with us. I confess I would rather resign than stay on Morris Island, or any other garrison."⁹¹ The first was sent "as a basis of an application that this regt., the 52ⁿᵈ Pa. Vols, may be returned to the Army of the Potomac, or at least, from its present Department & Brigade connection.

"We participated in the siege & reduction of Forts Wagner & Gregg, from the inception of the operation, & to this date have been daily on picket & fatigue duty, faithfully & conscientiously. Our record, in the trenches, during the siege is all we desire. At the projected final assault, Maj. Genl. [Quincy A.] Gillmore assigned the 52ⁿᵈ P.V. to the assault on Ft. Gregg, decidedly the post of honor, at the battle of 'Fair Oaks' in May, 1862, at which we lost in killed and wounded one half of our men & officers, less one. We were the victims of 'Gen McClellan's dispatch' on [Silas] Caseys Division, since thoroughly corrected in his official reports; but it still is a source of chagrin to us. I confidently appeal to our record for all this campaign, including the 'Seven days battles' as exhibited in the official reports. We earnestly beg to be relieved from our position on mere garrison duty & are sincerely anxious to go into the Field among our old comrades in the Army of the Potomac. In December last we received recruits, making our aggregate, 1040, all well armed with Springfield rifles, thoroughly drilled, & I think, in high condition of discipline. With this machinery I submit we are entitled to a wider field of activity.

"I beg to disclaim any attempt to interfere with the distribution of troops & am reluctant in making this application outside of the regular channels. But I can see no relief, except at the hands of our own Governor. I assure you, we are in just that condition of obscurity & inactivity which will crush the spirit out of us."⁹²

Having gained no satisfaction from his complaints and request for a transfer, Hoyt again wrote Governor Curtin on April 17, 1864, "The disaster and, maybe, disgrace, which I feared has overtaken us. All the white troops in this Department, except Genl. [Alexander] Schimmelfenig's

[Schimmelfennig's] Brigade of Germans, & 'Col. [William W. H.] Davis['s] Brigade' . . . consisting of 104th P.V. & 52 P.V. have been ordered North. On the face of it, this is a state of facts which should only be explained to our discredit & shame. It <u>looks</u> as though our regiments were unworthy of participation in active service and to stand by the side of the horde of ravenous, selfish, & whining troops from Maine, Mass., N.H. & Conn. who constitute the Department. From the beginning it has been a Dept. of cliques & favoritism. . . . I <u>know</u>, that my officers are, as a body, an unusually skilled & conscientious roster of good soldiers & gentlemen—with a far more than ordinary spirit of stubborn, bitter-end, loyalty. Men who are in earnest about this rebellion & who <u>never</u> utter a sentiment, this side of its utter overthrow & suppression, with all its causes. From the comd'g officer down to the drummers they burn to get to a wider field of service & honorable distinction. . . . It stings in to the soul, to be left here with Negroes. . . . If we are to waste our time, I would rather be at home."[93]

Hoyt found the combat action he clamored for on the night of July 3, 1864, as he led the 52nd PVI by boat against James Island, for an attack on Fort Johnson and Battery Simkins in Charleston Harbor. They successfully made their amphibious landing, captured a battery and, with Hoyt leading the way while brandishing his sword, fought their way into the fort. Union reinforcements did not arrive in time to support them, however, and Hoyt and his men were captured by the Confederates. His capture was only the second time a future governor of Pennsylvania became a prisoner of war, the first occurring during the American Revolution, when Joseph Hiester (1752–1832) was taken prisoner by the British. Hoyt and fellow officers were first held at a prison in Macon, and afterwards in Charleston, where they were exposed to Union artillery fire. Hoyt and four other officers attempted to escape during their transfer, but they were tracked down by bloodhounds and recaptured. The enlisted men who were captured with Hoyt were sent to Confederate prisons at Andersonville and Columbia, where many died from inadequate food and care. Brigadier General Schimmelfennig, Union district commander, complimented Hoyt on his bravery in the attack on Fort Johnson and felt certain the assault would have succeeded if properly supported.

While held in a Confederate jail in Charleston, Hoyt wrote a report on August 2 that detailed the events of the previous month. "On 3d July we carried Fort Simkins, the Brooke gun battery, and with 135 men (all who had landed) pushed over

Andrew Gregg Curtin (1817–1894)—whose posthumous portrait was painted in 1904 by Philadelphia artist Albert Rosenthal (1863–1939)—was the two-term Republican governor of Pennsylvania, from 1861 to 1867, to whom Hoyt wrote during the Civil War. (30 x 25 inches)

H.O. 52d P.V. Morris Island. S.C.
1st Sept. 1864.

Col Saml. B. Thomas,
    A.D.C. Harrisburg. Pa.

    My dear Sir, I beg leave to recommend the following promotion to fill a vacancy in this regiment. Corporal William Phillips, (Co D.) of Union County to be 2d Lieut in his Co. vice George Scott, Killed in assault on Ft. Johnson.

    My reason for this promotion is this: None of the Sergeants in this Co are "Veterans" & none of them desire to remain after 5th Nov. when our time expires. Phillips is a most worthy & useful man. He will be 1st Serg.t upon Muster-out of his Co. & is a "Veteran". His Company now musters more than 90 men.

    I congratulate myself upon my release from captivity among the rebels, upon special exchange by Maj Genl. Foster. I shall also be most happy, at some future day, to lay before His Excellency Gov. Curtin, the facts of this most desperate enterprise on Ft. Johnson, which only failed because of gross misconduct in those who failed to land & support us.

It is my present intention to be "mustered-out" on 5th Nov. with my regt. I beg your influence in furthering my intentions. The regt. will still be about 650 strong.

Very respectfully
Your obt. servt.
Henry M. Hoyt
Col. 52d P.V.

Colonel Hoyt wrote about his capture and exchange by the enemy to Colonel Samuel B. Thomas, on September 1, 1864. Safeguarded by the Pennsylvania State Archives, the correspondence files in many regiments' muster rolls offer information about regimental and company history, as well as the history of individual soldiers. "I shall also be most happy, at some future day," wrote Hoyt to Thomas, "to lay before His Excellency Gov. Curtin, the facts of this most desperate enterprise on Ft. Johnson, which only failed because of gross misconduct in those who failed to land & support us."

the parapets of Fort Johnson, and the garrison had actually begun to leave. The battery (Tynes) was in our possession. Nothing but the failure of the other boats to land prevented our capture of the works. All who landed (five boat-loads, 135) were captured. I trust the most thorough investigation will be made, let the responsibility fall where it may."[94]

Engraving of Union officer Colonel Henry M. Hoyt. He served as lieutenant colonel of the 52nd PVI from November 5, 1861, until he was promoted to full colonel of the regiment on January 9, 1864. Hoyt was given the rank of brevet brigadier general on March 13, 1865. His capture by Confederate troops on July 3, 1864, distinguished him as the second governor of Pennsylvania to ever have been held as a prisoner of war.

On August 21, Hoyt wrote a more descriptive report about the action on July 3. "The distance between that bar and the leading boat did not exceed six hundred yards. Hereupon, cannonading & musketry were opened upon us, from Simkins along the beach and from Fort Johnson with considerable rapidity, but entirely over our heads. A landing was immediately and successfully effected by the leading boats at the Brook gun battery which was readily carried & no halt whatever occurred at it. Five boats were now ashore . . . being a total of one hundred & thirty-five men all of the 52nd P.V. It was now apparent that not only were no other boats landing but that the entire expedition were retiring in the boats, not only without orders, but in disobedience to the most explicit orders to the contrary. Neither then nor since have I been able to arrive at any satisfactory knowledge of the causes & facts connected with their failure to land.

"So much of the expedition as disembarked pushed with all the vigor possible upon Fort Johnson & its connected line of high earthen parapets. The parapet was entered near the main Fort with a brisk movement of about thirty of the advance, who exchanged shots within the work but were compelled to retire. The whole of our force was then conducted along the entire line from the rebel left to the right, with repeated efforts to enter it until at the extreme right another assault was attempted. It was only partially successful & resulted in the capture of most of the troops that joined in the attempt. At this time my force was very largely outnumbered. The controversy was prolonged some little time but in a feeble & desultory manner, & the undertaking was of necessity abandoned. The entire party was taken prisoners. . . . The casualties on shore were *Killed . . . 7 Wounded . . . 16.*"[95]

It was reported under War Department General Orders Number 255, dated September 12, 1864, that Hoyt and other officers were returned to the Union Army through a special prisoner exchange with the Confederates and allowed to return to their respective regiments.[96] This exchange took place on August 3, 1864, one month to the day after his capture. Hoyt mentioned his release in a letter to Colonel Samuel B. Thomas in Harrisburg, dated September 1. "I congratulate myself upon my release from captivity among the rebels, upon special exchanges by Maj. Genl. [John G.] Foster. I shall also be most happy, at some future day, to lay before His Excellency Gov. Curtin, the <u>facts</u> of this most desperate enterprise on Ft. Johnson, which only failed because of gross misconduct in those who failed to land & support us."[97]

In an effort to protect his reputation by vigorously defending his actions at James Island, Colonel Hoyt wrote to Governor Curtin from Morris Island, South Carolina, on September 18, attempting to set the record straight about his capture by the Confederates. "Since my return from captivity among the rebels, I have noticed several theories and mis-statements in print, relative to the assault on Ft. Johnson by the 52nd P.V. & 127 N.Y.V. I have the honor to transmit to you, as the Governor of the State, my official report; and solely for the purpose of proving that whatever may have been the unfortunate cause of a failure, it was in no way attributable to Pennsylvanians. The whole subject has been carefully investigated upon my request, made while in the Charleston Jail.

Like many veterans entering the political arena after the Civil War, Hoyt capitalized on his military record. An 1878 gubernatorial campaign poster reminded voters that he served with distinction during the war. (24 x 19 1/8 inches)

Photograph of Governor Hoyt (center, wearing white top hat) inspecting National Guard of Pennsylvania troops at Fairmount Park in August 1880. Photographed by prominent Philadelphia photographer Frederick Gutekunst (1831–1917), the image is entitled "Camp First City Troop, N.G.P. Inspection by Gov. H. M. Hoyt and Staff."

We had too glorious results in our very grasp to permit it to be passed over. The truth is, with the handful of men (140) who did land we almost wrested Ft. Johnson itself from their possession. The situation of this work in Charleston Harbor and the conduct of these men & officers who assaulted it, attest the very desperate nature of the enterprise. I but repeat what General [John Gray] Foster has said publicly & privately 'that it was the most hazardous & desperate attempt made in this war and that the work done by those who landed was as gallant & well done, as any in record.' This is a great satisfaction to us who were unfortunately gobbled at it & who returned from captivity to find the really responsible parties to the failure putting their after thoughts & inventions & lies in circulation. . . . The truth is, it was the business of Col [William] Gurney, 127 N.Y.V. Comd'g this post, to have been with the expedition instead of remaining at Paine's Dock two miles off—he was in command—would have taken all credit of success & now complains that it was my business, not to have landed as I did, but to have remained in the rear & drove the expedition ashore. I did pass up & down the line of boats & until his pilot failed me, then I was compelled to go ahead myself or order a retreat. The 127 N.Y. were to attack Battery Simpkins—why did they not land and do it? They were then at the Fort & could have carried it by simply landing—indeed the 52nd did carry it—while my regt. had a 1000 yds further to row in boats. There you have the whole case. Our supports failed us & I only complain of one officer in my regt. who could have landed & did not. So much, pardon me in saying in vindication of Pennsylvania soldiers. Success in this affair would have given us Charleston & been glory enough for ourselves & the country. Yet I know that myself & my regt. did all there was to do & all human effort could accomplish."[98]

Hoyt was mustered out of service on November 5, 1864, and returned home to Wilkes-Barre. At the end of the war he was brevetted brigadier general, backdated to March 13, 1865. After the war, he resumed the practice of law, served on Wilkes-Barre's school board in 1866, and was appointed as a judge in Luzerne County by Governor John White Geary in 1867. Two years later, he was appointed collector of internal revenue for Luzerne and Susquehanna counties. In 1875–1876, Hoyt served as state chairman of the Republican Party; he next decided to run for governor. Since the country was in a wide depression while he ran for the governor's office,

Henry M. Hoyt returned to his law practice after leaving the governor's office. He retired to Wilkes-Barre, Luzerne County, several years later, where he died on December 1, 1892.

he campaigned under the slogan, "Professing to be an honest man, and the candidate of an honest party, I believe in honest money."[99] Hoyt was also not above waving the bloody shirt in his gubernatorial campaign of 1878, using his status as a Civil War officer to aid his campaign.

One of Hoyt's friends and advisers was Governor John F. Hartranft, to whom he wrote on April 27, 1878, complaining about his campaign for the Republican nomination and seeking advice. "I am persuaded an amount of hostility to my nomination is being created thru the state to render it inexpedient. Much of it I fear will survive the convention and remain to be fought during the campaign."[100] Hoyt won the Republican primary, and then the general election by twenty-two thousand votes in defeating Democrat Andrew H. Dill. He served as governor from January 21, 1879, to January 16, 1883. He was the third Civil War general in a row to serve as governor of Pennsylvania.

Hoyt's administration reduced the state debt by roughly one and a half million dollars. During his term in office, school segregation was banned throughout Pennsylvania by an 1881 Act of Assembly, and the state militia system was formally merged into the National Guard of Pennsylvania. One of his first acts as governor was to appoint John F. Hartranft, former governor, as major general of the National Guard of Pennsylvania for a five-year term. "The reorganization of the National Guard conceived and partly carried out by General Hartranft, when Governor, has been perfected, and is now complete," he reported to the general assembly in 1881. "The Guard contains eight thousand officers and enlisted men. The morale of the body is most excellent. The officers are efficient, prompt, intelligent, and earnest in their duties. The rank and file are composed of citizens, the very best types and representatives of the real people of the State."[101]

The soldiers' orphan school system concerned Governor Hoyt and, in his biennial message to the state legislature in 1881, he championed the work of the orphan schools. He praised those in charge and reminded legislators why they existed. "The conduct of these schools calls for no abatement in the pride with which all have watched their organization and growth. The supervision over them has been intelligent and rigid. The inspections have been thorough as to the physical surroundings and material well-being of the inmates of the several schools. Children admitted under existing laws must belong to one of three classes: 1. Those whose fathers were either killed or died of disease while in the army. Only one hundred of this class remain. 2. Those whose fathers have died since the close of the war of wounds or disease contracted while in the service. 3. Those whose fathers are living, but are so disabled by wounds or disease contracted while in the army, that they are unable to support their families; and in all the cases, the children must be under sixteen years of age, and in destitute circumstances."[102]

On March 24, 1881, Governor Hoyt sent a message to the state legislature, urging members to pursue the settlement of claims that Pennsylvanians had made against the federal government for payment for supplies taken from them by United States troops during the Civil War.[103] However, there is no evidence to suggest that Hoyt's plea on behalf of these claimants produced the desired results.

In early November of the following year, outgoing Governor Hoyt spoke out in the press against Republican Party bosses and in favor of the state's independent Republican movement. His stance hurt the Republican Party's endorsed candidate that year, James A. Beaver, who was soundly defeated. In late 1882, Hoyt remarked about that year's gubernatorial election, the defeat of his party, and its Cameron-Quay Republican machine. "This change marks the beginning of a new epoch in our political life. Those who cherish it argue that thousands of our best citizens, relieved of the pressure of national anxieties, and unwilling to live forever in the past, are beginning to study the nature and details of State and municipal government as never before; are awakening to the business and scientific character of political problems, and have determined to thrust aside every individual, and every contrivance, that stands between them and the management of their own affairs. They will no longer be content with the automatic activity in politics; they demand a conscious share in this noblest pursuit of intelligent men. The people have come to claim their own, without the intervention of middlemen."[104]

Hoyt returned to his law practice in Philadelphia, at 423 Walnut Street, soon after leaving the governor's office.[105] In poor health since the days of his military service, he retired to Wilkes-Barre and died on December 1, 1892. He is buried in the historic Forty Fort Cemetery in Luzerne County.

An article appearing in The Philadelphia Press *on November 4, 1882, discussed and reprinted Governor Hoyt's letter concerning his support of the Independent Republican movement and his dissatisfaction with Pennsylvania's Republican machine controlled by political power brokers Simon Cameron and Matthew S. Quay. His criticism of this political machine contributed to the Republican Party losing the 1882 gubernatorial election and providing the Keystone State its first Democratic chief executive, Robert Emory Pattison, since the administration of William Fisher Packer, who served from 1858 to 1861.*

Governor
James Addams Beaver
in office from 1887 to 1891

Born on October 21, 1837, in Millerstown, Perry County, to Jacob and Ann Eliza Addams Beaver, James Addams Beaver was their third child, having two older sisters and a younger brother. His father died in 1840, when James was three years old. His widowed mother married a Presbyterian clergyman, the Reverend S. H. McDonald, and in April 1846, the combined family moved to Belleville, Mifflin County. After graduation from Jefferson College in Canonsburg, Washington County, in 1856, Beaver settled in Bellefonte, Centre County, where he studied law and was admitted to the bar in January 1859. He practiced law with business partner Hugh N. McAllister.

During the period in which Beaver studied law, he joined the Bellefonte Fencibles, a volunteer militia company, in May 1858, as a private. That year, he wrote to his only full brother, Jacob Gilbert "Gib" Beaver, "The chief excitement here now is the attempt on the part of the young men to raise a military company—the iniatory steps have already been taken."[106] On September 2, Beaver wrote to his brother about the first public appearance of the new military company. "The Fencibles made their first appearance on Saturday last—The ladies presented us with a magnificent flag—and altogether—not withstanding the rain—we had a pretty magnificent display. . . ."[107]

James Addams Beaver (1837–1914) served as governor of Pennsylvania from 1887 to 1891. The Republican Party machine, led by boss Matthew S. Quay, supported and directed Beaver's campaign.

Andrew Gregg Curtin was the captain of the Fencibles before becoming governor of Pennsylvania in 1861. Beaver was promoted several times while in the organization: on October 8, 1858, to sergeant, on September 3, 1860, to 2nd lieutenant, and on April 18, 1861, to 1st lieutenant. At the time of Curtin's funeral in 1894, Beaver noted that the militia company to which they once both belonged, "was intended to embrace most of the young men of the town and to give point to the social life of the community as well as to provide military instruction and training for its members. . . . The Bellefonte Fencibles became, under his [Curtin's] leadership, not only a crack military company but a great social agency. . . . His efforts to provide entertainment for the people were probably quite as striking as his success as a military officer, but the combination was such as to win the enthusiastic admiration of all of his soldiers."[108]

While preparing to attend Curtin's inauguration on January 15, 1861, Beaver was aware that his militia unit was soon likely to be called into active service. He wrote his mother Ann on January 11,

"Governor Curtin assures me that if a requisition is made upon this State, ours is the first company to be called out. . . .

"Since writing the above I have just been to the telegraph office. A dispatch rec'd from Washington says that hostilities have actually begun. The South Carolinians fired upon the 'Star of the West' which contained supplies for Maj. [Robert] Anderson. . . . If this is true, which God forbid, war has actually commenced. Where will be the end? The Union must be preserved & who can mistake his duty in the emergency. I have prayed for direction, guidance and clear revelations of duty and I cannot now doubt where the path of duty lies. If required, I will march in it trusting in God for the result. There are few men situated as I am. No person <u>dependent</u> upon me, and a business which I leave in able hands. If we have a nationality it must be continued, supported, upheld."[109] The firing on the *Star of the West*, on January 9, was not the start of the Civil War, however, because Major Anderson did not instruct the guns of Fort Sumter to return fire, due to his lack of orders.

On February 16, Beaver wrote his mother, "The peace conference now in Washington is likely to effect an amicable arrangement with the border states and then unless the cotton states come into the harness nicely there may be some little difficulty which must be settled with the sword—but it will be a small affair compared with what it would have been had all the slave states united. We will not be called to Washington I think—not for the present at all events."[110] The uneasy lull in the action in South Carolina was shattered on April 12, 1861, when Confederate forces began bombarding Fort Sumter and the United States troops that garrisoned it. With that action, the American Civil War began.

On April 17, he again wrote his mother, "Need I say that that direction points to the defence of our Nation in this hour of her peril. We march tomorrow for Harrisburg—remain there until ordered into actual service—thence to whatever port may be assigned us. We march with at least 100 men— The officers of our company laid down their commissions and entered the service as volunteers— We were reelected—I am therefore in a position of comparative ease and comfort—but of course not without its trials and difficulties."[111]

The Bellefonte Fencibles traveled to Harrisburg on April 18 and were sent to Camp Curtin. Beaver, then twenty-three years old, was mustered into active military service two days later. He was elected first lieutenant of Company H of the 2nd Pennsylvania Volunteer Infantry (PVI)

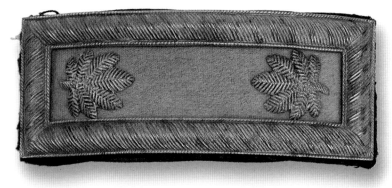

Lieutenant colonel shoulder straps worn by James Addams Beaver during the Civil War. Beaver served as lieutenant colonel of the 45th PVI from October 19, 1861, until he was promoted to full colonel of the 148th PVI on September 4, 1862.
(1 1/2 x 4 inches each)

A sketch of Camp Curtin, at Harrisburg, the largest training camp for Union soldiers during the Civil War, by Jasper Green (1829–1910), illustrator and war correspondent, originally appeared in the May 11, 1861, edition of Harper's Weekly. *More than three hundred thousand soldiers passed through this military training facility during the war.*

Regiment, a three-month regiment that included the former Bellefonte Fencibles. The unit stayed at Camp Curtin only two days, April 19–20, 1861.

By April 23, the 2nd PVI was encamped at Camp Scott, York, Pennsylvania. Two days later, Beaver was appointed adjutant of the 7th Pennsylvania Regiment, but after many of the men in his company expressed their dismay at losing him, he was able to decline the promotion while in Harrisburg, on April 25. On May 27, while still at Camp Scott in York, Beaver wrote his mother, "The suspense of our men becomes greater every day—the deepest anxiety to be marched— marched anywhere possesses every one of them. But it is impossible to tell where we will go."[112] Due to Captain John B. Mitchell's illness, Beaver acted as captain during much of his company's encampment at Camp Scott. In the same letter, Beaver noted his interest in drilling the men, "I am really becoming much interested in our company and if they took half as much pride in themselves as I do—they would be the best drilled company on the ground."[113]

On June 18, Beaver and his regiment were encamped three miles from Hagerstown, Maryland, where he wrote his mother about the war. "A rebellion the only real result of which will be to establish this government upon a foundation which cannot be moved by the too violent uprisings of factious and designing demagogues—and in this view of it, I doubt not but this movement on the part of the South will demonstrate itself to be the most important and fortunate in its results which could possibly have happened. The government will have proved itself to be self sustaining."[114]

The 2nd PVI, thereafter, took part in minor engagements in Virginia at Falling Waters (now West Virginia) and Bunker Hill. The 2nd Regiment was mustered out of service at the end of its three-month term on July 26, in Harrisburg. On July 22, Beaver was enrolled into service for three years and began assisting in recruiting a new regiment, the 45th Pennsylvania Volunteer Infantry (PVI) Regiment. "I am to be Lieut. Col. of one of the new Penna. Regiments," he wrote to his brother on August 17.[115]

Beaver was back at Camp Curtin by September 8. "I entered upon my duties here on Monday morning," he wrote his mother on September 10. "My special duty being to muster in the troops as they arrive—to frank soldiers letters in the peculiar manner fixed by Congress and take command in the absence of Col [Thomas] Welsh. We have over 5000 men here now and have them constantly arriving. It is becoming rather unwieldy and we will make an effort to dispatch two or three regiments this week and thus reduce the number of men and give us more room. . . . Governor Curtin is anxious to have us remain here until all these regiments are organized. We will remain sometime but cannot stay so long."[116] The 45th PVI was mustered into service on October 19, at Camp Curtin, the same day Beaver received his commission as lieutenant colonel of the three-year regiment. Beaver and his new regiment left Harrisburg for Washington, D.C., two days later.

Beaver and part of the 45th PVI occupied Fort Seward overlooking Hilton Head, South Carolina, by December 11. "We are here—away here on the soil of South Carolina in the den of rebels or rather at the mouth of the den," he wrote his mother that day. "In command of five companies of our regiment I occupy Fort Seward late Fort Beauregard a very nice little earth work overlooking the sea and almost directly opposite Hilton Head the Head Quarters of the Army here. . . . Colonel Welsh and the balance of the Regt. have gone up to occupy Otter Island about midway between here and Charleston."[117] On December 26 he wrote to his mother about the unanticipated reaction of local African Americans to the 45th's occupation, "The negroes are not offering their services as fast as was expected. As long as they can plunder their masters homes and plantations and live on corn and sweet potatoes which are left they will stay where they are. Nothing will bring them to us to work but starvation."[118]

Beaver and five companies of the 45th PVI, A, C, D, E, and I, occupied part of Hilton Head Island on January 6, 1862. On January 20, he was put in charge of the defense of Otter Island, because Colonel Welsh of the 45th was on sick leave. Along with others in his regiment, Beaver enjoyed catching and eating crabs from the sound near their outposts. Bored, however, with the assignment of occupying the islands off the coast of South Carolina, Beaver wrote on March 19 to his brother, Lieutenant Jacob Gilbert Beaver, serving in Colonel John F. Hartranft's 51st PVI. "As for our 'Expeditionary Corps' I scarcely know what to say. It is toiling away erecting batteries at night in deep swamps. . . . I like active operations, pushing energetic movements and we have been anything else. I am almost tempted to think sometimes that I would be of as much use at home sitting in my office as here. However it's no part of a soldier's duty to complain or do anything else but <u>obey</u>. So I take it all as the fortune of war and make the best of it."[119]

On April 7, he wrote to one of his sisters about reinforcements and the possibility of an active campaign. "I hope it will be soon, for I am sick, tired, disgusted with this humdrum existence— Enemy in sight all the time—and we in effect saying, 'If you let me alone I'll not hurt you.'"[120] In an April 21 letter to his brother, he again complained about outpost duty, noting that his brother's regiment had seen more action at Roanoke and New Bern.[121]

Beaver wrote to his mother on May 12 about his dislike of Major General David Hunter's "Negro imbroglio," emphasizing "I verily believe that Genl Hunter is insane on the subject."[122] On May 9, Hunter had issued a directive declaring slaves in Georgia, Florida, and South Carolina "forever free." Hunter also sent a circular to his officers ordering them to send to headquarters all the "able bodied negroes capable of bearing arms." According to Beaver, the African Americans "are to be organized into a regiment or regiments and serve in this Dept. . . . Were it not for my overwhelming sense of duty in this crisis and the implied pledge to the boys to stand by them to the last I

The North's Major General David Hunter (1802–1886) declared three southern states to be forever free and authorized a regiment of African Americans to be raised along the coast of South Carolina in 1862, which offended Lieutenant Colonel James Beaver's sensibilities and countered President Abraham Lincoln's policies.

would resign without a moment's hesitation. I have as yet made few sacrifices in the discharge of my duty and perhaps this sacrifice of personal feeling and dignity is to be the test of my devotion to my country. No greater one could be required. In addition to our being kept here inactive to guard the negroes in their farming operations—now that the crops are in the ground the additional indignity of serving with them is to be heaped upon us. Henceforth a white Northern soldier is to be as good as a negro one if he behaves himself. . . . My colored boy Ike came to me a little while ago and asked for the loan of my saddle cloth and spurs—he said he wanted to be 'Lieut. Col of de darkey division.'"[123] Beaver wrote to his mother about the issue of slavery on June 10. "The fact is much as we despise the name of abolitionist, we are all practically abolitionists, differing only perhaps as to the time and the means of carrying our views into effect. If we could colonize all the slaves of the rebels I would at once confiscate them."[124] Major General Hunter's African American regiment, raised on the South Carolina sea coast, was disallowed by the War Department in Washington and disbanded by August 1862.[125]

In mid-July, Beaver's regiment was ordered to reunite and sail to Newport News, Virginia. The 45th was ordered to guard a military railroad between Aquia Creek and Fredericksburg, Virginia. This was not the type of active duty for which Beaver longed. "This kind of duty although exceedingly important," he wrote from Brooke's Station on August 6, "is not generally considered very honorable for the reason that however well performed very little honor attaches to the performance by reason of the quiet and peaceful nature of the duty."[126]

In late August, Governor Curtin offered the twenty-four-year-old Beaver the colonelcy of the 148th Pennsylvania Volunteer Infantry (PVI) Regiment, a new regiment from Centre County. Beaver tendered his resignation as lieutenant colonel of the 45th PVI regiment on September 3 and returned to Washington, D.C. He then traveled

A pass dated September 6, 1862, allowed Colonel Beaver to freely move in and out of Camp Curtin whenever he wished during his second stay, as he organized the 148th PVI.

to Harrisburg, arriving at Camp Curtin the following day to take command of his new regiment. His promotion to colonel of the 148th was dated September 4. The 148th PVI was organized as a three-year regiment in Harrisburg, on September 8. Beaver and his regiment left for the field the next day. The 148th was promptly given the task of guarding twelve miles of the Northern Central Railway—one of the main rail lines between the nation's capital and Union troops—during and after the Antietam Campaign. Beaver whipped his new regiment into shape through discipline and strict adherence to the rules of conduct. While there, Beaver and the regiment were formally mustered into federal service at Cockeysville, Maryland, on October 8.

A great personal tragedy befell Colonel Beaver later that month as his twenty-two-year-old brother, Lieutenant Jacob Gilbert Beaver of Company H, 51st PVI, was killed at the Battle of Antietam on September 17, during Colonel John Frederick Hartranft's dramatic charge for Burnside Bridge. "My heart has been sore—my reason confused my nerves all mustering," Beaver wrote to a friend, on September 26, after learning of his brother's death. "I have been fit for nothing. Oh! how carefully how intensely I scanned the papers all of last week. Almost afraid to read the lists and yet disappointed if I did not see them. Gradually apprehension gave way to

Battle of Antietam: Gallant Charge of Gen. Burnside's Division at the Bridge, *an engraving by Alonzo Chappel (1828–1887). Beaver's brother, Lieutenant Jacob G. Beaver, was killed during the 51st Pennsylvania Volunteers' capture of this bridge on September 17, 1862. (8 5/8 x 11 inches)*

hope and by Saturday morning hope yielded to a feeling of security. . . . On Saturday came home in the evening and found the evening paper on my table. The first glance at the local column revealed the sad—sad truth that I was brotherless. Earth and Heaven seemed to be swept from under me at a blow. I seemed to stand on grief to be surrounded with bitter anguish to be covered with a great black cloud of sorrow. My noble father—my sainted blue eyed sister died before I knew what sorrow was. My life since then has been a never changing continuity of bright unclouded sunshine until this great calamity fell upon me with a crushing might against which I wrestled in vain. Whilst I can bow submissively beneath the rod with which our Heavenly Father has seen fit to chastise us. Whilst I can rejoice at the thought that the ransomed spirit of my heroic brother is now among the saints in life joining in the 'song of Moses and the Lamb' I cannot repress the natural emotions of the heart or stifle the cry of my wounded affections. Few are called to mourn the loss of such a brother—few have such a brother to lose.

"Oh! how many sad hearts have cause to mourn the invasion of Maryland."[127] Beaver drew a rectangular black mourning ribbon in his 1862 diary for the date his brother was killed in action. His diary also noted that Jacob's remains were sent home on October 1.

Not long after the Battle of Fredericksburg, in December, the 148th was assigned to the 1st Brigade, 1st Division of the 2nd Corps of the Army of the Potomac. The 148th PVI's appearance, after less than three months of service, was an exemplary sight at that time and was commended by other officers.[128] Beaver directed the 148th to construct winter quarters beginning on December 21.

Beaver proved to be an excellent officer. He was renowned for his disregard for his personal safety. On February 27, 1863, he explained his reason for not fearing death in battle. "If my life can atone for any National evil," he wrote, "if I were satisfied that the result of this struggle is to be Union—Purity—Liberty how gladly would I resign life. . . . It seems like doubting God, to hesitate for an instant, I never doubt, I have therefore no anxious thoughts as to the future."[129]

On April 27, the 148th left its winter quarters and moved with the Army of the Potomac toward Chancellorsville, Virginia. Its main action at the Battle of Chancellorsville, fought from May 1 to May 6, occurred after the Confederate forces had gained the rear of the Union Army. Major General Joseph Hooker, commander of the Army, ordered the 148th PVI into woods near a ford in the Rappahannock River. The 148th regiment found the woods filled with Confederate troops and an engagement at close range erupted, during which Beaver received the first of his battle wounds. Hit in the abdomen by a bullet, which tore a large hole in his coat, Beaver initially thought the wound was mortal. He ordered his men to leave him where he fell, urging them, "Go to your places, it will be time enough to bury the dead when the battle is over."[130] Fortunately for Beaver, a pencil that he carried had turned the course of the bullet away from vital organs and caused it to come to rest in the fleshy part of his abdomen.

While recuperating back home in Bellefonte, Centre County, Beaver learned of the South's invasion of Pennsylvania. His wound had not yet healed, but he could not resist traveling to Harrisburg to offer whatever assistance he could provide. Major General Darius N. Couch, commander of the Department of the Susquehanna and in charge of the defense of Harrisburg, assigned Beaver to command Camp Curtin on June 18.[131] This was a time of great activity at Camp Curtin—thousands of men were arriving to volunteer for emergency militia service during the Gettysburg Campaign. Beaver wrote to his mother on June 21 of his experience as camp commandant, "a position of much thankless labor and vexatious toil. I feel so much better now that I shall ask to be relieved here in a few days and will then join my Regiment which I know needs my presence and a little stirring up. . . . The militia force here is immense and untamed. I have never seen anything to equal it."[132]

Beaver requested to be relieved of his duties at Camp Curtin near the end of June 1863. Because of the emergency in Harrisburg, however, Couch declined to relieve Beaver until July 15, causing him to miss the 148th PVI's participation in the Battle of Gettysburg, July 1–3.

Major General Couch commended Beaver in his special order number 35, relieving him of his Harrisburg duty on July 15. "The Major-General commanding tenders his thanks to Colonel Beaver for the important service rendered him in the organization of the troops," Couch wrote, "which were hurried to the Capitol, and placed under his command at Camp Curtin, notwithstanding he was absent on leave in this Department, on account of wounds received in battle. The zeal and energy he manifested in the cause is worthy of emulation." Years later, Couch wrote to Beaver's biographer, Frank A. Burr, about his service at Harrisburg, "When Governor Curtin, in June of 1863, made his call for men to hurry to Harrisburg, and organize in defence of their homes against Lee's advancing army, General, then Colonel James A. Beaver, was among the first who presented themselves for service.

"His previous good record and sterling character induced me at once to place him upon my staff, where he showed so much ability that upon the re-establishment of Camp Curtin, near the Capitol, he was selected as one possessing the necessary

Field desk, often called a campaign desk, used by Beaver—a prolific letter writer and diarist—during the Civil War. The desk, which disassembles into two pieces for travel, was acquired by The State Museum of Pennsylvania from Beaver's descendants in 1988. (top: 20 1/8 x 29 3/4 x 15 1/16 inches; bottom: 28 x 29 1/2 x 14 3/4 inches)

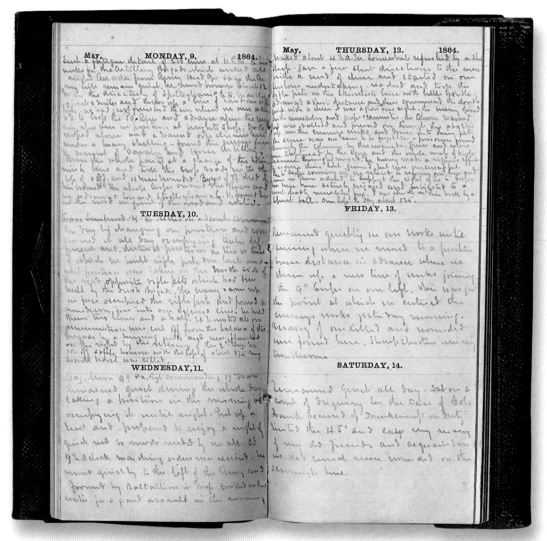

Beaver kept diaries throughout his service with the Union Army. His 1864 diary is especially fascinating because it stopped a spent enemy bullet as he carried it in his breast pocket during the Battle of Spotsylvania Court House on May 12, 1864. This particular diary also contains entries describing his serious wounding on August 25 at Reams' Station, which caused the amputation of his right leg. (7 1/16 x 7 3/16 inches as shown)

qualifications for the trying position of commandant. Moreover the confidence reposed in him was not misplaced, he earning the gratitude of all for the way in which he applied common sense to strictly soldierly duties. In other words he was a soldier who could be trusted morning, noon, and night. I could not add to that if I should write a whole week."[133]

Beaver returned to the 148th PVI to resume command on July 19, near Woodgrove, Virginia.[134] He and his regiment participated in the Battle of Bristoe Station, on October 14, and in the Mine Run Campaign, in November. Because of his training as an attorney, he was frequently detailed to take part in courts martial when not actively campaigning, which he noted in his wartime letters and diaries. On August 24, 1863, Beaver wrote to his mother about the fate of one deserter, "We had a military execution in the 2nd Division of our Corps on Friday last. I did not go to see it and even at this distance from it I shuddered when I heard the discharge of musketry which hurried a fellow being into eternity. He was shot for 'Desertion.' His eyes bandaged and sitting on his coffin. I felt more over the death of this poor fellow than if ten thousand had been slain in battle and yet his punishment was just and at this time when conscripts are arriving so rapidly and making all sorts of efforts to desert it was necessary for an example."[135]

Fighting at the battles of The Wilderness and Spotsylvania, Virginia, in May 1864, he garnered further reputation for bravery under fire. At Spotsylvania, he and the 148th were part of the 2nd Corps force that broke the rebel line. Brevet Brigadier General John R. Brooke, Beaver's brigade commander, praised him for his actions in this battle. "In this assault Beaver was conspicuous for his great bravery—bravery accompanied by coolness, which is the highest attribute of an officer of the highest stamp. For hours, in the midst of the dreadful carnage, he gallantly held his men in their most trying position. . . . It is hard to realize the terrible work done that morning in that bloody spot; the bayonet was freely used, and a large number of men were afterwards found to have been killed by it.

"In the shock of the assault Beaver led his regiment and displayed the most daring courage, and in the hours of desperate, tenacious fighting which followed he was conspicuous for his gallantry. In the days succeeding this day of particularly hard fighting, the usual story of gallantry and devotion to duty was the daily life of this man."[136]

Beaver wrote of the May 12 Battle of Spotsylvania Court House, in a letter to his future wife on May 20, describing it as "a terrible and at the same time a glorious day for our Corps. We moved silently at midnight in front of the enemy's works—snatched a few hours sleep and at the early dawn advanced steadily until their works appeared in view and there with a soul inspiring cheer rushed through a perfect storm of bullets and canister up to the very mouths of their cannon staggered for a moment under their terrible discharges and then rallied and the works were won. My Regiment was in the first line and behaved as they always do magnificently. They captured

DESPERATE FIGHT ON THE ORANGE C.H. PLANK ROAD, NEAR TODDS TAVERN, MAY 6TH 1864.   COPYRIGHTED 1887 BY KURZ & ALLISON, ART PUBLISHERS, 76 & 78 WABASH AVE, CHICAGO U.S.A.

BATTLE OF THE WILDERNESS.

An 1887 Kurz & Allison color lithograph entitled Battle of the Wilderness. Desperate Fight on the Orange C. H. Plank Road, Near Todd's Tavern, May 6th, 1864. *Fought May 5–6, 1864, the Battle of the Wilderness was the initial encounter in Lieutenant General Ulysses S. Grant's Overland Campaign of 1864, and the first time Grant and Confederate General Robert E. Lee led armies in battle directly against one another. The Wilderness area was known for its dense undergrowth which caused limited visibility during the battle. (21 ⅞ x 28 inches)*

three flags—three cannon and hundreds of prisoners. We gained their works before they were thoroughly awaked. I had the satisfaction of having Brig. Genl G. H. [George H.] Steuart surrender to me soon after I entered the works. We did not stop to count our prisoners but ordered them to the rear by wholesale to be cared for by the Provost Guard. This is the cheerful side of the picture, I have no heart to give you a glimpse of the other side. I was struck twice but was not injured. One ball when force was spent struck me on the breast but my memorandum book received the shock. It sounded exactly as if it had entered the flesh and being very near the line the boys heard it. I heard the intelligence carried all along the line—and almost feared for the result. I sat down but a moment to assure myself that the ball had not entered and then overtook the advancing line."[137] Beaver's diary entry for May 12 also described the Battle of Spotsylvania and commented on his near wounding that day, "I was struck on this book by a spent ball."[138] His bravery at the Battle of Spotsylvania was cause for him to be offered brigade command of the 3rd Brigade, 1st Division, 2nd Corps, but he declined it, preferring to stay with his 148th PVI Regiment.

In the Battle of Cold Harbor, Beaver's regiment was part of the Union 2nd Corps that reached close to the Confederate line on June 3, 1864. Beaver related in his diary what occurred just outside of the rebel lines that day. "Advanced several hundred yards and came upon the enemy's works, the outside of which we gained. The 2nd Div. not affording prompt support we failed to enter and dropped under the hill. Pushed up gradually and got a little earth thrown up which soon grew into a rifle pit some 100 yds from the enemy. Had a warm time all day which closed at night with a horrendous fusillade. Was struck with a spent ball on the hip."[139]

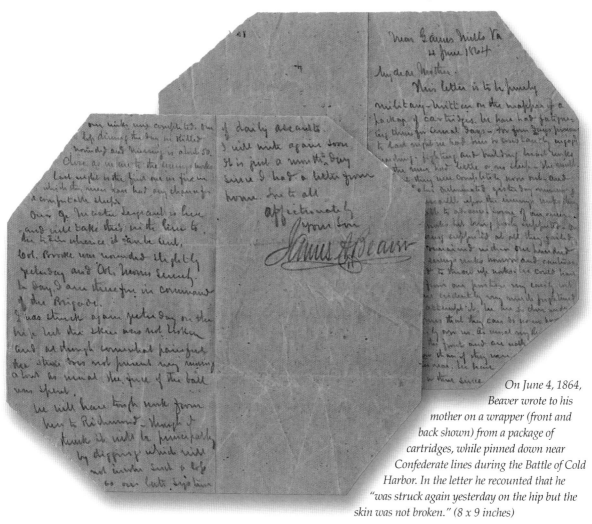

On June 4, 1864, Beaver wrote to his mother on a wrapper (front and back shown) from a package of cartridges, while pinned down near Confederate lines during the Battle of Cold Harbor. In the letter he recounted that he "was struck again yesterday on the hip but the skin was not broken." (8 x 9 inches)

M. J. and C. Croll, of Philadelphia, manufactured Beaver's Model 1851 general officer's coat, for his use in the National Guard of Pennsylvania in the 1870s. The firm, appearing in Philadelphia city directories of the period, was listed as merchant tailors and included Martin J. and Christian Croll as principals.

Beaver likely wore these gilt brigadier general epaulettes (above) with his officer's dress coat. He stored the epaulettes in a tin case (below), which also contained a spare pair of general officer's stars and a small brass buckle.

Colonel James A. Beaver, depicted during the Civil War era, was given the brevet rank of brigadier general on November 10, 1864, for highly meritorious and distinguished conduct, particularly at the Battle of Cold Harbor. The promotion was effective from August 1 of that year.

The rudimentary shelter his men dug allowed the 148th PVI to stay near the enemy lines. In the 2nd Corps attack, Beaver had again been hit by a spent bullet, this one slowed by passing through the body of an aide with whom he was speaking. In a letter to his mother on June 4, Beaver related some of the action from the 2nd Corps' failed attack at Cold Harbor the previous day. "We remained within one hundred yards of the enemy's works however and cautiously commenced to throw up works," he wrote. "We could have been driven from our position very easily but the enemy were evidently very much frightened and did not attempt it. We are so close under the enemy's guns that they can do us no harm firing entirely over us. As usual my Regiment is in the front and are much safer here <u>now</u> than if they were a mile in the rear. We have lost but two or three since our works were completed. . . . Close as we are to the enemy's works last night is the first one in five in which the men have had any chance for a comfortable sleep. . . . I was struck again yesterday on the hip but the skin was not broken and although somewhat painful the strike does not prevent my moving about as usual, the force of the ball was spent."[140] Beaver wrote this letter on "the wrapper of a package of cartridges" while in his regiment's works near the Confederate lines at Cold Harbor.

At Petersburg, Virginia, on June 16, 1864, Beaver commanded the 4th Brigade in Brigadier General Francis C. Barlow's 1st Division, 2nd Corps. Beaver led his brigade in a charge late in the day, and W. M. Mintzer, lieutenant colonel of the 53rd PVI, in Beaver's brigade, later described what he had witnessed: "There was an open plain between our position and the earthworks of the enemy which was swept by their guns, and over this cleared field we were to charge for several hundred yards. . . . He (Beaver) was first over our works, and I shall never forget him as he looked that beautiful June afternoon when he turned towards us, removed his sword from its scabbard, and shouted for the charge in clear, ringing tones. He was the picture of a soldier, and he had the confidence of the command as few men had. The men followed him with a shout, and over the plain they swept, under his lead, amidst a perfect shower of shot and shell. When we were well on toward the Confederate works and the charge was at its height, with every prospect of victory, I saw a shell strike beneath General Beaver's feet, bury itself in the ground, and explode. It threw him into the air, and he fell, as I and all of us then supposed, dead. He was quickly picked up by some of the men and carried to the rear with a severe wound in his side. Deprived of his inspiring leadership, despite the efforts of the officers the brigade fell into confusion and retired."[141] This third serious wound that Beaver received in battle caused him to be granted two leaves of absence. Nonetheless, he was anxious to get back to his brigade in the field and returned to action before his second leave expired.

A copper engraving plate, mounted on wood, of a portrait of James Addams Beaver in military officer's uniform. Before the widespread use of photography, copper plates were used to print images for cards, books, and periodicals. (4 ³/₄ x 3 ¹/₂ x 1 inches)

Shoulder straps worn by Colonel Beaver during the Civil War. Beaver served as colonel of the 148th Pennsylvania Volunteers from September 4, 1862, until he was promoted to brevet brigadier general on November 10, 1864, a promotion that was retroactive to August 1 of that year. (1 ³/₄ x 4 inches each)

By this time the 2nd Corps had been given the task of destroying the Weldon Railroad, a major line of communication and supplies connecting Petersburg, Virginia, and Wilmington, North Carolina. An overwhelming Confederate attack hit the 2nd Corps at Reams' Station, on August 25, 1864. Just before the attack began, Beaver arrived on the field by ambulance. Major General Winfield Scott Hancock, commander of the 2nd Corps, welcomed him and sent him out to lead his brigade, noting that a battle was soon to occur. Colonel Beaver had just reached his troops and was reviewing their position when the Confederates attacked, wounding him again. It was only thirty minutes after Beaver reported to Hancock that he was hit in his right thigh by a minie ball at the Second Battle of Reams' Station. The day after the battle, it was determined by division surgeons that Beaver's shattered right leg should be amputated at the hip. Surgeon J. W. Wishart performed the operation, which essentially ended Beaver's active military career.

Beaver's diary entries from this time are brief but poignant: August 25, "To Reams Station Shot through the right leg"; August 26, "Right leg amputated near the body"; and August 27, "Carried on stretcher to Burchett House into which I was carried." Four days passed without any entries, but on the first and second days of September, he noted that friends had come to see him. On September 3, Beaver reached the nadir of his spirit during his recovery when he wrote, "Commenced to die. Stimulants ruined me."[142] Fortunately for Beaver, and the Commonwealth of Pennsylvania, his demise was still many years away.

On September 17, Beaver wrote his first letter in his own hand since his wounding. "I scarcely know what to say of what is generally regarded as a very great calamity," he wrote to his mother, "the loss of my leg. I have yet to feel any great regret or to have the first feeling of sadness in regard to it. . . . The feeling which has been uppermost in my mind and heart ever since my wound has been one of thankfulness that my life has been spared and that I am left in a condition in which my usefulness in the community need not in the slightest degree be impaired. The loss of either arm would have unfitted me in a great degree for the exercise of my profession. . . . I have not had a desponding hour in all thru three weeks and more that I have laid here on my back. . . . The surgeons here are quite enthusiastic this morning over the improvement in my stump. . . . My case has excited quite a degree of interest among the medical fraternity and is regarded as one in a thousand."[143]

One of Beaver's surgeons, Uriah Q. Davis (1821–1887), of the 148th PVI described Beaver's wounds to his mother, Ann Eliza Addams Beaver McDonald, of Belleville, in a letter dated August 27, 1864. Dr. Davis described the extent of Beaver's injury, subsequent amputation, and the beginning of his recuperation. After the war, Dr. Davis practiced in Milton, Northumberland County, and died at the age of sixty-six after being struck by a train.

Beaver paid one dollar for each of the thirty-two days he stayed at the 1st Division Hospital, 2nd Corps, from August 29 to September 29, 1864. The receipt was signed by Dr. James E. Pomfret, the field hospital's surgeon in charge.

Regiment Infantry, N. G. of Penn'a.

484

Company, Rank, Name, Residence, Date of Commission. Rank from	Original Entry into Service, Subsequent Service and Commission	Service of other States and of the United States	Born	Received Military or Medical Instruction
Brigadier General James A. Beaver, Bellefonte Centre Co. Penna. Commissioned January 21st 1879. To Rank from October 12th 1870.	11 May 1858 enlisted – Private Bellefonte Fencibles 10 July 1858 mustered " " 8 Oct 1858 Sergeant " " 5 Sept 1860 2 Lieut " " 13 April 1861 1 Lieut " 24 March 1871 Maj. Genl. 14th Div. N. G. of Pa. Rank 12 Oct 1870. 31 March 1875 Maj. Genl. 5. Div. N. G. of Pa. Rank 12 Oct 1870. 22 Oct 1878 – Brig. Genl. N. G. of Pa. Rank 12 Oct 1870.	" 1861 April 18 1st Lieut. Co H. 2nd Reg. Pa. Vols. " 1861 July 22 Lieut. Col. 45 Reg. Pa. Vols. Com. dated 19 Oct. 1861 mustered 21 Oct. 1861. " 1862 Sept 4 Col. 148 Reg. Pa. Vols. Com. dated 22 Jany 1863. mustered 8 Oct 1862. remustered to date 8 Sept 1862. Aug 1st 1864 Bvt. Brig. Genl. U.S. Vols. com. mission dated 28 March 1865.	1837 Oct 21 Millerstown Perry Co Pennsylvania	Was one of the original members of the Bellefonte Fencibles whose preliminary organization took place in May 1858 of which A. G. Curtin afterwards Govnr. of the Comth. was Captain. The Co. was mustered 10 July 1858 & Brigade Inspector Major Genl. R. Fisher 3rd Brig. 14 Division Penna. Militia.

I hereby certify, on honor, that the above is a full and correct statement of my military record.

Date, 10 July 1880

Station, Bellefonte Pa

James A. Beaver
Brigadier General N. G. of Pa.
Bellefonte Penna.

I do solemnly swear, that to the best of my knowledge and ability, I will support and defend the Constitution of the United States, and of the Commonwealth of Pennsylvania, against all enemies, foreign and domestic; and that I will well and faithfully discharge the duties of the office on which I am about to enter. So Help me God.

James A. Beaver

Sworn and subscribed this 14th
day of December A. D. 1883.
before me.

J. F. Hartranft
Major General

Beaver's military record (top) from the National Guard of Pennsylvania enlistment records. Beaver completed the form on July 10, 1880, which documented his militia, federal, and National Guard service up to that time. Oath of Allegiance (above) dated December 14, 1883, signed by Beaver and countersigned by Major General John F. Hartranft, who had served two three-year terms as governor, from 1873 to 1879, and was then commander of the National Guard of Pennsylvania.

After weeks of recovery in army hospitals, Beaver was moved to his home in Bellefonte to continue recuperating. While there, he received notice from Secretary of War Edwin M. Stanton, dated November 10, that he had been promoted to the rank of brevet brigadier general. Nevertheless, in December, Beaver requested to be mustered out of military service. The War Department inquired, at Major General Hancock's behest, if Beaver would instead approve of light duty that would allow him to stay in the army. Beaver responded, "I have no taste for court-martial, or other inactive military duty. Being unfit for service in the field, I prefer to attend to my business at home, rather than burden the government with the care of a useless soldier."[144] He was mustered out of service on December 22, 1864.

Like many officers and soldiers, 2nd Corps Commander Major General Winfield Scott Hancock thought highly of Beaver. In a letter to Beaver's biographer, Frank A. Burr, in 1882, Hancock lauded his gallantry. "I considered him one of the most intrepid, intelligent and efficient young officers in our service during the war, and on several occasions mentioned him in my official reports for valuable services and distinguished bravery. He was wounded at 'Chancellorsville,' again while gallantly leading his fine regiment and brigade in an assault upon the enemy's works at Petersburg, Va., June 16th, 1864, and at 'Ream's station,' August 25th, 1864. On this latter occasion he had just joined his regiment, on the battle-field, and taken command of the brigade to which it belonged, after an absence caused by former wounds, when he was struck by a musket ball which shattered his thigh, and disabled him for life by the loss of a leg. He was brevetted brigadier-general for highly meritorious and distinguished conduct, and for valuable services, especially at 'Cold Harbor,' Va., where he commanded a brigade."[145]

Hancock lauded his gallantry. "I considered him one of the most intrepid, intelligent and efficient young officers in our service during the war."

After being mustered out of military service, Beaver resumed his law career. His military reputation no doubt aided in the business of his law firm. In the fall of 1865, the Republican Party nominated him as a candidate for the state legislature. He accepted the nomination with the understanding that he would not campaign. He lost the election by 141 votes.

On December 26, he married Mary Allison McAllister, the daughter of his law partner, Hugh N. McAllister. The couple had five sons, the youngest of which, James Jr., died in 1887 while Beaver served as governor of Pennsylvania.

Beginning in 1870, Beaver was active as an officer in the National Guard of Pennsylvania, serving as major general of its 14th Division upon Governor Geary's appointing him on October 12, and as major general of the 5th Division after Governor Hartranft appointed him on March 16, 1875. Subsequently, Beaver was one of the first brigade commanders appointed by Governor Hartranft for the newly reorganized National Guard of Pennsylvania, on January 16, 1879. He loved the National Guard and devoted much of his time to training new recruits.

He also had a great fondness for Pennsylvania State College, now the Pennsylvania State University, located just over a mountain from his home in Bellefonte. From 1873 to 1914, Beaver served on its board of trustees, twice as board president. He also helped the school obtain funding from the Commonwealth between 1891 and 1893. From 1906 to 1908, he served as president of the institution. The university's nationally renowned football team's Beaver Stadium is named for him.

Beaver refused the Republican Party's nomination for Congress in 1877. In 1880, he chaired Pennsylvania's delegation to the Republican National Convention. He ran unsuccessfully for governor in 1882, losing to Democrat Robert E. Pattison, after his party split into factions during the campaign. He was elected governor in 1886, defeating Democrat Chauncey F. Black by more than forty thousand votes.

The front page of the November 5, 1886, edition of The Keystone Gazette, *published in Bellefonte, Centre County, hails the election of local resident James A. Beaver as the new governor-elect of Pennsylvania. The newspaper headline describes Beaver as "The Gallant Soldier." (22 x 15 inches)*

Medal celebrating Beaver's inauguration (right) as governor of Pennsylvania on January 18, 1887, depicts his likeness on the obverse and an American eagle with banners heralding "Protection to American Industry" on the reverse. (2 x 1³/₈ inches dia.)

Not above capitalizing on his war wound to further his political career in the post-war years, Beaver preferred to be addressed as "General" because, he cited, "that office cost me the most." He eschewed wearing military ribbons and medals in the post-war period, because he believed his crutches were the only military decorations he needed. He did, however, have a "staff of military officers around him always and in the receiving lines they sparkled and glistened in the gold lace and braid on their resplendent uniforms."[146]

A medal made for Beaver's unsuccessful 1882 gubernatorial campaign (left), which he lost to Democrat Robert Emory Pattison (1850–1904), depicts a bust of the candidate on the obverse and crossed crutches with a cloverleaf, the 2ⁿᵈ Corps badge, beneath them on the reverse. The inscription, "The Only Medal He Wears Won At Reams Station," shows how Beaver conspicuously used his military service and his amputation to garner support from Pennsylvania's voters. (1 inch dia.)

In his gubernatorial inaugural address, Beaver spoke out in support of the Pennsylvania Soldiers' and Sailors' Home in Erie. "A new institution," he said, "providing for a class which appeals especially to our sympathy and demands our help, has been established at Erie for the care and support, under immediate State supervision, of the Soldier's and Sailor's rendered destitute by reason of their service in the defense of the country, who do not come within the technical provisions of the laws regulating our national homes established for this class of unfortunates. It seems to be conceded that our alms houses are not proper places for them. The beginning which has been made at Erie demonstrates the entire feasibility of the plan, and the attention of the public is called to the institution in the hope of awakening interest and inquiry in regard to its management, and of calling forth a wider sympathy in behalf of the unfortunate class gathered, and yet to be gathered within its hospitable walls."[147]

Governor Beaver favored reconciliation with the South and welcomed Confederate veterans to the twenty-fifth anniversary of the Battle of Gettysburg on July 2, 1888. He delivered the gubernatorial address at Gettysburg on September 12, 1889, when the monuments ordered by the state's Gettysburg Commission were installed by the Commonwealth. He also delivered the address by which the Commonwealth transferred the monuments to the Gettysburg Battlefield Memorial Association.[148]

Entrance to Soldiers' and
Sailors' Home, Erie, Pa.

A circa 1917 postcard of the main entrance of the Pennsylvania Soldiers' and Sailors' Home in Erie, dedicated on February 22, 1886. Beaver supported the establishment of the facility for indigent and disabled veterans. The twenty-six acre complex, administered by the Adjutant General's Department (now the Pennsylvania Department of Military and Veterans Affairs), contains a veterans cemetery which was established in 1896. The postcard depicts Civil War era cannon flanking the walkway.

An early twentieth-century postcard image of a group of military veterans and residents of the Pennsylvania Soldiers' and Sailors' Home, Erie, bears the description "A discussion underneath the Old Pension Tree" on the reverse.

Medal created for President Benjamin Harrison's inauguration, at which Beaver served as chief marshal of the president's inaugural parade, on March 4, 1889.

Beaver was the chief marshal of President Benjamin Harrison's inaugural parade on March 4, 1889. One future and one former governor of Pennsylvania were also involved in the inauguration. Future governor Daniel H. Hastings, adjutant general of Pennsylvania, served as Beaver's chief of staff, and former governor John F. Hartranft, major general of the National Guard of Pennsylvania, served as marshal of the 2nd Division in the parade.

In a gesture of national reconciliation, Beaver announced his intentions to include not only Union veterans on his staff at Harrison's inaugural, but also Confederate veterans as well. He was inundated with letters from fellow Republicans who recommended former Confederates as potential staff members. Governor Beaver's adjutant general, Daniel H. Hastings, convinced him to appoint Confederate Lieutenant General James Longstreet to his staff for President Harrison's inaugural. "I had it in my mind to tender a Staff appointment to General Longstreet," Beaver wrote to Hastings on February 27, 1889, "but felt some delicacy in doing so—thinking that a gentleman who had served as Lieutenant-General, and occupied a place of such high rank and influence in the Confederate Army, might hesitate about riding behind a Brevet-Brigadier-General. I am glad he has signified his willingness to join us on the occasion. It will be historically and dramatically an event in the exercises of the day."[149]

Governor James A. Beaver led President Harrison's inaugural parade in Washington, D.C., on March 4, 1889. Riding next to (and a little behind) Beaver is State Adjutant General Daniel Hartman Hastings, followed by the mounted National Guard of Pennsylvania.

Beaver delivered a speech in June 1892, at the unveiling of the High Water Mark monument at the Gettysburg battlefield, during which he commented extensively about his desire for remembrance and reconciliation. "As the years go by," he said, "I become more and more convinced of the duty which devolves upon the survivors of our late war to smooth the way for the complete union, in sentiment and feeling, of the people of all sections of our common country, and for the destruction of sectionalism in all its forms and phases.

". . . An irrepressible conflict no longer separates us into necessarily contending factions. The house is no longer divided against itself. Our aims, our hopes, our ambitions for our country are one. Upon this field, where the division was so bitterly emphasized, let us make the effort for union."[150]

The 1889 Johnstown Flood, on May 31, devastated the Cambria County community. Governor Beaver responded immediately in the wake of the catastrophe, dispatching the National Guard of Pennsylvania, headed by Adjutant General Daniel H. Hastings, to reestablish order after the floodwaters subsided. Governor Beaver's and Adjutant General Hastings' rapid and vigorous response to the disaster helped to ameliorate conditions in Johnstown as speedily as possible.

After leaving office in January 1891, Beaver returned to practicing law and managing the Blubaker Coal Company. He was appointed to the first Superior Court of Pennsylvania in 1895 and remained on the bench until his death at the age of seventy-seven, on January 31, 1914. Even as a judge, Beaver was concerned about his place in history with the National Guard of Pennsylvania. He wrote to the state's adjutant general, Thomas J. Stewart, on July 21, 1904, inquiring why his name no longer appeared on the retired list of the National Guard's directory. Beaver was also active in various Civil War veterans groups, including the 148th Pennsylvania Regiment Association, and also served on the Governor Curtin Monument Commission.

Governor James Addams Beaver (seated front row, far right) and State Adjutant General of Pennsylvania Daniel Hartman Hastings (seated front row, far left), photographed with National Guard of Pennsylvania staff members at an encampment at Conemaugh Lake, circa 1888.

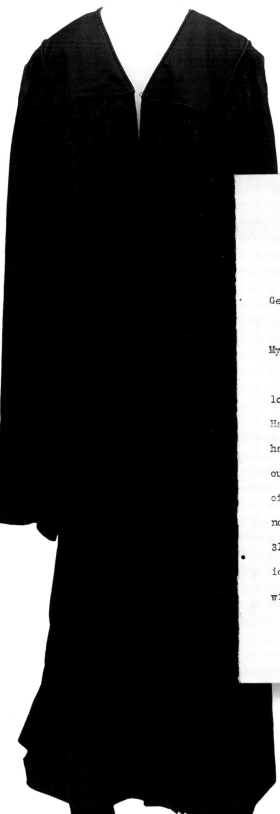

Black cotton judicial robe likely worn by James A. Beaver while he was a member of the Pennsylvania State Superior Court, circa 1895–1914.

The Superior Court of Pennsylvania.

Bellefonte, Penn'a.,

July 21st, 1904.

Gen. Thomas J. Stewart,

Adjutant General, etc., Harrisburg, Pa.

My dear General:-

What has happened to me that I am no longer in the National Guard of Pennsylvania? Have I done anything which I ought not to have done or left undone anything which I ought to have done? In a late directory of the National Guard of Pennsylvania I do not find myself in the retired list on page 31. I have always been under the impression that I was there. If I am in default, will you kindly let me know.

Very cordially yours,

Judge Beaver wrote to Adjutant General of Pennsylvania Thomas J. Stewart on July 21, 1904. His pointed question about his status as a member of the National Guard of Pennsylvania illustrates his concern for his continued association with the organization.

Governor
William Alexis Stone
in office from 1899 to 1903

William Alexis Stone was born in Delmar Township, Tioga County, on April 18, 1846, to Israel and Amanda Howe Stone. The farmhouse in which he grew up, near Wellsboro, was used as a stop along the Underground Railroad, where a spare room was used to temporarily hide escaped slaves. As Stone told the story, it was between 1856 and 1860 when he discovered that his father was a conductor on the Underground Railroad. "I slipped outside and saw through a hole in the window curtain, a black man and woman sitting there. I had never seen a colored person before. I asked my mother about it, but only succeeded in getting from her a command to keep quiet. But I was watchful. That night about 9 o'clock my father took these people away in the sleigh. There were no bells on the horses, as usual, and no lantern. The next day my father came home. I was full of curiosity, and beseeched my mother to explain. She finally did so, after pledging me to secrecy. These colored people were on their way to Canada and freedom. They had been brought to our house the night before by the keeper of the underground railroad station twenty miles south of us, and my father took them to the next station twenty miles north. After that escaping slaves at our house were frequent. My father was an anti-slavery man."[151]

This engraving depicts Republican William A. Stone (1846–1920) who served four terms in the U.S. House of Representatives before being elected governor of Pennsylvania in 1898.

Stone was fifteen years old when Abraham Lincoln was inaugurated president in 1861. Two of his half-brothers enlisted in the Union Army in response to Lincoln's first call for volunteers. They both became members of the First Pennsylvania Bucktails, also known as the 42nd Pennsylvania Volunteer Infantry (PVI) Regiment. An impressionable youth, Stone wanted to enlist and leave the family farm as well, but as

Carte de visite of abolitionist John Brown (1800–1859), whose October 16, 1859, raid on Harpers Ferry is believed by many historians to have exacerbated sectional differences between the North and the South and propelled the country closer to the irreconcilable divisiveness that caused the outbreak of the Civil War. Lieutenant Colonel Robert E. Lee, United States Army, commanded the forces which captured Brown and ended the raid. Brown was tried and convicted for crimes committed during the raid. He was executed on December 2, 1859.

he described, "I was big enough, but not old enough. They were more careful about enlistments in the early days of the war."[152] Speaking of the first year of the American Civil War, Stone remarked, "The men who volunteered went South to abolish slavery and revenge John Brown and Uncle Tom. If there had been only the question of division of States at issue, I doubt whether the war would have occurred. The North was fired with a hate of slavery. It was a curse upon the land. I have always thought that Harriet Beecher Stowe and John Brown did more to rouse the patriotic spirit of the North than any other persons."[153]

In July 1863, Stone—although not yet of age—ran off with a number of other local boys to join the Union Army in Harrisburg. However, his father discovered where he had gone and nipped his young son's military venture in the bud. Stone related his first underage attempt to join the Union Army, "In July, 1863, the great battle of Gettysburg was fought. I was then seventeen years old and was anxious to enlist. There was a battalion of Pennsylvania volunteers organized to defend the State under a six months' enlistment. George W. Merrick was the Captain of Company A, and I, with four other boys went to Harrisburg and enlisted in Captain Merrick's Company. We were to be mustered in and get our uniforms in a few days, and in the meantime were given a tent and rations. Before I was mustered an order came to discharge me and send me home. My father had telegraphed Senator Simon Cameron, and he had obtained my discharge. I had neglected to get my father's consent to my enlistment, or tell him about it, for I was afraid that he might object."[154] Stone was quickly turned out of the camp of the 1st Battalion, Pennsylvania Infantry, and returned home to his family.

On February 4, 1864, Stone again enlisted, this time at Wellsboro, for a three-year period as a private in Company A of the 187th Pennsylvania Volunteer Infantry (PVI) Regiment. This time Stone had dutifully received his father's permission in advance, a requirement because he was still only seventeen years old. "I can't say that it was any excess of patriotism that led me to do this," Stone recalled. "I suppose that I was as patriotic as the average boy of my age, but my recollection is that I felt ashamed to stay at home when so many boys were going."[155] He was mustered into service with his regiment at Camp Curtin, Harrisburg, on February 25. His company's muster roll describes him as being 6 feet 1½ inches tall, with blue eyes, light-colored hair, and a fair complexion. "Our company lay at Camp Curtin through March and April. We were in an enclosure called the Bull Penn, which had a high board fence all around it. Two or three gates gave access to it, which gates were guarded."[156] While at Camp Curtin, Stone received his first promotion, and later recalled, "I was made a corporal, and I was more proud of it than of any office I have ever received."[157]

> *"The North was fired with a hate of slavery. It was a curse upon the land."*

The 187th PVI was ordered to the front in May, and one of the regiment's most noted engagements began that month at Cold Harbor, Virginia. Stone at the time, however, was a patient at Carver Hospital in Washington, D.C., on sick leave with chronic diarrhea. The 187th also participated in the siege of Petersburg, Virginia, from June to September. Stone rejoined his regiment in August, in front of Petersburg. His company had suffered extreme losses at Forts Hell and Damnation during an attack on Confederate lines at Petersburg. Because of this, in part, on June 18 he was promoted to sergeant.[158]

Stone participated in his regiment's successful attack, capture, and defense of the Weldon Railroad's line, on August 18. Shortly afterward, he and his tent mate, Sergeant David Bricker, went out in front of the regiment's main line to gather some shingles from an old house that had been torn down. They planned on using the shingles as flooring for their tent because the ground was damp and muddy. "We found the shingles and piled them on two poles," Stone recounted. "Then I took the front ends of the poles and he the rear end and we started slowly to camp. We had gotten about half way back when the confederates began their attack. Cannon balls and shells were flying

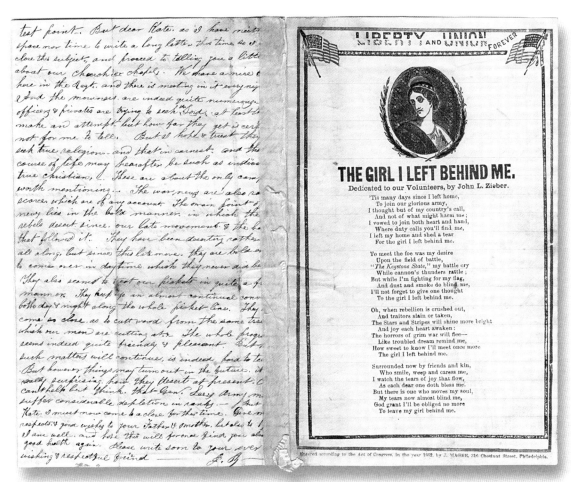

Songs, poetry, and envelopes and letterhead with patriotic imagery were used by both soldiers and civilians in their correspondence during the Civil War. "The Girl I Left Behind Me" became especially popular with Union soldiers. From a camp near Petersburg, Virginia, Jacob Bomgardner of Company D, 93rd Pennsylvania Volunteer Infantry Regiment, wrote to Kate Musser of Lebanon, Lebanon County, on February 14, 1865. To his letter he attached the lyrics for the song, written by John L. Zieber and copyrighted in 1862 by James Magee, Philadelphia. Bomgardner mustered into service as a private on December 20, 1861, and reenlisted in the company as a veteran volunteer on January 1, 1864. He mustered out of service on June 27, 1865, with the rank of corporal.

through the air from both sides. We got back to our tent but we brought no shingles. He beat me back. I remember thinking I did not know that he was such a sprinter. . . ."[159]

Stone described letter writing in camp. "The envelopes coming to us and those we sent had little patriotic songs upon them in fine print, covering sometimes two-thirds of the envelope," he recounted. "It required some taste and skill to select the envelope. It would not do to send a letter to your mother with the song of 'The Girl I Left Behind Me' or to write to your best girl with the song on the envelope of 'Who Will Care for Mother Now?'. . . These envelopes were of all colors, scarlet, pink, white, blue, and grey. They were very popular at home and in the army, and many a poor letter writer was helped out very much by the selection of an envelope that bore the proper song. It was wonderful how patient the folks were at home, and how they cheered us with their letters. Boys wrote letters to girls at home that they scarcely knew, and the girls were very nice to answer them. Of course, as poor speakers make the most speeches, the poorest writers wrote the most letters."[160]

On September 22, 1864, the 187th PVI was ordered to Philadelphia and was posted at Camp Cadwalader. Stone immediately recognized the difference between officers who had remained stationed at home and those in his regiment who had tasted combat at the front. "Our regiment was

PENNSYLVANIA.

Executive Office--Military Department,

Harrisburg, August 2nd 1865

SECRETARY OF THE COMMONWEALTH,

Let Commissions issue for 187 *Reg't P. V., as follows, viz:*

NAME.	COUNTY OF RESIDENCE.	RANK.	Co.	DATE FROM WHICH TO RANK.
Timothy B. Culver	Tioga	First Lt:	A	Mch: 10. 1865.
William A. Stone	do	Second Lt:	A	" " "

By order of the Governor,

J. B. Thomas

a d c

A commission order, by the directive of Governor Andrew Gregg Curtin, dated August 2, 1865, promoted William A. Stone from sergeant to 2nd lieutenant of Company A, 187th PVI. The promotion was retroactive to March 10, 1865. (6 1/2 x 8 1/2 inches)

ordered on dress parade the day after we got there. Of course we came back when ordered and were in our fighting clothes. We had no extra clothing as we had thrown it away on the march. The average man had a woolen shirt, a pair of trousers, a hat, blouse, and shoes. I had owned for a time while in front a pair of socks, but I had none when we went to Philadelphia. We had no trouble with dress parade at the front, but neither our appearance nor our evolutions satisfied these gorgeous military officials who commanded Camp Cadwalader. A stranger could not tell the rank of all of our officers. Some of them had no shoulder straps, but we knew them, for they had led us in battle. There was no mistake about these camp officers for they had braid on their trousers, coats, and caps, and shoulder straps large enough for shelter when it rained. . . . We got into position and paraded before this brilliant bunch. When it was over a little fellow read an order or composition which was a criticism on our personal appearance. If they had given us time we could have improved it. They evidently thought that the officers at the front looked as they did. . . . Our comparison to them was unfavorable to us. So they told us, in the order, that we were not soldierly and neat. Now, if there is anything that offends it is a criticism of personal appearance. Neither we, nor our officers liked the order. They marched up to headquarters and denounced it."[161] Several of the 187th PVI officers were arrested and court-martialed for their insubordination. Stone was promoted from 1st sergeant to 2nd lieutenant, effective March 10, 1865.

The 187th remained at Camp Cadwalader for the winter and early spring of 1865, and therefore, Stone was in Philadelphia when Lincoln's funeral train arrived. He described the event in his autobiography. "When Lincoln's body was brought to Philadelphia on his way to Springfield, our regiment acted as escort. The people had the greatest desire to see him. His casket was placed on a high vehicle, trimmed in black and drawn by ten black horses all caparisoned with crape, each horse was led by a colored man dressed in mourning. It was with the greatest difficulty that we kept the crowd from pressing upon the vehicle. Occasionally, we were delayed for ten or fifteen minutes. We finally reached Independence Hall where his casket was placed on wooden rests, and his face exposed to view. It was shrunken and relaxed. I had seen him when alive, but his face did not have much resemblance to the face I had seen in Washington. All night the people poured through Independence Hall passing on each side of him until early morning when he was taken to Kensington Station. It seems difficult to believe that one can have any real grief for a person he has never seen, but on this occasion I saw men and women weeping and in great grief and sorrow. Lincoln was loved by the people as no man in this country has ever been loved. Washington was respected and admired but not loved as Lincoln was."[162]

After the assassination of President Abraham Lincoln (right) on April 14, 1865, the 187th PVI, including William A. Stone, served as escorts for the slain president's body while it was in Philadelphia. Lincoln's funeral train was photographed by David C. Burnite at Harrisburg's train station (below) a week after the murder, on Saturday, April 22. The coat of arms of the United States was affixed to the car bearing his body.

The New York lithographic firm of Currier and Ives—which advertised itself as "Publishers of Cheap and Popular Pictures"—published The Funeral of President Lincoln, New York, April 25, 1865, *which depicts the president's ornate funeral carriage passing through New York City's Union Square. Built by New York undertaker Peter Relyea, the carriage was pulled by sixteen horses. Several days earlier, on April 22–23, more than three hundred thousand people viewed Lincoln's casket in Philadelphia, where William A. Stone and the 187th PVI regiment served as official escorts. (11 x 15 inches)*

Four months later, on August 3, 1865, Stone was mustered out of service with the rest of his regiment. "We went home to find that we were not nearly as great heroes when the war closed as we had been during the war. The thoughts of the people were again turned to farming and other pursuits."[163] After the war, Stone attended Mansfield State Normal School (now Mansfield University of Pennsylvania), in Tioga County, graduating in 1868. Following graduation, he initially—but unsuccessfully—attempted to find employment as a store clerk. He was eventually hired as the principal of Wellsboro Academy. During this time, he also studied law and was admitted to the bar in 1870.

On July 19, 1871, Stone was appointed assistant adjutant general and lieutenant colonel of the 13th Division of the National Guard of Pennsylvania. He held this position until his extensive business interests prompted him to resign on August 20, 1873.

Stone married Ellen Stevens on August 18, 1870, with whom he had two children. Ellen died in 1878, and the following year Stone married Elizabeth White. Stone and his second wife had six additional children.

In 1872, Stone was appointed transcribing clerk for Pennsylvania's House of Representatives. In 1874, he was elected district attorney of Tioga County, an office he held until 1876, when he resigned to move to Allegheny County. He then established a successful legal practice in Pittsburgh. In 1880, President Rutherford B. Hayes appointed him United States District Attorney

Oath of allegiance (right), dated July 19, 1871, for Stone's appointment as assistant adjutant general of the 13th Division, National Guard of Pennsylvania, giving him the rank of lieutenant colonel in the National Guard.

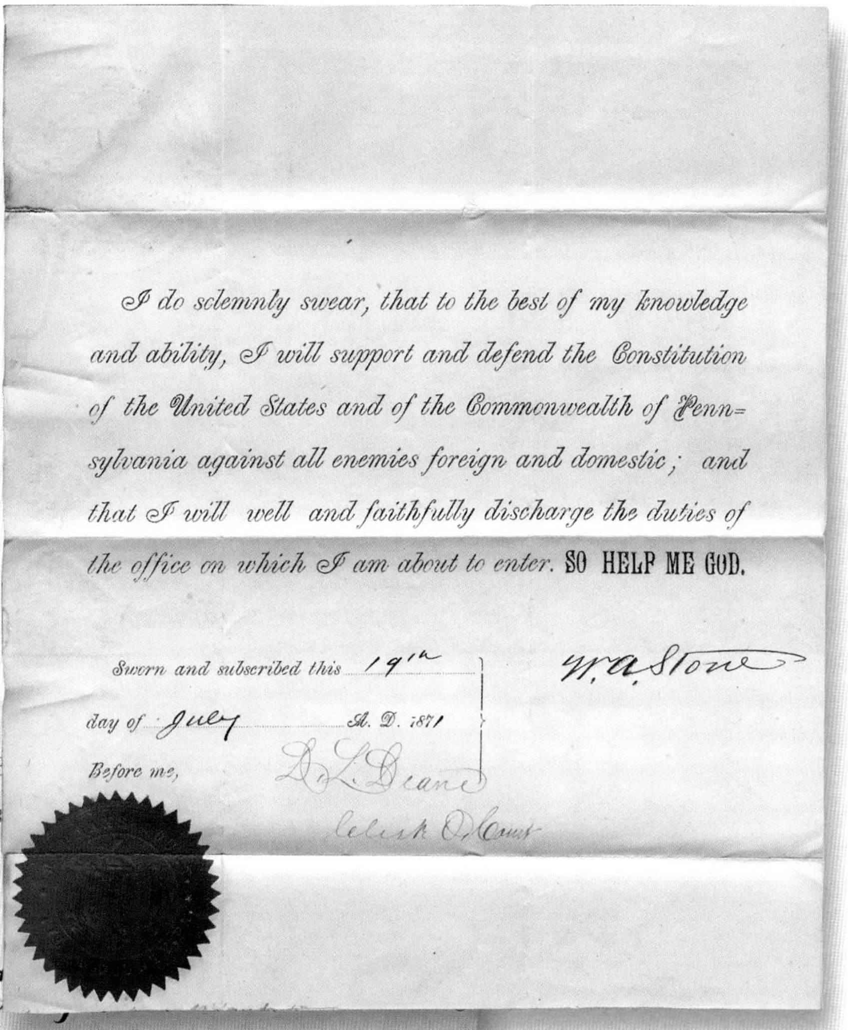

I do solemnly swear, that to the best of my knowledge and ability, I will support and defend the Constitution of the United States and of the Commonwealth of Penn= sylvania against all enemies foreign and domestic; and that I will well and faithfully discharge the duties of the office on which I am about to enter. SO HELP ME GOD.

Sworn and subscribed this 19th
day of July A. D. 1871
Before me,

W. A. Stone

D. L. Dean
clerk O Court

Head-quarters 13

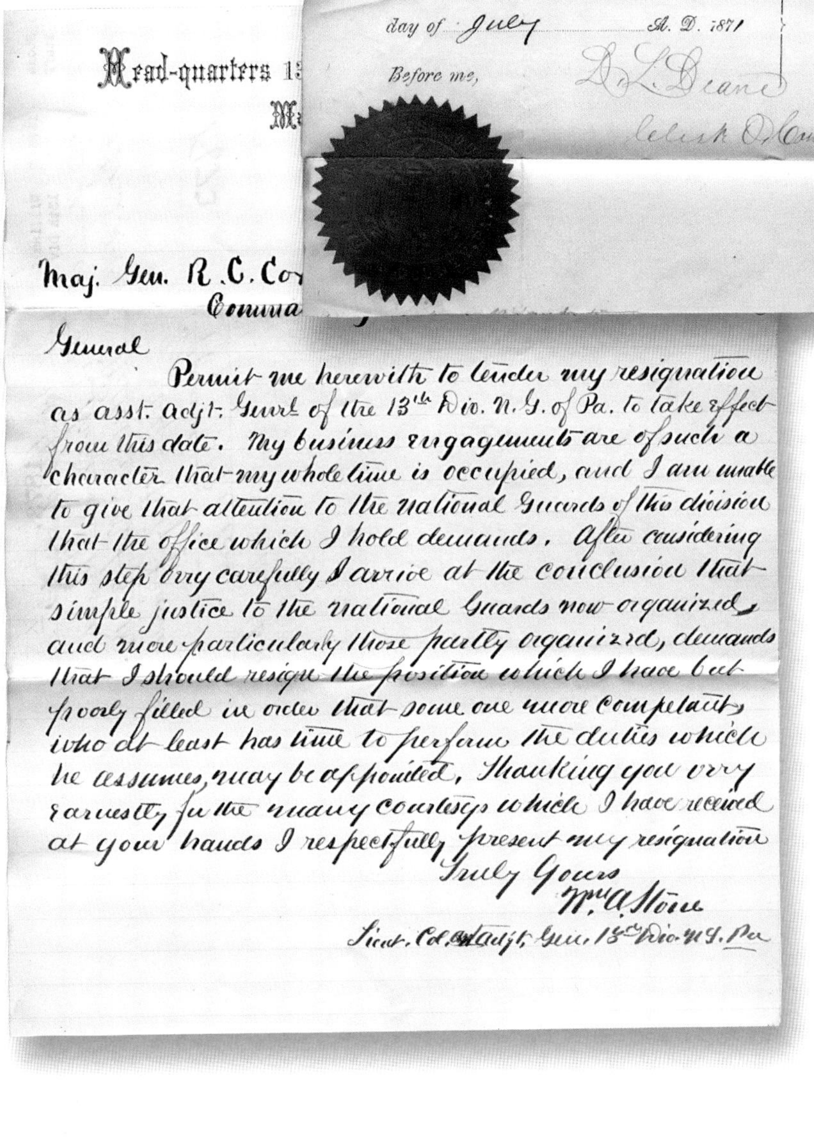

Maj. Gen. R. C. Co
Comma

General

Permit me herewith to tender my resignation as asst. adjt. Genrl of the 13th Div. N. G. of Pa. to take effect from this date. My business engagements are of such a character that my whole time is occupied, and I am unable to give that attention to the National Guards of this division that the office which I hold demands. After considering this step very carefully I arrive at the conclusion that simple justice to the National Guards now organized, and more particularly those partly organized, demands that I should resign the position which I have but poorly filled in order that some one more competent, who at least has time to perform the duties which he assumes, may be appointed. Thanking you very earnestly for the many courtesies which I have received at your hands I respectfully present my resignation

Truly Yours
Wm. A. Stone
Lieut. Col. & Adjt. Gen. 13th Div. N. G. Pa.

In his letter (left) of August 20, 1873, to Major General Robert C. Cox, Commanding General of the 13th Division of the National Guard of Pennsylvania, Stone resigned as assistant adjutant general of the division because of his "business engagements."

for the Western District of Pennsylvania. President Chester A. Arthur reappointed him four years later, but in 1886, President Grover Cleveland removed him from office because he had campaigned for political candidates, including Republican James Addams Beaver. Stone resumed his law practice until he was elected to Congress from the 23rd District, in 1890. He served four terms in the U.S. House of Representatives, from 1891 to 1899.

House of Representatives U. S.,

Washington, D. C., Jan. 23rd. 189 5.

His Excellency Danl. H. Hastings,

    Governor of Pennsylvania.

Dear Sir;-

    Among the appointments which you will have to make is that of Agent of the State of Pennsylvania here at Washington.   I desire to recommend the appointment of Hon. Henry M. Foote of Wellsboro, Tioga Co. Pa.   Mr. Foote was a former member of the legislature, and was appointed one of the assistant Attorney Generals under Harrison's administration, a position which he held with great credit, discharging his duties with entire satisfaction to the administration, and which qualifies him to discharge the duties of agent here, he having had experience and practice, and is thoroughly acquainted with the duties of that appointment.

    Mr. Foote was a member of my company in the war and I have known him all my life.   He is a good lawyer and would make an honest, faithful, efficient agent of the State, and I believe would secure more money for the state and better represent her interests than any one that I can now think of.

        Very truly yours, Wm. A. Stone

U.S. Representative Stone wrote to Governor Daniel H. Hastings on January 23, 1895, to recommend that his former Civil War comrade in Company A, 187th PVI, Henry M. Foote, of Wellsboro, Tioga County, be appointed as "Agent for Pennsylvania" in the nation's capital. The position was responsible for collecting money from the federal government that the state claimed it was due from the Civil War. In 1903–1904, the Commonwealth collected more than nine hundred thousand dollars from the federal government for the funds it "expended in arming the state under the Act of May 15, 1861," and for the money the Keystone State "paid to owners of buildings and grounds, used for the purpose of equipping troops for the service of the United States in [the] War of the Rebellion."

In 1898, Stone sought the Republican nomination for governor. Republican political boss Matthew Stanley Quay (1833–1904) supported his campaign. Another candidate who had sought Quay's support for the Republican nomination assured Quay, "I'll do what you tell me, the same as Bill Stone would." "I know" replied Quay, "but I would have to tell you, and I don't have to tell him."[164] Quay used the outbreak of the Spanish-American War to tout Stone as a well-qualified "war governor," due to Stone's past military service. Stone defeated Democrat George Jenks and Prohibition candidate Silas Swallow in the 1898 general election for the governor's office by more than 110,000 votes.

After his inauguration, on January 17, 1899, Governor Stone served as commander-in-chief of the National Guard of Pennsylvania. He attended a number of events with the Guard, including dedications of military monuments and presidential inaugurations. His term as governor was not always so peaceful, though.

A political cartoon from the 1898 gubernatorial election entitled "At the Same Old Game" ridicules Stone's assertion that "I Own Myself" by showing his likeness being pushed forward by Matthew S. Quay and William Andrews, a state senator and longtime Quay ally. In the balcony throwing charges shaped like stones at Quay are his archenemies, wealthy Philadelphia retail merchant John Wanamaker and Dr. Silas Swallow, the Prohibition Party candidate for the governor's office. In the lower left hand corner, with his back turned away, is Christopher L. Magee, Pittsburgh, a state senator and Quay opponent. To the right of Magee is Governor Daniel H. Hastings, in military uniform, and David Martin, Hastings's secretary of the commonwealth and one-time Quay ally in Philadelphia. To the right is President William McKinley, awaiting the outcome of Pennsylvania's gubernatorial fight.

Portrait of Matthew S. Quay *(circa 1896) by artist William A. Greaves (1847–1900) of Warren, Warren County. A recipient of the Medal of Honor for his actions at the Battle of Fredericksburg during the Civil War, Quay was a successful and controversial Republican Party boss and politician in Pennsylvania. He was a United States senator representing the Keystone State at the time Greaves painted his likeness. (51 x 34 inches)*

Delegate's badge and ribbon (right) for the Republican League of Pennsylvania's eleventh annual convention held in Pittsburgh on September 7–9, 1898. The badge would have been worn by a delegate supporting Stone in his quest for the governorship.

Stone's gubernatorial campaign badge and handbill (below and left) emphasized his military service by using the title colonel, a reference to his position with the National Guard of Pennsylvania. Republican Party boss Matthew S. Quay urged candidates seeking political office to capitalize on their Civil War service.

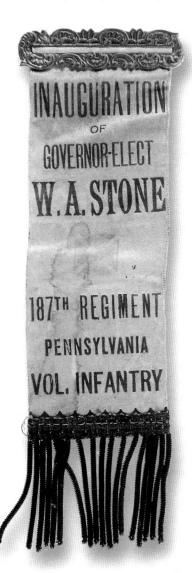

Inaugural ribbon for Stone (above), whose swearing in as governor took place in Harrisburg on January 17, 1899. The ribbon was most likely worn by one of Stone's former Civil War comrades in the 187th Pennsylvania Volunteer Infantry. Stone served in this regiment from February 1864 to August 1865.

Gubernatorial campaign badge for Stone (left) distributed in Philadelphia on October 26–27, 1898, during the Peace Jubilee, an observance of thanksgiving proclaimed by Governor Daniel H. Hastings to celebrate the success of the United States armed forces, the end of the Spanish-American War, and the return of victorious American troops to Pennsylvania.

Governor Stone (wearing civilian clothes and riding a white horse) led the National Guard of Pennsylvania at the second inauguration of President William McKinley in Washington, D.C., on March 4, 1901. Adjutant General of Pennsylvania Thomas J. Stewart rode next to him. The event was captured by William H. Rau (1855–1920), a leading Philadelphia photographer who documented the Lehigh Valley and the Pennsylvania railroads in the late nineteenth century.

In 1902, Stone called out 90 percent of the National Guard to restore order in a sweeping anthracite miners' strike that crippled Schuylkill, Carbon, Columbia, Lackawanna, Luzerne, Northumberland, and Susquehanna counties. "The State troops are sent to the scene of disturbance for the sole purpose of protecting life and property and preserving order when the county authorities are unable to cope with the difficulty," he declared. "The owner of a mine claims the right to stop work at any time. The miner claims the right to stop work at any time. If capital can shut down, labor can shut down. If capital can strike, labor can strike. No greater right is claimed for one than for the other and no right can be withheld from one that is conceded to the other. But neither has the right to resort to public violence. No one, under any circumstances, has a right to commit a breach of the peace."[165] The strikes did not end until President Theodore Roosevelt intervened and appointed a commission to study the dispute.

Governor Stone supported the mission of Pennsylvania's soldiers' orphan schools. The 1902 *Annual Report of the Pennsylvania Commission of Soldiers' Orphan Schools*, headed by Governor Stone, read, in part, "The time is now rapidly approaching when we can commence to see the beginning of the end of this most worthy charity upon the part of this great State towards the children of the men who upheld the honor of the flag upon many a battlefield in the War of the Rebellion. While it will take some years yet to bring about that result, because of the extreme youth of the children in the schools, the Commission most earnestly point out the advisability of preparing for that event by concentrating all the children at one of the schools where the buildings, ground and all the property belongs to the State.

"With a very small amount of money the Commission feels that they could erect sufficient buildings of the proper character at Scotland, Franklin County, Pa., to accomplish that end."[166]

Photograph entitled "Girls' Calisthenics, Soldiers' Orphan Industrial School," depicts a class at Scotland, Franklin County, in 1898. At their zenith, orphan schools in Pennsylvania numbered twenty-three primary and fifteen advanced schools. By June 24, 1912, Pennsylvania's soldiers' orphan school system had consolidated into one school at Scotland. Governor Stone strongly supported the schools and was proud of their accomplishments.

"Male Pupils, Soldiers' Orphan Industrial School," depicts, in 1899, young men wearing military-style uniforms which corresponded with the military training they received at the Soldiers' Orphan School in Scotland. The institution—the last of Pennsylvania's orphan school system—was eventually renamed the Scotland School for Veterans' Children and was administered by the Adjutant General's Department (now the Pennsylvania Department of Military and Veterans Affairs), until the school's closing in 2009.

The report further recommended that the consolidation of schools at Chester Springs, Uniontown, and Scotland be completed by 1905. As of May 31, 1902, the three schools housed a total of 654 boys and 421 girls. "Pennsylvania has at all times shown a generous spirit towards her soldiers and sailors," the report continued, "but never has it been more observant than the splendid care and protection that she has accorded the children of the men who in their youth did so much on many desperate battlefields for the good of our common country."

"There have been over 17,000 of these boys and girls discharged at the age of sixteen years since the inception of this system, and all over this State and all over this land are men filling positions of responsibility and trust, men of affairs who owe their success in life to the careful training they received in the Soldiers' Orphan Schools of Pennsylvania, who never tire in sounding the praises of this grand old Commonwealth."[167]

Governor Stone was also keenly interested in the Pennsylvania Soldiers' and Sailors' Home, opened in Erie, Erie County, in 1886. The report for the quarter ending March 31, 1899, during Stone's first year as governor, showed an average of 479 patients present in the home with an additional average of 26 absent with or without leave from the facility.[168] As a veteran, Stone endorsed the idea that such a home was a necessity for Pennsylvania.

During his administration, Stone managed to wipe out the state debt. After leaving office, he joined his son, Stephen, in a Pittsburgh law practice, Stone and Stone.[169] In 1915, he served as prothonotary of the state Supreme Court and, in 1916, the state Superior Court. William A. Stone died on March 1, 1920, and is buried in Wellsboro Cemetery, Tioga County.

Circa 1910 penny postcard bearing an image of part of the grounds of the Pennsylvania Soldiers' and Sailors' Home in Erie, published for S. H. Knox & Co. of Erie. (3 ³/₈ x 5 ³/₈ inches)

Governor
Samuel Whitaker Pennypacker
in office from 1903 to 1907

Samuel Whitaker Pennypacker was born in Phoenixville, Chester County, on April 9, 1843, to Dr. Isaac Anderson Pennypacker and Anna Maria Whitaker Pennypacker, the daughter of successful iron maker Joseph Whitaker. His father, a professor at the Philadelphia College of Medicine, died of typhoid and erysipelas on February 13, 1856. Thereafter, Pennypacker, his widowed mother, and three siblings, went to live with their mother's father, Joseph Whitaker, in Mont Clare, Montgomery County.

While working as a druggist's apprentice in Kensington, in 1857, Pennypacker began studying to enroll at Yale University. Financial concerns thwarted his plans, however, and in the winter of 1861–1862, he worked at a Philadelphia firm owned by relatives that sold iron. In the winter of 1862, Pennypacker taught school in a one-room schoolhouse in Mont Clare.

He took note of an ominous movement during the 1860 presidential campaign. "At the political meetings held by the Republicans, clubs called 'Wide Awakes,' never before known, wearing oilcloth caps and capes as a sort of uniform, carrying torches upon the edge of long staffs often used as bludgeons, drilled to march and go through the maneuvers of the manual of arms in a semi-military way, appeared all over the North and were everywhere greeted with enthusiastic approval. I do not know that their significance was recognized, but a philosophical observer could well have forecasted that when men instinctively turned to military organization, war was approaching."[170]

Pennypacker and his maternal grandfather witnessed President Lincoln's visit to Philadelphia in the spring of 1861, which he described in his autobiography. "When Lincoln came to Philadelphia on his way to Washington to be inaugurated, my grandfather and I went to the city and from a second-story window watched him as he passed in a barouche bowing to the crowds, anxious but earnest, who lined the streets. The next morning we heard him make his speech in which he alluded to the possibility of assassination, and saw him raise the flag over Independence Hall. He took off his coat, rolled up his sleeves and pulled at the rope, hand over hand, in a way which led my grandfather to ejaculate, 'I think he will do.'"[171]

Samuel Whitaker Pennypacker (1843–1916), who served as Republican governor of Pennsylvania from 1903 to 1907, enlisted in the 26th Pennsylvania Emergency Militia when General Robert E. Lee's Army of Northern Virginia threatened to invade Pennsylvania in June 1863.

An 1860 ambrotype, a positive photographic image on a sheet of glass, of a Wide Awake man holding a parade torch to which is affixed a flag supporting Abraham Lincoln (1809–1865) for president and Hannibal Hamlin (1809–1891) as vice president in the election of 1860. The Wide Awakes was a pseudo-military organization affiliated with the Republican Party, whose members wore a uniform consisting of a black oilcloth cape and cap. (3 ¹/₄ x 2 ³/₄ inches)

A circa 1856–1860 parade or campaign torch similar to this one would have been carried by Wide Awakes during political rallies. The torch is comprised of a gimbel-mounted oil lamp attached to a long pole. (49 1/2 inches)

A Wide Awake ribbon and stovetop hat, circa 1860. The symbolism of a stovetop hat was often associated with Abraham Lincoln. The hat and the ribbon for the West Chester Wide Awake Club may have been combined after the era in which they were created. (12 x 10 3/4 inches)

His cousin, Galusha Pennypacker (1844–1916), entered the American Civil War as a sergeant in the 9th Pennsylvania Volunteer Infantry (PVI) Regiment on April 24, 1861, emerging at the end of the war as a brevet major general of volunteers and, later, a recipient of the Medal of Honor. Samuel Pennypacker claimed that his patriotic sentiments were also stirred in 1861. "The military impulse had arisen and I wanted to enlist," he wrote, "but I was my mother's dependence, and she persuaded me to wait."[172] Instead, he sought an appointment to the United States Military Academy at West Point, which went unrealized.

Two years later, on June 15, 1863, President Lincoln issued a call for fifty thousand volunteers from Pennsylvania to help repel the pending invasion of the Commonwealth by Confederate forces. Governor Andrew Gregg Curtin issued a proclamation the same day: "An army of rebels is approaching our border. I now appeal to all the citizens of Pennsylvania, who love liberty and are mindful of the history and traditions of their revolutionary fathers, and who feel that it is a sacred duty to guard and maintain the free institutions of our country, who hate treason and its abettors, and who are willing to defend their homes and their firesides, and do invoke them to rise in their might and rush to the rescue in this hour of imminent peril. The issue is one of preservation or destruction."[173]

Curtin's call for troops to thwart the 1863 Confederate invasion was met at first with a mixed response from Pennsylvania's citizenry. A similar call the year before, during the Antietam Campaign, raised many troops that were never needed for the defense of the Commonwealth and, as a result, many Pennsylvanians initially turned a deaf ear to the 1863 call for emergency militia troops. Pennypacker, however, began looking into enlisting the day after Curtin's call was made.[174] In mid-June, he joined a number of other Phoenixville area men and volunteered for service. Even though his mother opposed his enlistment, she assisted him in "tying up a red horse-blanket with a piece of clothes line so that it could be thrown across the shoulder, prepared some provision consisting of a piece of cheese, several boiled eggs, with sundry slices of bread and butter which were put in one of the boys' school satchels and a tin cup fastened upon the strap. . . ."[175]

They left the Phoenixville depot for Harrisburg shortly after four o'clock on the afternoon of June 17, arriving at about 10:30 p.m. at the State Capitol, where they discovered "the Copperhead

Carte de visite of Andrew Gregg Curtin, two-term Republican governor of Pennsylvania, from 1861 to 1867. A staunch supporter of Lincoln's administration, he was so well liked by Union soldiers that he acquired the sobriquet "The Soldiers' Friend."

[Democratic Party] Convention, which had assembled for the purpose of nominating a candidate for Governor, had just chosen Judge [George W.] Woodward and held possession of the hall and seats of the House of Representatives, shouting, hurrahing and making inflammatory speeches while the pavement, the stone porch, and the floor of the galleries were covered with militia trying to sleep amidst the din. The thought was enough to anger a Saint. The Capital of the State threatened by the rebels, the Governor almost beseeching men to come to the rescue, and those who respond compelled to lie outside upon the stones and listen to the disloyal yells of the enemies of the country comfortably quartered within."[176] Pennypacker slept on the steps of the State Capitol, covered by his red horse blanket. "About one o'clock they adjourned and came out, stepping over us, and went to their hotels all of which they had previously engaged and crowded. The men groaned and cursed them, damned Woodward, [George B.] McClellan, and traitors generally and there were several fights in consequence."[177]

The following day, the volunteers marched to Camp Curtin and, according to Pennypacker, were "taken to one corner of the camp, very near to the railroad, and by the side of a small tree which stood there. A wheat field was within a few rods, and it answered the same purpose for which an out house is used generally. On the opposite side of the Rail-road and some distance off was a farm house where we got water, went to wash, and sometimes bought milk. It had also attached to it, a fine orchard the shade of whose trees afforded a pleasant spot to loll and rest upon."[178]

On Saturday, June 20, Pennypacker and several other men "went into Harrisburg, and crossing over the tottering wooden bridge which spans the Susquehanna, climbed up the very steep hill on the western bank of that river, upon which they were busily engaged throwing up fortifications. A large number of men employed and the plan of operations was, after placing a line of hogsheads filled with gravel forming the enclosure, to dig a deep ditch on the outside and bank the earth up against them. The back of the fort, toward the river and town, terminated on a very steep bank in some places like a precipice."[179] Pennypacker's description was of the construction of Fort Washington, which together with Fort Couch were both constructed in June 1863 as part of a defensive system designed to protect Harrisburg from the Confederate invasion.

Concern grew among the men who had traveled to Harrisburg with Pennypacker as to whether or not they should be sworn into service for six months. The majority refused to do so, even after Governor Curtin promised that they would be sent home as soon as the emergency ended. The employer of many of the men in Pennypacker's company, the Phoenix Iron Company, sent word that none of its employees should be sworn into federal service under penalty of losing their promised bonuses and jobs. Most of Pennypacker's compatriots returned home without ever formally being

JUDGE WOODWARD
On the War!

PHILADELPHIA, Oct. 2, 1863.

" On the 7th of July last, the Tuesday after the battle of Gettysburg, I left my home in this city for the purpose of visiting the battle-field. At Wrightsville, I took the stage, and found myself in company with several gentlemen, one of whom was the Hon. George W. Woodward, who had just been nominated for the office of Governor. I rode with him from Wrightsville to Gettysburg, and I also returned in his company from Gettysburg to York.

" As we were journeying toward the battle-field the conversation was naturally of the war, and at Oxford, in Adams county, there was quite a discussion between Judge Woodward and the Rev. Edward Strong, of New Haven, Conn., who was one of the party. Judge Woodward denounced the Administration and the war in very strong and decided terms. He said that it was an unconstitutional war and an abolition

war, and that he had no interest whatsoever in the result, let this result be what it might ; that it was a contest in which the North could gain neither credit nor honor, and this he believed would be the verdict of history.

" I was with Judge Woodward for a good part of three days, in going and returning, and there was much more said by him to the same effect as the above; and there was not one word of sympathy uttered by him, in my hearing, for the Government or for those who were sacrificing their lives for its support. As a loyal citizen, who has always voted for Democratic nominees, I was shocked at the sentiments which were uttered by one who held a high judicial position, and who aspired to receive yet higher honors from the State.

GEORGE W. HART,
NO. 666 NORTH EIGHTH STREET.

"I further stated that I had been informed, upon most respectable authority, by citizens of my own town, that Judge Woodward, in a conversation with the Hon. H. B. Wright, had defended the constitutionality of the doctrine of secession, and denied the power and authority of the General Government to coerce a State into obedience to its obligations under the Constitution ; that Judge Hale had expressed himself as being shocked at the sentiments avowed by Judge Woodward in a

conversation on the subject ; and that Judge Lorin, who knew him intimately, whilst recently on a visit to Carlisle, had characterized Judge Woodward as a disciple of the extreme Calhoun school of politics, and by far a more dangerous man than Vallandigham himself."

LEMUEL TODD,
CARLISLE, PA., Sept. 28, 1863.

Judge Woodward in a recent letter, attributes "this unconstitutional Abolition war" to the "malignant fanaticism" of the North. The following letter written by ex-President Pierce to Jefferson Davis bel leaders were induced to revolt, by promises of **Demo-** North:

Clarendon Hotel, Jan. 6, 1860.

Washington D. C.

not believe that our friends at of the state of feeling hurrying intense exasperation between ical obligations and those who power, but which fanatical estic slavery imparts. Without t—of abstract power to secede actual disruption of the Union

can occur without blood; and if through the madness of Northern Abolitionists that dire calamity must come, the fighting will not be along Mason and Dixon's line alone. *It will be within our own borders, in our own streets, between the two classes of citizens to whom I have referred. Those who defy law and scout constitutional obligations, will, if ever we reach the arbitrament of arms, FIND OCCUPATION ENOUGH AT HOME. . . .*

Ever and truly your friend,

FRANKLIN PIERCE.

aitors lured to destroy their country, and now the promise is to be redeemed y giving the government "occupation enough at home."

Although he lost in Pennsylvania's gubernatorial campaign of 1863, Judge George W. Woodward (left), served as Chief Justice of the Pennsylvania Supreme Court from 1863 to 1867. During the Civil War, he opposed allowing the Commonwealth's soldiers to vote outside their home precincts. A campaign poster (above) was published in opposition to Democratic candidate Woodward, an avowed Copperhead who believed the Civil War was unconstitutional and called slavery an "incalculable blessing." He lost to Republican incumbent Andrew Gregg Curtin. Woodward was later elected to the U.S. House of Representatives and served from 1867 to 1871. (23 3/4 x 18 3/4 inches)

TRENCHES MADE BY UNION ARMY DURING THE CIVIL WAR 1861 AT FT. WASHINGTON. HARRISBURG. PA.

Post-war postcard entitled "Trenches Made by Union Army During the Civil War." The card depicts the earthworks of Fort Washington, constructed in June 1863 under the direction of Major General Darius N. Couch. The fort was on the west shore of the Susquehanna River to protect Harrisburg from a Confederate invasion. Fort Washington was built on the east end of a ridge called Hummel Heights in present-day Lemoyne, Cumberland County.

mustered in. Pennypacker "disliked the idea of going home in that manner, considering it dishonorable and discreditable in itself and dreading the jeers which I knew must be endured and, to a certain extent, would be merited."[180] He and a few of his friends eventually joined the Pottstown Company led by Captain George Rice, Company F of the 26th Pennsylvania Emergency Militia Regiment. The 26th Pennsylvania Emergency Militia had ten companies, including Company A, which was made up mostly of Gettysburg area residents and college students. Pennypacker recalled that on June 22, "about five oclock we went to the mustering officer, were each called by name, told to take off our hats and hold up our right hands, and were sworn 'to serve the United States in the department of the Susquehanna, during the existing emergency against all enemies whatsoever'—a remarkably short and simple ceremony—but five minutes before we were our own men, now we belonged to Uncle Sam."[181] With that "simple ceremony," Pennypacker was mustered into the Union Army as a private, at the age of twenty. According to Pennypacker, the emergency regiments were "believed to be the only body of troops during the entire war, unless we may except the Veteran Corps, who committed themselves to the control of the government for a period of uncertain duration."[182]

A pump from Camp Curtin, Harrisburg, was used to supply water to soldiers encamped at the military facility, circa 1861–1865. The Grand Army of the Republic Post 58, of Harrisburg, donated the pump to the Commonwealth of Pennsylvania in 1929.
(61 1/2 x 14 inches diameter)

126

MUSTER–IN ROLL—Continued.

Muster-In Roll of Company F, 26th Pennsylvania Emergency Militia Regiment records Pennypacker's enrollment in the unit as a twenty-year-old private from Pottstown, Montgomery County, on June 22, 1863.
(10 5/16 x 17 inches as shown)

A postcard image of Harrisburg's Market Square as it appeared during the Civil War. Thousands of Union soldiers, including Samuel W. Pennypacker, passed through the state capital and would have undoubtedly been familiar with Market Square, the city's economic and cultural center.

The day after his mustering in, Pennypacker had a half-hour liberty while returning old militia arms in downtown Harrisburg, after being issued new Springfield muskets earlier in the day. Accompanied by a friend, Pennypacker "purchased a shirt from a rascally Harrisburg skin-flint who, seeing my private's uniform, gave me a great deal more impudence than I would have borne, had I not been under the necessity of getting the article."[183]

The 26th Militia left Camp Curtin by train on June 24, commanded by Colonel William W. Jennings. The following night, Pennypacker and about one hundred men were detailed to march into Gettysburg under the command of a lieutenant. They spent their first night in Gettysburg, according to Pennypacker, at the railroad "depot upon the platform of which we passed the remainder of the night. It was an extremely filthy place but sheltered us from the rain."[184]

At nine o'clock in the morning, on June 26, the rest of the regiment arrived by train. At about ten o'clock, Major Granville O. Haller of Major General Darius N. Couch's staff, Department of the Susquehanna, ordered the entire regiment —except Company C, which remained in Gettysburg—numbering approximately 743 men, to march three miles west on the Chambersburg Pike. They were dispatched to take up a position

General Robert E. Lee (1807–1870), Commander of the Army of Northern Virginia, like many Confederate officers, was a graduate of the United States Military Academy at West Point, New York, and a United States Army officer before the Civil War.

west of Gettysburg. After Jennings set out a picket line along the road, the majority of the 26th Pennsylvania Emergency Militia entered woods near Marsh Creek, about seventy-five yards to the right, or north of the road, and pitched their tents. Despite receiving only two days of training as a regiment—and the majority of the men being in the Army for only four days total—they were among the first forces to engage Confederate troops at Gettysburg. "The men upon whom this duty was imposed," Pennypacker claimed, "coming from the field, the college, and the home, had been in the service just four days; not long enough to have acquired a knowledge of the drill, hardly long enough to have learned the names of their officers and comrades. . . . These young men, in their unsoiled uniforms, and flushed with enthusiasm, were to be thrown as a preliminary sacrifice to the army of Northern Virginia for the accomplishment of a military end."[185]

Confederate Colonel Elijah V. White's cavalry battalion encountered the 26th Pennsylvania Emergency Militia on their way from Cashtown to Gettysburg. Forty soldiers of the 26th Militia were captured trying to cover the rest of the regiment's retreat, but most simply fled. Colonel William W. Jennings of the 26th Militia, after seeing the oncoming Confederate force, ordered his troops to turn back towards Harrisburg. They fled across fields between Mummasburg and Gettysburg, heading towards Hunterstown. Pennypacker described the retreat. "We crossed three or four fields until we came to one of the numerous back roads which we entered and along which we proceeded in a rapid march."[186] In the confusion of the retreat, the 26th Pennsylvania Emergency Militia became widely scattered. At about four o'clock, while resting near the Henry Witmer farmhouse on the Goldenville Road, Pennypacker saw his first Confederate soldiers, "the rebel cavalry first made their appearance and commenced picking up the stragglers in the rear.

Major General George Gordon Meade (1815–1872), Commander of the Army of the Potomac from June 28, 1863, to the end of the war, was victorious at the Battle of Gettysburg, waged July 1–3, 1863. This posthumous portrait was painted in 1904 by Philadelphia artist Albert Rosenthal (1863–1939). (40 x 30 inches)

Seeing all of our men jumping over fences on the right, I followed suit and found myself in a corn-field. Nearly all were in the adjoining wheat field further on, so I directed my steps thither. . . . In this field there was the greatest imaginable confusion. The officers were running around, waving their swords, shouting and swearing but no one even dreamed of obeying them; the men having previously been all mingled together were separated from their companies and each fellow did as he thought proper. In fact they were compelled to do so, for the commands from half-crazy Captains and Lieutenants were often unintelligible and perfectly contradictory. Collected together in little knots or standing alone they commenced firing off their pieces as rapidly as possible. Some were falling in behind the fences and others streaking off over the fields. I believe every man was shouting or yelling. . . . After firing off one load and ramming down another I began to look around for Co F but could not see one of them. About half a company were drawn up behind the next fence, and thinking I might find some of them there I went over to them. The great bulk of the regiment were much farther off and the balls from their muskets and the rebel carbines whistled over our heads very rapidly. We were rather between the two there and had the benefit of all of the firing. . . . Our regiment were now nearly all collected together and were drawn up in line some two or three fields distant. Supposing the idea was to await an attack there we concluded we had better go over and join them which we did. . . ."[187] This line of battle was formed in the field of the William Wirt house. "Upon taking my position in rank and waiting for a short time, we commenced a retreat toward the mountains. . . . Here we halted to have the roll called and among quite a number who were missing. . . . Although an hour previous I had felt excessively tired, the excitement of the skirmish had completely removed all fatigue and had so refreshened and invigorated my spirits that I seemed to be as elastic as in the morning. . . . Crossing creeks and fields, tearing down the fences and tramping grain and corn, over gullies and hills, but keeping principally to the woods and mountains we continued our retreat."[188]

"We had lost all the regimental baggage, drums, tents, blankets, & c.—over two hundred men, and the remainder were dirty, stiff and foot sore, limping along like so many cripples."

The engagement, according to Pennypacker, lasted about twenty to thirty minutes. Approximately 136 members of the 26th Pennsylvania Emergency Militia Regiment were captured in and around the Witmer farm, totaling 176 captured that day. Pennypacker overstated the 26th Militia's actions as having held back Confederate Major General Jubal A. Early's division an entire day.[189] In his autobiography, Pennypacker argued that his regiment "had fired the first shots and drawn the first blood upon the battlefield of Gettysburg."[190] After this precursor to the Battle of Gettysburg had ended, the 26th Militia continued its march towards Harrisburg.

"In circumstances in which there is anything like an equality of force, running is properly considered disgraceful; but as we were situated, our strength was entirely inadequate for successful opposition and we found ourselves drawn into a trap from which we could only be extricated by skill and celerity," Pennypacker asserted.[191] "There was something very thrilling and romantic to me then in the idea of our position and the resemblance we had to hunted game endeavoring to elude their pursuers—a sense of danger gave intensity to the interest with which we watched the chances of being captured. It soon after became very dark which caused us to feel more secure but increased the unpleasantness of travelling."[192]

The regiment passed through Dillsburg, York County, on the evening of June 27. Before dawn the following day, it reached Major General Darius N. Couch's outer picket lines approximately thirteen miles from Harrisburg. Major General Couch was in charge of the Department of the Susquehanna during the Gettysburg Campaign. The 26th continued to press on toward Harrisburg.

130

Hermann J. Meyer, of New York, published an engraving entitled Columbia Bridge (Susquehanna) *in the mid-nineteenth century, which depicts the Columbia-Wrightsville Bridge. Built in 1834 to link the communities of Wrightsville, York County, and Columbia, Lancaster County, the bridge was a casualty of the Civil War. Measuring more than a mile in length, it was the longest covered bridge in the world at the time. On June 28, 1863, nearly fifteen hundred Union troops retreated eastward across the bridge from Wrightsville to Columbia after skirmishing with a Confederate force of about eighteen hundred soldiers, led by Brigadier General John B. Gordon. The Union soldiers, consisting primarily of Pennsylvania militia, led by Colonel Jacob G. Frick, set fire to the span to prevent it from falling into enemy hands. The Confederates were thereby halted from entering Lancaster County and heading to the state capital at Harrisburg from the river's east side. (7 x 9 inches)*

Near Fort Couch, one of the forts constructed on the west shore of the Susquehanna River during the Gettysburg Campaign to protect Harrisburg, the 26th Pennsylvania Emergency Militia "passed several regiments of militia who crowded about us inquiring who we were and where we had come from. Some of them said, 'They look hard don't they? As if they had been out for a year' and I expect we did present a pretty rough appearance. We had lost all the regimental baggage, drums, tents, blankets, & c.—over two hundred men, and the remainder were dirty, stiff and foot sore, limping along like so many cripples. We were destitute of everything pertaining to comfort or convenience."[193] Pennypacker and his comrades continued on until they marched into the fort and stacked arms. They had marched continuously for about fifty-four hours. On the afternoon of June 28, Pennypacker recounted, "the rebels came to within three miles of the fort which was the nearest point they had reached when ordered back by Lee for the purpose of concentrating his forces to oppose Meade. In my opinion there is not the least doubt that in one day more they would have entered Harrisburg."[194] The 26th Militia spent most of the next few weeks at Fort Couch.

During their time in and around Fort Couch, members of the 26th were reunited with a number of their regiment believed to have been captured at Gettysburg. Pennypacker recalled that about fifty members of Company F took part in the defense of the Wrightsville-Columbia Bridge, during which nine members were wounded.[195] Company F was put in charge of guarding the gate at Fort Couch, while the rest of the regiment garrisoned the fort.

On July 12, Pennypacker's regiment received orders to leave Fort Couch. The soldiers boarded a train and were taken through the Cumberland Valley, through Mechanicsburg and Carlisle, to Shippensburg, where they disembarked because the railroad south of that community had been destroyed. They marched to Chambersburg, arriving near twilight and camped in a clover field owned by Colonel Alexander K. McClure. The next day, Pennypacker and a friend decided to walk into town to look around. "Following the pike for some distance we turned to the left, crossed

"The rails were lying in heaps along the road."

the Conecocheague, a rapid stream which runs directly through the centre of the town, and went to the hospital where we saw a number of Grey back prisoners who were confined there. . . . We then concluded to go to the depot and take a view of the depredations which the rebels had committed there. All the buildings belonging to the rail road company were in ruins. The plan adopted for their destruction was to batter in the walls with heavy bars until the structure fell. I was at a loss to understand why they had not applied fire and thus saved themselves from what must have required a great deal of labor. All the machinery which could be injured had been rendered useless and even the large masses of iron exhibited the marks of blows from sledge-hammers."[196]

On July 14, Pennypacker recollected, "The camp was only a few rods from the rail road, and early in the morning I went to see what was the method of destroying the track. The rails were lying in heaps along the road, all of them bent in the middle at an angle of about one hundred and thirty degrees. The manner in which this is effected is to lay them across gutters or hollow places so that both ends are supported upon the bank, then heaping the sills underneath the centre and setting them on fire, when the iron becomes hot and soft it bends from its own weight. In this way both sills and rails are rendered useless. In one place we saw some rails which while hot had been wound around a tree. We were told that the track was in this condition for seven miles and that several thousand men were engaged in the work. How those fellows managed to make such long daily marches and at the same time scour the country so effectually for miles and accomplish so much hard labor was more than I could understand."[197]

The 26th Militia, now 467 men strong, marched west towards Greencastle, in Franklin County, later on July 14, and made camp about a mile outside of the community. Early in the morning of July 16, news reached the 26th that General Robert E. Lee had successfully retreated across the Potomac River at Williamsport, Maryland. This stopped any further forward movement of the regiment. Pennypacker visited Greencastle later that day, buying food from townspeople. Upon returning to camp he learned, "Governor Curtin was on the ground addressing the men, and soon afterward he came over to our regiment and though he was very hoarse made a short speech. He said among other things that there was every prospect of the 'Emergency' being over and our being sent home in a few days; that he sympathized with us in all we had endured but being of one Commonwealth no Pennsylvanian had a right to sleep quietly at home while these people of the border were driven from their habitations and their property despoiled; that when they had returned with the probability of remaining undisturbed, we might consider our services finished. Upon the conclusion of his remarks we gave him three cheers and he drove off."[198]

On Saturday, July 18, Pennypacker and a tent mate went out on a foraging expedition. "For two or three miles we kept pretty closely along the pike, which had been terribly broken up by the heavy baggage trains and artillery. . . . We found in that distance three or four wagons and caissons whose spokes had been cut and wheels destroyed after they had given way on the retreat. Shells, rebel clothing, haversacks, &c were scattered about plentifully. . . . On our way back we stopped in a barn where some of the rebels had slept and gathered up a number of letters and other documents left behind by them."[199] On July 21, they struck their tents and began the march back towards Chambersburg, stopping at their previous camp near the community. Two days later, "a large squad of rebel prisoners went by under guard. We all ran out to see them and as we stood along the edge of the road, one of them said to another 'there's that 26th that we drove from Gettysburg.'"[200] Early on July 26, Pennypacker's regiment departed Chambersburg by train for Harrisburg, arriving near Fort Couch in the afternoon. They pitched their tents in a field near the fort. The 26th Pennsylvania Emergency Militia Regiment began mustering out on July 27, and on the following day marched to Camp Curtin, where the soldiers deposited their muskets. By July 30, their muster-out papers had been completed. On August 1, they returned their "tents, blankets, haversacks, and canteens, and were left with nothing but our clothing of those things with which we were supplied by government."[201] Later that afternoon they were paid; Pennypacker received $19.26. After supper, they boarded a freight car in Harrisburg bound for home and arrived in Pottstown between two and three o'clock the next morning.

A monument to the 26th Pennsylvania Emergency Militia Regiment was erected in Gettysburg on September 1, 1892. This bronze statue depicts a young soldier, bearing a musket, striding atop a boulder. The soldier faces west at the point Chambersburg Street splits at a Y in the road leaving the downtown area. It was Pennypacker, "who suggested that the statue should show the trousers tucked into the boot-legs to indicate the sudden change from peaceful life to the battlefield."[202] At the dedication of the memorial, Pennypacker delivered an address to his old comrades that ended with the words, "it is still enough to preserve your memories green forever that in Pennsylvania's time of trial, you, her sons, were there to show that her resentful arm was raised to smite the foe, and that you, the first of all the troops of all the states, unaided and alone, met the rebel army upon the battlefield of Gettysburg."[203] During 1910–1911, Pennypacker was instrumental in selecting the site for the additional stone marker monument to the 26th Militia. It was placed on the Chambersburg Pike near Marsh Creek, where the 26th Militia had first encountered Confederate troops in 1863. He also played a significant role in determining the inscription that was placed on the tablet, as he was friendly with John P. Nicholson, chairman of the Gettysburg National Park Commission and former brevet lieutenant colonel of the 28th PVI.[204]

Shortly after returning home from his emergency service, Pennypacker was drafted. "I had no idea of returning to the service in this way and my grandfather," he wrote, "who was much pleased with the outcome of my military experience, paid $300 for a substitute at Norristown only too willing to go to the front in my stead. I do not know of his name or his fate."[205] Following his brief military service, Pennypacker began reading law in 1864 in the office of Peter McCall of Philadelphia.

Pennypacker was a member of the 26th Pennsylvania Emergency Militia Regiment, organized in response to the Army of Northern Virginia's invasion of Pennsylvania in June 1863. The monument to the regiment is one of more than fourteen hundred memorials erected at Gettysburg. This image was extracted from a photographic print in the collections of the Pennsylvania State Archives.

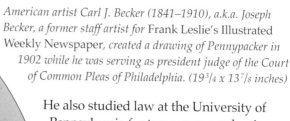

American artist Carl J. Becker (1841–1910), a.k.a. Joseph Becker, a former staff artist for Frank Leslie's Illustrated Weekly Newspaper, *created a drawing of Pennypacker in 1902 while he was serving as president judge of the Court of Common Pleas of Philadelphia. (19³/₄ x 13⁷/₈ inches)*

He also studied law at the University of Pennsylvania for two years, graduating with a Bachelor of Laws degree. He was admitted to the bar in May 1866.

Pennypacker, living at the time in Philadelphia, described the impact of President Lincoln's assassination in April 1865. "No such event had ever before occurred in America," he wrote. "Its effect was to arouse all the undercurrent of animal passions. Along with the warm glow of love for one who had been so gentle, considerate and wise, arose the desire to tear into pieces those who had harmed him. Personally I felt that I wanted to set my teeth in the throat of some rebel and that the inability to gratify the impulse was a deprivation. In a remarkable way the war revealed to men how thin is the gloss of civilization and how below seethe the primary passions which have ever swayed them.

"Perched on the roof of a building on south Broad Street, the catafalque that bore his body passed before me and thousands of others and the next morning I arose early to go to Independence Hall. Forming in line, we walked two by two along the north side of Chestnut Street from Fifth Street to the Delaware River and there crossed over to the south side of Chestnut and after hours reached Fifth, only to find that there the line had been broken up by the undisciplined crowd. Not to be balked, I fought my way with some of the more fortunate to the hall where the body lay in state, and so it happened that I saw Lincoln both upon the first and the last time that he came to the Pennsylvania State House."[206]

Pennypacker married Virginia Earl Broomall on October 20, 1870, and together the couple had four children. Governor John White Geary appointed Pennypacker a notary public in Philadelphia, on March 17, 1869.[207] He was also appointed to the Philadelphia Board of Education in 1885. In 1889, Governor James Addams Beaver appointed Pennypacker judge of the Court of Common Pleas of Philadelphia. He became president judge of the court in 1897 and was reelected two years later. Pennypacker was keenly interested in community service and history, and in 1900 became president of the Historical Society of Pennsylvania. He also served as a trustee of the University of Pennsylvania, beginning in 1886.

Pennypacker joined Post Number 19 of the Grand Army of the Republic in Philadelphia, following its creation, and was elected its commander in 1869. This position gave him the rank of colonel in the organization, with which he remained affiliated for the remainder of his life. At the post's Memorial Day Services on May 30, 1898, Pennypacker delivered the main oration, astutely speaking out against attempts occurring in the late nineteenth century, to modify the causes of the Civil War. "The underlying cause of the war was the determination of those whose commercial and political importance was based upon the ownership of labor to maintain and extend the institution of human slavery," he said. "I am well aware that under the softening influence of time and the restoration of kindly feeling there is a growing disposition to regard the struggle as involving solely the interpretation of the Constitution and the settlement of the question of the sovereignty of the States. . . . If our purposes be really to ascertain the truth, we will turn away from the mere comment of a later day and look at the records of the time, and the conduct of the parties while in action, and see what this examination discloses."[208] To bolster his argument, Pennypacker cited six clauses in the Constitution of the Confederate States of America, adopted March 11, 1861, related to preserving and extending slavery into new territories.

He became a member of the Valley Forge Commission in 1893, the year it was created, charged with acquiring and protecting the site of the important Revolutionary War encampment. Pennypacker's participation on this commission presaged the commemoration of Civil War soldiers observed during his term as governor.

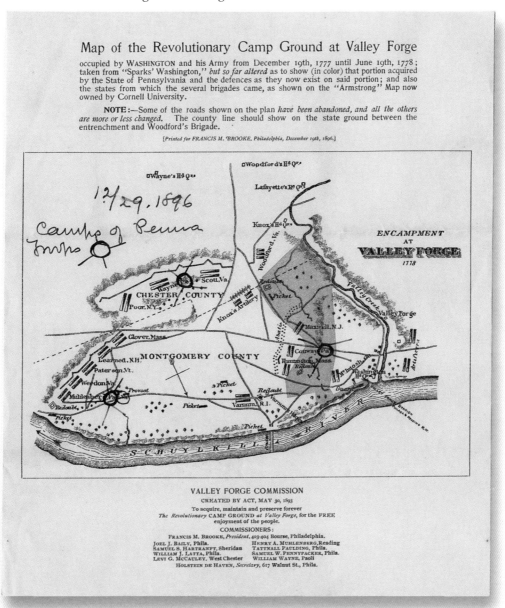

Map of the Revolutionary Camp Ground at Valley Forge, occupied by Washington and his Army from December 19th, 1777 to June 19th, 1778, *was created in 1896 for the Valley Forge Commission, of which Pennypacker was a member. The commission was charged with acquiring and preserving the grounds of this famous Revolutionary War site. (9³/₄ x 8³/₈ inches)*

Poster for Pennypacker's 1902 gubernatorial campaign. Pennypacker's appearance at the First Annual Lawton Farmers' Club Fair in Susquehanna County was scheduled between a foot race and a horse race. (41⁵/₈ x 28⁷/₈ inches)

Buttons for Pennypacker's 1902 gubernatorial campaign in which he opposed Democrat Robert Emory Pattison, who was seeking a third non-successive term. President Theodore Roosevelt publicly proclaimed that Pennypacker's defeat would be a "national calamity."

Pennypacker defeated John P. Elkin, state attorney general, for the Republican Party's gubernatorial nomination in 1902. In his initial campaign speech after securing the nomination, he said, "When the Republican party came into control in 1861, there was great opposition to its theory of national unity and to the conduct of the war for the maintenance of that theory, but before a quarter of a century had elapsed even the defeated as well as the Democrats of the North were willing to concede that the overthrow of the Confederacy and the institution upon which it was based was well worth the struggle and the sacrifice.

"The great achievement of the Republican party in national affairs has been rendered possible only because of the attitude of the proud Commonwealth in which you and I live. For the success of the efforts of that party and the enforcement of its policy, she deserves more credit than any other of the states. To other states it has been necessary to give great rewards in order to win their favor and ensure their fealty, but she has been ever strong and steadfast. Of the four potent states,—New York, Pennsylvania, Ohio, and Illinois,—she alone since the first election of Lincoln has never given an electoral vote against a Republican candidate for President."[209]

Pennypacker claimed the nomination for governor came to him without his seeking it. "It came to me without the lifting of a finger, the expenditure of a dime or the utterance of a sigh," he elaborated.[210] Handpicked and supported by his cousin Matthew S. Quay's powerful political machine, Pennypacker easily won the general election by defeating Robert E. Pattison, who was seeking a third nonconsecutive term as governor. Support from Pennypacker's fellow Civil War veterans proved vital to his election.

Pennypacker's candidacy was supported by former governor James Addams Beaver, the Philadelphia Grand Army of the Republic, and the Philadelphia Brigade Association. To the delegates of the Republican State Convention on June 6, 1902, the association announced, "The surviving members of the old Philadelphia Brigade . . . which held the 'Bloody Angle, the high water mark of the Rebellion,' against the world-renowned Charge of Pickett's Division at Gettysburg, July 3, 1863, carry an appeal to the Republican State Convention for the nomination of a candidate for Governor free from recent and dangerous factional differences.

Pennypacker (standing, center) reads his speech during his inauguration on January 20, 1903, in Harrisburg. During his campaign, the Republican Pennypacker won the enthusiastic endorsements of veterans, farmers, and James Addams Beaver, Civil War hero and former governor.

"Faction lost us a Governor in 1882, and two years later Cleveland succeeded to the Presidency. It lost us a Governor again in 1890, and Cleveland—and defeated in 1888, in an interim of party peace—succeeded to the Presidency in 1892. . . .

"Let us avoid the folly which sickens, and seek the unity which preserves. We can do it by nominating for Governor one who is without political offense to any element of the party. Such a one is Judge Samuel W. Pennypacker, the offspring of an old Chester County family, himself a soldier in the ranks of the Union, and of a most distinguished family group, which itself contributed to that great war—and wholly to the right side of it—116 privates and non-commissioned officers, three generals, five colonels, four surgeons, nine captains and eight lieutenants.

"Surely a character like this will, if placed upon the ticket hush all faction, and unite all patriots. We, therefore, bespeak the good offices of every delegate, and of all who can influence the result in behalf of our Comrade Judge Pennypacker, whose election will mean a promising future for the party and the people of the State and Nation."[211]

Artist O'Donel Seigfreids painted a portrait of Pennypacker in 1903 during his first year as governor. (29 3/4 x 24 1/4 inches)

Pennypacker was even given the opportunity for celebrity by the Cumberland Cigar Company, which offered to name a cigar brand for him. The Republican State Committee encouraged him, in August 1902, to allow the company to proceed.[212] This provided a novel opportunity for free advertising during Pennypacker's gubernatorial campaign.

During his time in office, Pennypacker brought about the creation of the Pennsylvania State Archives, and dedicated the present-day State Capitol, a monumental beaux-arts style building which dominates downtown Harrisburg. He also dedicated and presented Pennsylvania Civil War monuments at Andersonville, Georgia, Antietam, Maryland, Chattanooga, Tennessee, Fredericksburg, Virginia, and Vicksburg, Mississippi, among others, to the federal government.

The great monument and memorial movement of the 1890s and 1900s was not without controversy for Pennypacker, however. Shortly after his inauguration, he received a number of letters from disgruntled Pennsylvania Civil War veterans, including one from James F. Dampman, who served from April 23, 1861, to July 19, 1865, informing the governor that they were unhappy with the proposed installment of a monument to a Confederate officer on Pennsylvania soil. "I have the honor to write to you in regard to the proposition of Col. McClure to erect a equestrian statue to the late Genl Lee of the Rebel Army, on the battlefield of Gettysburg," Dampman wrote. "As a private who served in the Pennsylvania Volunteers on that historic field, in the 109th Vet Vols. Genl [Thomas L.] Kanes Brigade Gearys Div 12th Army Corps on Culps Hill, I hereby earnestly <u>protest against</u> any action by my native state in <u>honoring</u> a man who done his best to break up our Union.

"To my way of thinking statues are erected to commemorate some noble action or career of a man, to him that tries to build up not tear down in his public life. Lee was a would be destroyer. Take his contemporary Genl [George H.] Thomas. He was a Virginian and he risked all to serve the Union cause. Even ostracized by the people of his state; yet that did not swerve him from his paramount duty to his country. . . . No your Excellency I am deadly opposed to such a move, and instead of healing old sores, this action of Col McClures stirs up strife.

"I am no Collegian but I have never yet read of a country or people that would go so far as to do homage or honor to one that tried to overthrow the Govt. As charitable as old Abe was he would never countenance such a move. Lee's escape from the hangmans noose was honor enough for him and the other leaders to my way of thinking."[213]

Flanked by officers of the National Guard of Pennsylvania, Governor Samuel W. Pennypacker (center) attended the dedication of the 73rd Pennsylvania Volunteers monument at Chattanooga, Tennessee, on November 11, 1903. The regiment fought in the Battle of Missionary Ridge (Chattanooga-Ringgold Campaign) on November 25, 1863, suffering tremendous casualties. Governor Pennypacker strongly believed in honoring the valor and memory of the Keystone State's soldiers, by memorializing their military feats.

Governor Pennypacker's speech at the dedication of the Antietam monuments was a brief but solid example of his vast knowledge of the history of Pennsylvania and the Civil War. "Comrades: It is a noteworthy fact that the State which was settled by a people devoted to the ways of peace; who taught the doctrine that a civil answer turneth away wrath; who opposed every aspect of warfare, and who tried to carry their principles even into their dealing with savage tribes, should have reached highest fame and distinction in battles on sea and land. No other State save Virginia can vie with Pennsylvania in the number of distinguished military commanders given to the national government.

"We have come now from our Northern State into this, our sister State on the borderland of the South, to commemorate here the achievements of Pennsylvania's sons. The boundary line which separates our State from yours is the most famous in all this Union. It is only an imaginary line, however, and as our people and yours pass back and forth across it there has been bred in the heart of either a feeling of mutual love and respect.

Governor Pennypacker (top center, holding top hat), officers of the National Guard of Pennsylvania, various dignitaries, and veterans of the Battle of Antietam attended Pennsylvania Day at the Maryland battlefield on September 17, 1904. Pennsylvania Day commemorated the day on which monuments were dedicated to twelve Pennsylvania infantry regiments and a battery of artillery that had fought in the Battle of Antietam on September 17, 1862. Pennypacker's role in the program (above) was to accept the monuments from the Antietam Battlefield Commission on behalf of the Commonwealth and then transfer them to the federal government for perpetual care.

"...We have come here today to commemorate the part our soldiers played in the greatest battle of the Civil War, and here upon this field, where victory was won under the commandership of a son of Pennsylvania, we greet you.

"Antietam had a greater significance than any other battle of the war, for, when he heard the news of it, Abraham Lincoln issued his emancipation proclamation. It was due to what was done here that the pall which had hovered over our country for 157 years was dissipated.

"I accept these pretty monuments, beautiful and impressive as they are. . . . I now deliver them, to be cared for forever by the national government."[214]

Governor Pennypacker served on several Civil War monument commissions, including one established to erect a cavalry statue to commemorate the Battle of Hanover in York County, Pennsylvania. "It is a fact of which Pennsylvanians ought to be proud," he remarked in his autobiography, "and which has a significance, that this state was represented not only in all of the battles of the East, but likewise in those of the West. No other eastern state of the North had any part in Shiloh."[215] For this reason, Pennypacker supported erecting monuments to Pennsylvania troops at appropriate battlefields throughout the United States.

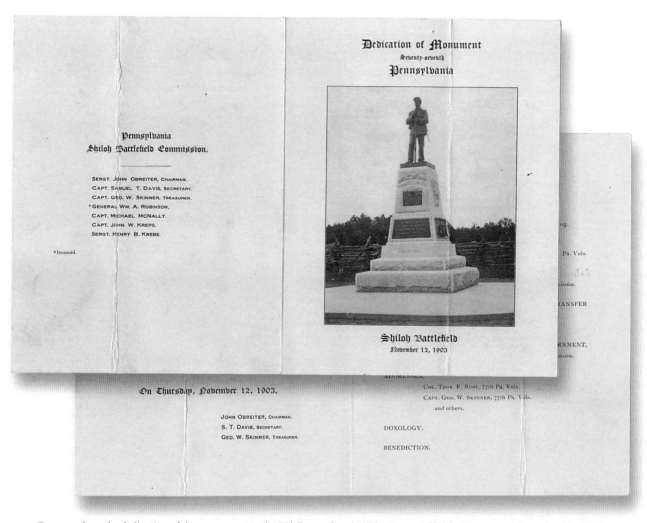

Program from the dedication of the monument to the 77th Pennsylvania Volunteers at Shiloh, Tennessee, November 12, 1903. Not only was the 77th Pennsylvania Volunteers the sole Pennsylvania regiment that fought at the Battle of Shiloh on April 6–7, 1862, but it was also the only Union regiment from states east of the Ohio River that took part in the engagement.

COMMISSIONERS:

Governor SAMUEL W. PENNYPACKER,
Harrisburg, Pa.

Lieut.-Colonel JOHN P. NICHOLSON,
1535 Chestnut Street, Phila.

REV. D. EBERLY, Hanover, Pa.

Commission to Erect a Monument
at Hanover, York Co., Pa.,

To Commemorate the Engagement which took place
there June 30, 1863, Prior to the Battle of Gettysburg.

——————— April 23d, ——— 190 4

Hon. S. W. Pennypacker

    Dear Governor

        We have received the Contracts from Mr. Eberly and will

forward to the Smith Granite Company at Westerly, R. I.

        Yours truly,

On April 23, 1904, John P. Nicholson advised Governor Pennypacker (above) on the progress of the Commission to Erect a Monument at Hanover, York Co., Pa. The governor actively participated in a number of commissions responsible for the erection of memorials paying homage to Pennsylvania's Civil War soldiers. A friend of Pennypacker, Nicholson also served as chairman of the Gettysburg National Park Commission. He had served as brevet lieutenant colonel in the 28th Pennsylvania Volunteers during the Civil War.

Governor Pennypacker was instrumental in the creation of The Picket *(above), an equestrian monument in Hanover, York County. The monument commemorates the Union Cavalry that took part in the Battle of Hanover, which was fought in the community's streets on June 30, 1863. The battle pitted the troops of Union Brigadier General Judson Kilpatrick against those of Confederate Major General J. E. B. Stuart.*

National Commander, COL. J. D. WALKER, Pittsburg, Pa.
National Vice-Commander, WILLIAM KELLY, Wilmington, Del.
National Chaplain, REV. JOHN S. FERGUSON, Keokuk, Iowa.

National Historian, GEN'L HARRY WHITE, Indiana, Pa.
Adjutant General and } STEPHEN M. LONG, East Orange, N. J.
Quartermaster General, }

THE NATIONAL ASSOCIATION OF

UNION EX-PRISONERS

OF WAR.

EXECUTIVE COMMITTEE.
AARON T. BLISS, Lansing, Mich.
O. A. PARSONS, Wilkesbarre, Pa.
CHARLES F. SHERRIFF, Pittsburg, Pa.
CHARLES G. DAVIS, Boston, Mass.
J. D. WALKER, Pittsburg, Pa.
STEPHEN M. LONG, East Orange, N. J.

CHIEF OF STAFF.
JOHN A. FAIRMAN, Allegheny, Pa.

SPECIAL AIDE FOR ENCAMPMENT
CHARLES G. DAVIS, Boston, Mass.

AIDES TO NATIONAL
COMMANDER.

John Kissane, Cincinnati Ass'n,
Cincinnati, Ohio.
Chas. E. Faulkner, Minnesota Ass'n,
Minneapolis, Minn.
E. H. Ripple, Lackawanna Co. Ass'n,
Scranton, Pa.
M. S. Kirby, New Jersey Ass'n,
South Amboy, N. J.
J. B. Cotty, Missouri Ass'n,
Moberly, Mo.
Walter Dull, New York City Ass'n,
No. 221 E. 126th St., New York City.
D. W. Howe, Chicago Ass,n,
Chicago, Ill.
J. Lane Fitts, Bedel Ass'n,
Manchester, N. H.
Lewis F. Lake, Winnebago, Co., Ass'n
Rockford, Ill.
Harry Palmer, Los Angeles Ass'n,
Los Angeles, Cal.
C. H. Colgate, Boston Ass'n,
Boston, Mass.
J. D. Walden, Fitzgerald Ass'n,
Fitzgerald, Ga.
A. H. Jones, Allegheny Co. Ass'n,
Pittsburg, Pa.
C. C. Shanklin, Cleveland Ass'n,
Cleveland, Ohio.
L. H. Rowley, Woodburn Ass'n,
Woodburn, Iowa.
H. D. Burkin, Wimington Ass'n,
Wilmington, Del.
C. H. Heald, Western Mass. Ass'n,
Northhampton, Mass.
Wm. H. Bricker, Beaver Co. Ass'n,
Beaver Falls, Pa.
David T. Davies, Philadelphia Ass'n,
Philadelphia, Pa.
Geo. W. Dunn, Dawes Co. Ass'n,
Chadran, Neb.
W. T. Ziegler, Gettysburg Ass'n,
Gettysburg, Pa.
John McElroy, Washington Ass'n,
Washington, D. C.
David Snell, New Jersey Ass'n,
Montclair, N. J.
D. G. Nesbitt, Cleveland Ass'n,
Cleveland, Ohio.
H. Lathrop, Lackawanna Co. Ass'n,
Scranton, Pa.

Pittsburgh, Pa., June 17, 1904.

Hon. Bromley Wharton,

Harrisburg, Pa.

My Dear Sir:--

Telegram announcing the appointment of myself by the

Governor a member of the Andersonville Monument Commission

received.

Kindly convey my thanks to the Governor for the same

and hoping that in the near future I may have the opportunity

of personally saying so to him, I remain,

Yours sincerely,

J. D. Walker

NATIONAL COMMANDER,
UNION EX. PRISONERS OF WAR.

On June 17, 1904, Colonel James D. Walker, National Commander of the National Association of Union Ex-Prisoners of War, wrote to Bromley Wharton, Governor Pennypacker's private secretary, to thank the governor for appointing him to Pennsylvania's Andersonville Monument Commission.

Circa 1905 photograph of the Pennsylvania Memorial at the National Cemetery in Andersonville, Georgia. The monument was dedicated on December 5, 1905, by Governor Pennypacker to honor Pennsylvanians who served in the Union Army and were held as prisoners of war at Andersonville. About 1,849 Pennsylvanians died while at Andersonville Prison (see page 20) between 1864 and 1865.

144

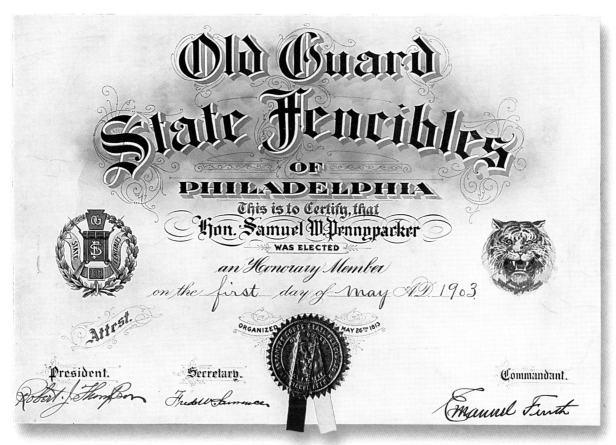

The Old Guard State Fencibles of Philadelphia conferred honorary membership on Governor Pennypacker on May 1, 1903. The veterans' organization was affiliated with the State Fencibles of Philadelphia, part of the Commonwealth's militia system from 1813 until about 1901, when it became a municipal unit. The State Fencibles did return to the Pennsylvania National Guard in 1920, during its reorganization following World War I. The Old Guard State Fencibles served as a social club for veterans. (14 x 18 3/4 inches)

Serving as commander-in-chief of the National Guard of Pennsylvania while governor, Pennypacker took a keen interest in the welfare of the organization and the guardsmen. He enjoyed the honor of commanding the 2nd Division, consisting of three brigades, at the inaugural parade of President Theodore Roosevelt in 1905.[216] He was also elected as an honorary member of the Old Guard State Fencibles of Philadelphia on May 1, 1903.

As governor, he served as the president of the board of trustees of the Pennsylvania Soldiers' and Sailors' Home in Erie and president of the Commonwealth's Commission of Soldiers' Orphan Schools. In those roles, he dealt with issues as mundane as filling vacancies on boards to overseeing the politically charged investigation of alleged mistreatment of students by faculty members at the Soldiers' Orphan Schools. In an affirmation of national reconciliation, he even entertained former Confederates at the Governor's Mansion. In a letter to his daughter, Josephine, on April 11, 1905, he wrote, "We had a rebel general with us over night recently, Genl. Fitzhugh Lee of Virginia and we all liked him very much."[217]

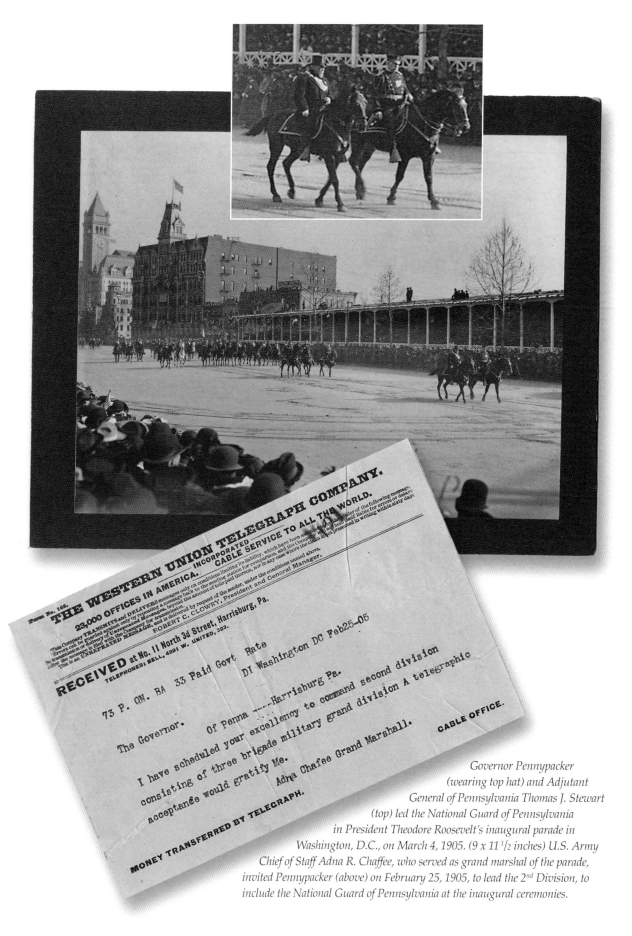

*Governor Pennypacker
(wearing top hat) and Adjutant
General of Pennsylvania Thomas J. Stewart
(top) led the National Guard of Pennsylvania
in President Theodore Roosevelt's inaugural parade in
Washington, D.C., on March 4, 1905. (9 x 11 1/2 inches) U.S. Army
Chief of Staff Adna R. Chaffee, who served as grand marshal of the parade,
invited Pennypacker (above) on February 25, 1905, to lead the 2nd Division, to
include the National Guard of Pennsylvania at the inaugural ceremonies.*

Following his term as governor, Pennypacker remained active with veterans groups and issues. As late as 1909, he attempted to persuade the federal government to give pension status to the emergency militia troops of 1863 and 1864. U.S. Senator Boies Penrose, of Pennsylvania, was committed to assisting in this pursuit. "I have presented in every Congress since I have been in Washington a bill to give the emergency troops of 1863 and 1864 a pensionable status, and such a bill I propose to again present at this session," he wrote to Pennypacker on December 15, 1909. "There are two difficulties in the way: 1. The men did not serve ninety days as required by law to establish a claim for pension. 2. The emergency militia regiments were not mustered into the service of the United States. It is true that pensions have been allowed to many persons who served in the emergency militia who could substantiate their claims to injuries received in the line of duty. . . . The failure to consider the bills I have presented is due to the fact that there is objection to opening the door for unlimited pensions."[218]

Pennypacker wrote extensively and returned to the practice of law, in the Philadelphia firm of Pennypacker and Thompson, after his term as governor. Samuel Whitaker Pennypacker died on September 2, 1916, in Schwenksville. He is buried in Morris Cemetery in Phoenixville, Chester County.

On July 20, 1905, Governor Pennypacker (top row, fourth from left) visited the Pennsylvania Soldiers' and Sailors' Home in Erie, an institution he ardently supported. Pennypacker is flanked by institution administrators, while residents and veterans stand below him.

*President Theodore Roosevelt (tipping his top hat) and (on his left)
Governor Samuel W. Pennypacker walk past the equestrian statue of
Civil War Brevet Major General and Governor John F. Hartranft at
the dedication of the new State Capitol on October 4, 1906.*

With his National Guard of Pennsylvania staff, Governor Pennypacker (center) was photographed during an encampment at Gettysburg, July 21–28, 1906. In addition to participating in National Guard events and activities, he held a number of offices in historical organizations, including president of the Historical Society of Pennsylvania and vice president of the Sons of the Revolution. He was also a member of the Colonial Society, Society of Colonial Wars, and the Society of the War of 1812. (9 3/4 x 13 inches)

Former Governor Pennypacker (center), with fellow veterans of the 26th Pennsylvania Emergency Militia Regiment, attended the fiftieth anniversary of the Battle of Gettysburg on July 3, 1913.

The American Civil War's Influence on Post-War Politics

An interesting parallel exists between Pennsylvania's gubernatorial elections and the nation's presidential elections in the post-Civil War era. Six of the first seven United States presidents during this period were Republicans and Union veterans, extending from the election of 1868 through the 1901 assassination of President William McKinley. The only exception, Democrat Grover Cleveland, won two nonconsecutive terms, first in 1884 and again in 1892. As a twenty-six-year-old, Cleveland had notably hired George Beniski, a thirty-two-year-old Polish immigrant, as a substitute in 1863 to avoid service in the American Civil War. In a speech delivered in support of Benjamin Harrison's presidential reelection campaign of 1892, Adjutant General of Pennsylvania Daniel H. Hastings facetiously compared Harrison with Cleveland. "Harrison was opposed to human slavery. Cleveland had the courage of his convictions and wanted it extended into the territories. Harrison thought it a blot upon our civilization. Cleveland believed it to be a divine institution. . . . Harrison was opposed to secession, believed in the union of all the states. He wanted one flag and he wanted it to hold all the stars. He volunteered for the Union and distinguished himself on the fields of battles. Cleveland had the courage of his convictions and when drafted, hired a substitute."[219]

Republican presidents of the period were Ulysses S. Grant (1869–1877), who had served as general-in-chief of Union forces from 1864 to the end of war; Rutherford

Cabinet card of Grover Cleveland (1837–1908), the Democratic Party's presidential candidate in 1884, 1888, and 1892. He is the only president in the nation's history to serve two nonconsecutive terms, from 1885 to 1889 and from 1893 to 1897. Cleveland, who lost the 1888 election to Benjamin Harrison, was the first Democrat to win the White House in the years following the Civil War.

B. Hayes (1877–1881), brevet major general; James Garfield (1881), major general of volunteers, assassinated in office and succeeded by Chester Arthur (1881–1885), quartermaster general of New York; Benjamin Harrison (1889–1893), brevet brigadier general; and William McKinley (1897–1901), brevet major, succeeded upon his assassination by Theodore Roosevelt, who was too young to have served in the Civil War. In these Republican victories, Union veterans—one and a half-million of them—played a critical role. Most veterans voted Republican, because they could not forgive the Democratic Party for its collective opposition to Lincoln's war policies.[220] Furthermore, the Republican Party, on both the state and national levels, became astute at

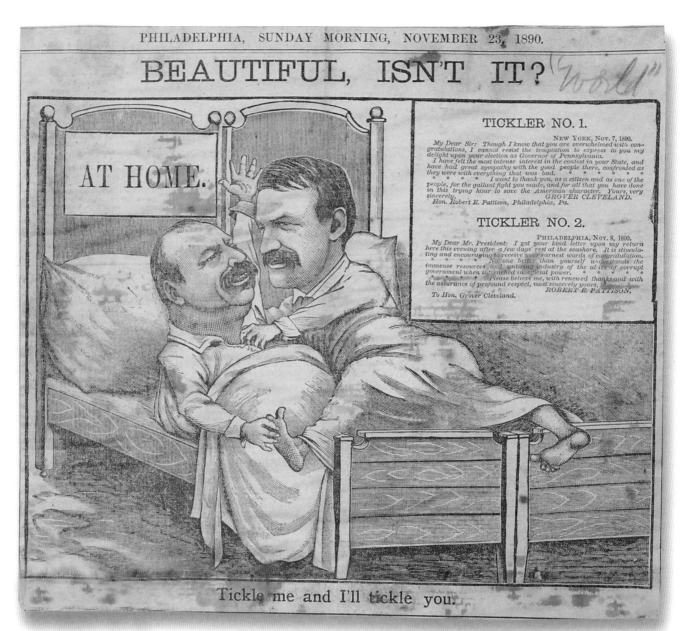

"Beautiful, Isn't It?" a cartoon published in a Philadelphia newspaper on November 23, 1890, depicts former President Grover Cleveland and Pennsylvania's Governor-elect Robert Emory Pattison tickling one another while in bed. Pattison had just been elected to his second nonconsecutive term as governor and Cleveland, who had served his first term as president, had lost his reelection bid in 1888. Pattison and Cleveland were the only Democrats who managed to break through the Republican Party's stranglehold in the late nineteenth century, of both Pennsylvania's governorship and the United States presidency, respectively.

waving the bloody shirt. This political tactic was used repeatedly to gain advantage in numerous elections in the post-war years, by reminding voters of the effusion of blood spilled during the recently concluded conflict, and encouraging them to vote as they had fought.

In Pennsylvania, Republican candidates in this era, both gubernatorial and presidential, were greatly assisted by the Republican Party machine developed by Simon Cameron, refined by Matthew S. Quay, and continued by Boies Penrose (1860–1921), another influential Pennsylvania politician and power broker. The machine was as powerful in Pennsylvania as was the well known Tammany Hall, the omnipotent Democratic machine in New York City. The Republican machine helped keep Pennsylvanians voting predominantly for its gubernatorial candidates from 1860 to 1934, with only the two nonconsecutive terms of Democrat Robert E. Pattison interrupting the streak.

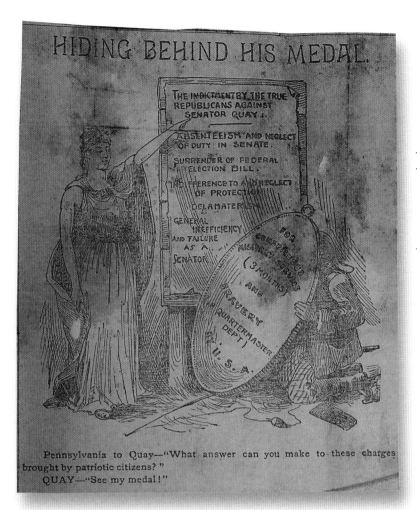

A circa 1890s cartoon attacked Matthew S. Quay for "Hiding Behind His Medal," a reference to Quay's deflecting criticism from fellow Republicans with the fact that he had received the Medal of Honor for his military service in the Civil War. Quay served as colonel of the 134th Pennsylvania Volunteer Infantry from August 23, 1862, to December 7, 1862, when he resigned because of illness caused by typhoid fever. A week after his resignation, on December 13, he volunteered as an aide on the staff of General Erastus B. Tyler of the 1st Brigade, 3rd Division, 5th Corps. In 1888, he was awarded the Medal of Honor for his conspicuous role in charging the heights at the Battle of Fredericksburg.

A pro-Matthew S. Quay political pamphlet, circa 1898, for one of Pennsylvania's most controversial political figures of the late nineteenth century. In addition to his active duty military service, Quay also served as one of Governor Andrew Gregg Curtin's wartime secretaries, and later held a number of influential positions, among them state legislator, secretary of the commonwealth, state treasurer, chairman of the Republican National Committee, and U.S. senator. He was among the Keystone State's most successful political leaders of all time, helping the Republican Party dominate state politics from the Civil War era, until his death in 1904.

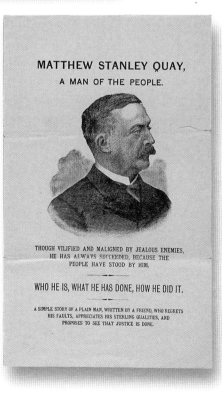

Because many Democrats in Pennsylvania had opposed the war and efforts to supply the Union armies with sufficient troops, it was relatively easy for the Republican Party to taint most Democratic candidates with the stain of being traitors or Copperheads. Countless stories about Ku Klux Klan atrocities in the South committed against Republican African Americans during the Reconstruction period pushed even more Pennsylvanians to vote Republican.[221]

The Grand Army of the Republic and its political ancillary group, the Boys in Blue, were overwhelmingly Republican. To many Pennsylvanians in the post-war period, the Republican Party came to represent loyalty to the federal government and the U.S. Constitution. Yet many Northern states did not experience the same decades-long Republican Party domination maintained in the Keystone State. Pennsylvania's Republican Party machine was at the forefront of politics during this era, strongly controlling nominations and heavily influencing elections. The machine's domination was based on controlling local leaders by offering them economic, political, and social power for their continued allegiance to the Republican Party bosses. Election fraud, in various forms, was also a tool used when the machine found it necessary.[222] During this time, Pennsylvania's Democratic Party suffered from a lack of central organization and leadership, inadequate financial resources, and by supporting unpopular stances on tariff and monetary reform during the financial depression of 1893.

An envelope from the Republican Party's successful 1868 presidential campaign depicts presidential contender Ulysses S. Grant (1822–1885) and vice presidential candidate Schuyler B. Colfax (1823–1885). Beneath Grant's portrait are crossed cannon, representing his Civil War service. A banner beneath the image of Colfax proclaims "Progress in Civilization" with a sheaf of wheat, symbolizing prosperity and growth. Speaker of the House from 1863 to 1869, Colfax was an outspoken opponent of slavery. (4 5/8 x 5 1/2 inches)

PICKING COTTON
ARKANSAS

THE PHILADELPHIA M

Life for many African Americans in the South—including those photographed picking cotton in an Arkansas field about 1893 —did not dramatically improve after the Civil War. In fact, with the end of Reconstruction, the South's African Americans suffered a reversal of their political, social, and economic lives, which would not be corrected for nearly a century.

In the immediate post-war period, the Reconstruction period of 1865–1877, African American rights were enforced by federal troops and championed by the Thirteenth, Fourteenth, and Fifteenth Amendments to the United States Constitution. A number of Union soldiers turned politicians, such as Governor John W. Geary, favored harsh treatment of their former Confederate enemies and the protection of increased rights for African Americans. It soon became clear, however, that many Union Civil War veterans and Northern politicians were more interested in binding up old wounds with their former foes, in an effort to reunite the country, rather than focusing on protecting the rights of African Americans. This desire to forgive former war adversaries is clearly evident in Pennsylvania as early as Governor John F. Hartranft's administration. In the effort to reconcile with the South, the North allowed former Confederates to reject the slavery issue as a main cause of the Civil War and to promote the "Lost Cause" myth. In doing so, the important role that the United States Colored Troops had played in helping the North win the war was also overshadowed and ignored.

Another turning point in the saga of Reconstruction in the South occurred in conjunction with the presidential election of 1876. This controversial election pitted Republican Rutherford B. Hayes of Ohio, a brevet major general during the Civil War, against Democrat Samuel J. Tilden of New York. The popular vote gave Tilden a majority just shy of 250,000 votes. However, the electoral votes were too close to call in the southern states of Florida, Louisiana, and South Carolina. A Congressional election commission was created in January 1877 to determine which candidate should be awarded the electoral votes in question, that would, in turn, determine who would become the next president of the United States. The commission, made up of both Republicans and Democrats, awarded all of the contested votes to Hayes, enabling him to win the electoral contest by a count of 185 to 184.

One of the primary reasons that the Democrats in Congress conceded the election to Hayes was that, in exchange, Republicans had agreed to remove the remaining few thousand federal troops stationed in Florida, South Carolina, and Louisiana to enforce Reconstruction. This deal was part of what is known as the Compromise of 1877. The troops were removed shortly after Hayes was inaugurated, thereby ending the military rule that had backed Reconstruction policies protecting African American civil rights in the South since the end of the Civil War. Without the presence of federal soldiers, whose withdrawal from the former Confederate states had begun in the late 1860s, many parts of the South quickly reverted to policies of African American disenfranchisement and white supremacy. In many Southern states in the 1880s, African Americans were officially stripped of their civil liberties by new state laws, supported by the Democratic Party, which were aimed at disenfranchising them by means of poll taxes, literacy tests, and new state constitutions adopted in the 1890s to the 1900s. In most areas of the South, the rights guaranteed to African Americans by the fourteenth and fifteenth amendments to the United States Constitution were taken away during the period from the 1870s through the 1890s. For many African Americans living in the South in the 1880s and 1890s, their political, social, and economic lives had reverted to levels that were little better than where they had been during the time of slavery. It would not be until the passage of the Voting Rights Act of 1965 that the fifteenth amendment was again enforced throughout the South.

Initially organized to combat the growth and expansion of slavery in the United States, the Republican Party had lost interest in protecting the rights of African Americans by the late nineteenth century and seemed content to be viewed as the party that saved the Union, rather than the party that had freed the slaves. At the same time, the national Democratic Party's desire to solidify its hold on white Southern voters obliged it to be complicit with Black Codes and Jim Crow laws. The era of reconciliation, a period of fifty years, from the 1880s through the 1930s, between former enemies, the North and the South, helped create a stronger national identity—but at the expense of African American civil rights.

Union and Confederate veterans met and shook hands in the sprit of reconciliation on July 3, 1913, during the fiftieth anniversary of the Battle of Gettysburg. Members of the Philadelphia Brigade Association (left), who fought for the Union, greeted members of Pickett's Division Association at the "Bloody Angle," the site of fierce hand-to-hand combat between the two former enemies on the third day of the grisly battle.

Scholarship devoted to the lives and military experiences of these six extraordinary individuals has been embarrassingly scant. There have been few recent studies written about any of them. Only John W. Geary and John F. Hartranft have been the subjects of book-length treatments published in the latter half of the twentieth century or the first decade of the twenty-first. Those works have largely neglected PHMC's collections relevant to these governors.

Most of the biographies and autobiographies of these prominent Pennsylvanians, published in the late nineteenth through the first quarter of the twentieth century, contain a number of factual errors, as well as faulty analyses of events and incidents that are no longer adequate or relevant for modern historiography or interpretation. In addition, a number of outstanding collections have shifted location over the years, such as National Archives and Records Administration's Record Group 393, Records of Brevet Major General John Frederick Hartranft as Special Provost Marshal for the Trial and Execution of the Assassins of President Abraham Lincoln, now on special deposit at the Pennsylvania State Archives. This nationally significant collection provides valuable primary source information documenting the imprisonment and execution of the conspirators in the aftermath of the assassination of President Lincoln in April 1865.

PHMC has been exceptionally fortunate over the years to have been entrusted with donations of premier historical collections by the descendents of the governors discussed in this book. The Commission is both honored and humbled that the families of these distinguished Pennsylvanians have recognized the agency as the appropriate permanent home for their cherished family collections of documents and artifacts related to their famous ancestors.

The Commonwealth of Pennsylvania began acquiring American Civil War artifacts and objects shortly after the war ended. In 1877, the General Assembly of Pennsylvania appropriated the funds for, and Governor John F. Hartranft approved the purchase of, the Joel Albertus Danner (1848–1904) Collection of Civil War artifacts from Gettysburg. An avid collector and dealer, Danner had amassed enough material to open a museum on Gettysburg's town square in the 1870s. His remarkable collection included, among many items, a musket owned by John L. Burns (1794–1872), a sixty-nine-year-old civilian who left his house and fought with the Union Army during the first day of the Battle of Gettysburg, and a chair used by Major General George Gordon Meade at his headquarters during the battle.

It is believed that Governor Geary's family donated the large collection of his military belongings, including uniforms, accoutrements, and equestrian equipment, to the Commonwealth shortly after his death in 1873. One interesting artifact that came into the possession of the Keystone State at a much later date—and in a most unusual way—is Geary's White Star identity badge, which was originally given to him by his staff in 1863. One hundred years later, in 1963, the badge was found in the dirt on the grounds of Fort Simcoe in Washington State and subsequently donated to the Commonwealth.

A substantial collection of artifacts chronicling the life of Governor James A. Beaver was donated to The State Museum of Pennsylvania by a member of his family, Jane K. Beaver, in 1986. The collection consisted primarily of military uniform items, rank insignia, and political and inaugural items. This donation is yet another example of PHMC being privileged to be chosen as the repository for artifacts associated with Civil War veterans who won the governor's office.

PHMC has also periodically pursued and purchased individual artifacts and collections associated with the careers of these soldier-governors. This book attempts to illuminate their stories, provide a venue for their voices to be rediscovered, and illustrate the vestiges of their exemplary lives and careers.

Several primary collections held by the Pennsylvania State Archives and utilized extensively in this book include:

Manuscript Group (MG)-56, John White Geary Collection, 1847–1873, which came to PHMC in 1957 through the Oregon Historical Society, consists primarily of letters written by John W. Geary between 1847 and 1873 to his brother Edward R. Geary, superintendent, from 1859 to 1861, of Indian Affairs in the Oregon Territory. This fantastic collection is integral to understanding Governor Geary's life during this era of extreme national turmoil and his own distinguished personal achievement.

MG-144, John F. Hartranft Papers, 1853–1897, consists principally of original commissions and appointments to the many military and political offices Hartranft held throughout his lifetime. They were donated to the Pennsylvania State Archives in 1965 by Hartranft Stockham (1902–1983), Governor Hartranft's grandson.

MG-171, Samuel W. Pennypacker Papers, 1703–1916, was donated, for the most part, in 1969 to the Pennsylvania State Archives by Margaret Haussmann Pennypacker (1906–1980), widow of Governor Pennypacker's grandson and namesake, Samuel W. Pennypacker II (1910–1968). This donation not only consisted of Pennypacker's gubernatorial and personal papers but also the gubernatorial papers of his predecessor, Governor William Alexis Stone, contained in MG-181. A smaller portion of the MG-171 collection was donated in 1971 by one of Governor Pennypacker's nephews, James A. Pennypacker.

MG-389, James A. Beaver Papers, 1790–1915, and undated, contains personal, political, and military documents, letters, and diaries related to his life, mainly written by Beaver himself. They were donated to PHMC in 1986 by Governor Beaver's descendants, Jane K. Beaver and James Beaver.

MG-461, Hartranft-Stockham-Shireman Family Photographs, 1860–1905, containing important photographic prints, was donated in 1996 to the State Archives by John F. Hartranft's great-granddaughter, Helen Stockham Shireman and her husband Ronald. These photographs document Hartranft's civil and military pursuits from 1853 until his demise in 1889, as well as the monuments and memorials erected to honor his memory following his death.

Record Group (RG)-19 Department of Military and Veterans Affairs, Civil War Muster Rolls and Related Records, 1861–1865, was transferred to the State Archives in 1965 by the Pennsylvania Department of Military Affairs. These records are critical in documenting the service of more than 362,000 Pennsylvanians who were part of the Union Army during the Civil War.

National Archives and Records Administration (NARA) RG-393 Records of Brevet Major General John Frederick Hartranft as Special Provost Marshal for the Trial and Execution of the Assassins of President Lincoln (Special Deposit at the Pennsylvania State Archives), transferred to the Pennsylvania State Archives in 1995 as a permanent loan by the National Archives and Records Administration, includes an order book, letter book, daily reports, and numerous letters, in addition to instructions written to Hartranft by Major General Winfield Scott Hancock and Secretary of War Edwin M. Stanton from April through July 1865.

Other PHMC collections used include:

Pennsylvania State Archives:

MG-17, Samuel Penniman Bates Papers, 1853–1895

MG-95, Daniel Musser Collection, 1861–1865

MG-145, Daniel H. Hastings Papers, 1877–1931

MG-168, Robert E. Pattison Papers, 1855–1904

MG-181, William A. Stone Papers, 1898–1903

MG-200, Poster Collection, 1854–1971, and undated

MG-213, Postcard Collection, [ca. 1880–1974]

MG-214, Warren J. Harder Collection, 1928–1968

MG-218, General Photograph Collection

MG-219, Philadelphia Commercial Museum Photograph Collection, ca. 1840–1954

MG-264, International Utilities Political Memorabilia Collection, 1789–1972

MG-474, John F. Hartranft-Shireman Family Papers

MG-485, T. Fred Woodley Collection, 1830–1937

MG-511, William Neel Collection, 1861–1878

RG-2, Department of Auditor General, Mexican War Accounts and Related Papers, 1846–1880

RG-2, Department of Auditor General, Chambersburg War Damage Claim Applications (Submitted Under Act of February 15, 1866), 1866–1868

RG-10, Office of the Governor, Governor John F. Hartranft Correspondence and Issues Files, 1870–1879 (Microfilm)

RG-15, Department of Justice, Board of Pardons, Death Warrants File, 1874–1899, 1912–1952

RG-19, Department of Military and Veterans Affairs, Adjutant General, General Correspondence, 1793–1934

RG-19, Department of Military and Veterans Affairs, Annual Reports of the Commission of Soldiers' Orphan Schools and the Superintendent of the Soldiers' Orphan School Department, 1870–1918

RG-19, Department of Military and Veterans Affairs, National Guard of Pennsylvania, Enlistment Records, Including "201 Files," 1867–1945

RG-25, Records of the Department of Special Commissions

PHMC Library

ENDNOTES

1 Frederick H. Dyer, *Compendium of the War of the Rebellion* (New York: Thomas Yoseloff, 1959), 12.

2 David L. Ladd, and Audrey J. Ladd, eds. *The Bachelder Papers: Gettysburg in Their Own Words.* Vol. I. (Dayton, Ohio: Morningside House Inc., 1994), 46.

3 Ladd and Ladd, Vol. I, 93, 95.

4 Ladd and Ladd, Vol. I, 200.

5 George Swetnam, *The Governors of Pennsylvania* (Greensburg, Pa.: McDonald/Swand Publishing Company, 1990), 33.

6 Harry Marlin Tinkcom, *John White Geary: Soldier-Statesman, 1819–1873* (Philadelphia: University of Pennsylvania Press, 1940), 35-36.

7 Letter from John W. Geary to brother [Edward R. Geary] on letterhead from the National Palace of Mexico, Sept. 21, 1847, Pennsylvania State Archives (PSA), MG–56.

8 Tinkcom, 36.

9 Letter from John W. Geary to brother, Sept. 21, 1847, PSA, MG–56.

10 Letter from R[ichard] Coulter to Uncle [Judge Richard Coulter], November 27, 1847, Westmoreland County Historical Society, Coulter Collection.

11 Letter from John W. Geary to brother, March 5, 1849, PSA, MG–56.

12 Letter from John W. Geary to brother, July 31, 1856, PSA, MG–56.

13 William C. Armor, *Lives of the Governors of Pennsylvania, with the Incidental History of the State, From 1609 to 1873* (Norwich, Conn.: T.H. Davis & Co., 1874), 474.

14 Letter from John W. Geary to brother, September 13, 1857, PSA, MG–56.

15 Letter from John W. Geary to brother, November 23, 1857, PSA, MG–56.

16 Letter from John W. Geary to Edward, November 10, 1860, PSA, MG–56.

17 Tinkcom, 115.

18 Samuel P. Bates, *History of Pennsylvania Volunteers, 1861–1865,* Vols. I–V (Harrisburg: B. Singerly, State Printer, 1869), Vol. I, 424.

19 Letter from John W. Geary to Mary [Church Henderson Geary, his wife], September 25, 1862, Historical Society of Pennsylvania (HSP), Geary Family Papers, Collection 2062.

20 Letter from Edward R. Geary [John W. Geary's son] to uncle [Edward R. Geary], May 30, 1863, PSA, MG–56.

21 Letter from John W. Geary to Mary, June 2_ , 1863, HSP, Geary Family Papers, Collection 2062.

22 Letter from John W. Geary to Mary, June 2_ , 1863, HSP, Geary Family Papers, Collection 2062.

23 Letter from John W. Geary to Mary, July 4, 1863, HSP, Geary Family Papers, Collection 2062.

24 Letter from John W. Geary to Mary, July 5, 1863, HSP, Geary Family Papers, Collection 2062.

25 Letter from John W. Geary to Mary, [October 25], 1863, HSP, Geary Family Papers, Collection 2062.

26 Letter from John W. Geary to Mary, November 2, 1863, HSP, Geary Family Papers, Collection 2062.

27 Letter from John W. Geary to Mary, November 6, 1863, HSP, Geary Family Papers, Collection 2062.

28 United States War Department, *The War of the Rebellion: a Compilation of the Official Records of the Union and Confederate Armies* (Washington: Government Printing Office, 1880–1901), Series I, Vol. 31, Part I, 94.

29 Letter from John W. Geary to Mary, December 4, 1863, HSP, Geary Family Papers, Collection 2062.

30 Letter from John Geary to brother, February 24, 1864, PSA, MG–56.

31 Letter from John Geary to brother, July 9, 1864, PSA, MG–56.

32 Bates, *History of Pennsylvania Volunteers, 1861–1865,* Vol. I, 434.

33 Letter from John W. Geary to Mary, September 3, 1864, HSP, Geary Family Papers, Collection 2062.

34 Letter from John W. Geary to Mary, December 23, 1864, HSP, Geary Family Papers, Collection 2062.

35 Resolution, PSA, RG–19, Civil War Muster Rolls and Related records, 1861–1866.

36 Letter from John W. Geary to Mary, April 19, 1865, HSP, Geary Family Papers, Collection 2062.

37 Letter from John W. Geary to Mary, April 29, 1865, HSP, Geary Family Papers, Collection 2062.

38 Ervin Stanley Bradley, *The Triumph of Militant Republicanism: A Study of Pennsylvania and Presidential Politics, 1860–1872* (Philadelphia: University of Pennsylvania Press, 1964), 258–261.

39 Tinkcom, 117.

40 Tinkcom, 115.

41 Bradley, 267.

42 Tinkcom, 119.

43 *Record of Hiester Clymer; and Historical Parallel Between Him and Major-General John W. Geary* (Philadelphia: T.K. Collins, 1866), 1.

44 *Record of Hiester Clymer,* 2.

45 *Record of Hiester Clymer,* 8.

46 Bradley, 274.

47 George Edward Reed, *Pennsylvania Archives,* Fourth Series, Volume VIII (Harrisburg: Wm. Stanley Ray, State Printer, 1902), 779–780.

48 Reed, Fourth Series, Vol. VIII, 781.

49 Reed, Fourth Series, Vol. VIII, 782.

50 Reed, Fourth Series, Vol. VIII, 795.

51 Letter from John Geary to brother on Executive Chamber letterhead, December 5, 1868, PSA, MG–56.

52 Letter from John Geary to brother on Executive Chamber letterhead, January 7, 1870, PSA, MG–56.

53 Reed, Fourth Series, Vol. VIII, 782.

54 Reed, Fourth Series, Vol. VIII, 943.

55 Reed, Fourth Series, Vol. VIII, 1020–1021.

56 Reed, Fourth Series, Vol. IX, 40.

57 Letter from John Geary to brother, February 1, 1873, PSA, MG–56.

58 A.M. Gambone, *Major-General John Frederick Hartranft: Citizen Soldier and Pennsylvania Statesman* (Baltimore, Md.: Butternut and Blue, 1995), 12.

59 *The War of the Rebellion: a Compilation of the Official Records of the Union and Confederate Armies*, Series I, Vol. 2, 406

60 Gambone, 70–72.

61 Gambone, 112.

62 *The War of the Rebellion: a Compilation of the Official Records of the Union and Confederate Armies*, Series I, Vol. 46, Part I, 348.

63 Hartranft's Commission to Major General, PSA, MG–144.

64 Gambone, 147.

65 Letter from Winfield Scott Hancock to John Hartranft, April 29, 1865, NARA Group 393, Special Deposit at PSA.

66 Letter from Edwin Stanton to John Hartranft, April 30, 1865, NARA Group 393, Special Deposit at PSA.

67 John Hartranft's letter book, NARA Group 393, Special Deposit at PSA.

68 Order from Winfield Scott Hancock to John Hartranft, July 6, 1865, NARA Group 393, Special Deposit at PSA.

69 John Hartranft's letter book, 88–89, NARA Group 393, Special Deposit at PSA.

70 John Hartranft's 1873 inaugural address, 5–6, PSA, RG–10, Microfilm.

71 Ibid., 6.

72 John F. Hartranft, *Message of His Excellency, John F. Hartranft, to the General Assembly of Pennsylvania, January 6, 1875* (Harrisburg: B. F. Meyers, State Printer, 1875), 10–11, PSA, MG–511.

73 Hartranft, *Message of His Excellency*, 23–24.

74 "The Result at Cincinnati," PSA, RG–10, Microfilm.

75 Telegram from M. S. Quay to Gov. Hartranft, July 21, 1877, PSA, RG–10, Microfilm.

76 Gambone, 267.

77 George P. Donehoo, *Pennsylvania: A History*. Volume III (New York: Lewis Historical Publishing Company, Inc., 1926), 1485.

78 Letter from William T. Sherman to John Hartranft, March 14, 1881, PSA, MG–474, Microfilm.

79 Letter from Fitz Lee to John Hartranft, August 1, 1884, PSA, MG–474, Microfilm.

80 Gambone, 280.

81 Ibid., 280.

82 Letter from Joseph F. Tobias to Governor Hartranft, October 17, 1873, PSA, RG–10, General Correspondence, Microfilm.

83 Letter from Governor James Beaver to R. A. Sprague, January 20, 1890, PSA, MG–474, Microfilm.

84 General Orders, No. 17, by Governor James A. Beaver, October 18, 1889, PSA, MG–474, Microfilm.

85 Invitation to Hartranft monument dedication, June 6, 1891, PSA, MG–474, Microfilm.

86 Letter from F. W. Ruckstuhl to Daniel Hastings, April 26, 1898, PSA, MG–145, Executive Correspondence.

87 Gambone, 294–295.

88 Letter from Henry M. Hoyt to Governor Andrew Curtin, June 1, 1862, PSA, RG–19, Civil War Muster Rolls and Related Records, 1861–1866.

89 Bates, *History of Pennsylvania Volunteers, 1861–1865* Vol. II, 56–58.

90 Letter from Henry Hoyt to Governor Curtin, February 29, 1864, PSA, RG–19, Civil War Muster Rolls and Related Records, 1861–1866.

91 Letter from Henry Hoyt to Governor Curtin, March 18, 1864, PSA, RG–19, Civil War Muster Rolls and Related Records, 1861–1866.

92 Ibid.

93 Letter from Henry Hoyt to Governor Curtin, April 17, 1864, PSA, RG–19, Civil War Muster Rolls and Related Records, 1861–1866.

94 *The War of the Rebellion: a Compilation of the Official Records of the Union and Confederate Armies*, Series I, Vol. 35, Part I, 86.

95 Report from Henry Hoyt to Capt. Jewatt, August 21, 1864, PSA, RG–19, Civil War Muster Rolls and Related Records, 1861–1866.

96 *The War of the Rebellion: a Compilation of the Official Records of the Union and Confederate Armies*, Series 2, Vol. 7, 805–806.

97 Letter from Henry Hoyt to Col. Thomas, September 1, 1864, PSA, RG–19, Civil War Muster Rolls and Related Records, 1861–1866.

98 Letter from Henry Hoyt to Governor Curtin, September 18, 1864, PSA, RG–19, Civil War Muster Rolls and Related Records, 1861–1866.

99 LeRoy Greene, *Shelter for His Excellency* (Harrisburg: Stackpole Books, 1951), 118.

100 Letter from Henry Hoyt to John Hartranft, April 27, 1878, PSA, RG–10, General Correspondence, Microfilm.

101 Reed, Fourth Series, Vol. IX, 781–782.

102 Reed, 760–761.

103 Reed, 805.

104 Greene, 119–120.

105 Letter from Henry Hoyt to Daniel Hastings, June 18, 1887, PSA, MG–145, General Correspondence.

106 Letter from James Beaver to his brother [J. Gilbert Beaver], 1858, PSA, MG–389.

107 Letter from James Beaver to his brother, September 2, 1858, PSA, MG–389.

108 James Beaver's Speech at Andrew Curtin's funeral, PSA, MG–389.

109 Letter from James Beaver to his mother [Ann Eliza Addams McDonald], January 11, 1861, PSA, MG–389

110 Letter from James Beaver to his mother, February 16, 1861, PSA, MG–389.

111 Letter from James Beaver to his mother, April 17, 1861, PSA, MG–389.

112 Letter from James Beaver to his mother, May 27, 1861, PSA, MG–389.

113 Ibid.

114 Letter from James Beaver to his mother, June 18, 1861, PSA, MG–389.

115 Letter from James Beaver to his brother, August 17, 1861, PSA, MG–389.

116 Letter from James Beaver to his mother, September 10, 1861, PSA, MG–389.

117 Letter from James Beaver to his mother, December 11, 1861, PSA, MG–389.

118 Letter from James Beaver to his mother, December 26, 1861, PSA, MG–389.

119 Letter from James Beaver to his brother, March 19, 1862, PSA, MG–389.

120 Letter from James Beaver to his sister, April 7, 1862, PSA, MG–389.

121 Letter from James Beaver to his brother, April 21, 1862, PSA, MG–389.

122 Letter from James Beaver to his mother, May 12, 1862, PSA, MG–389.

123 Ibid.

124 Letter from James Beaver to his mother, June 10, 1862, PSA, MG–389.

125 James M. McPherson, *The Negro's Civil War* (New York: Pantheon Books, 1965), 164.

126 Letter from James Beaver to his mother, August 6, 1862, PSA, MG–389.

127 Letter from James Beaver to a friend [Mary Allison McAllister], September 26, 1862, PSA, MG–389.

128 Letter from James Beaver to his mother, December 1, 1862, PSA, MG–389.

129 Letter from James Beaver to his mother, February 27, 1863, PSA, MG–389.

130 Frank A. Burr, *Life and Achievements of James Addams Beaver: Early Life, Military Services and Public Career* (Philadelphia: Ferguson Bros. & Co., 1882), 60.

131 James Beaver's 1863 diary, PSA, MG–389.

132 Letter from James Beaver to his mother, June 21, 1863, PSA, MG–389.

133 Burr, 64–65.

134 James Beaver's 1863 diary.

135 Letter from James Beaver to his mother, August 24, 1863, PSA, MG–389.

136 Burr, 154

137 Letter from James Beaver to a friend [Mary Allison McAllister], May 20, 1864, PSA, MG–389.

138 James Beaver's 1864 diary, PSA, MG–389.

139 Ibid.

140 Letter from James Beaver to his mother, June 4, 1864, PSA, MG–389.

141 Burr, 159–160.

142 James Beaver's 1864 diary.

143 Letter from James Beaver to his mother, September 17, 1864, PSA, MG–389.

144 Burr, 174.

145 Burr, 12.

146 Greene, 134.

147 James Beaver's Gubernatorial Inaugural Address, PSA, MG–389.

148 Donehoo, 1509.

149 Letter from James Beaver to Daniel Hastings, February 27, 1889, PSA, MG–145, General Correspondence.

150 James Beaver's speech at Gettysburg, June 1892, PSA, MG–389.

151 William A. Stone, *The Tale of a Plain Man* (Self Published, 1917), 28.

152 Stone, 58.

153 Stone, 64.

154 Stone, 68.

155 Stone, 69.

156 Stone, 70.

157 Stone, 72.

158 Stone, 72–73.

159 Stone, 78–79.

160 Stone, 83.

161 Stone, 85–86.

162 Stone, 92–93.

163 Stone, 93.

164 Swetnam, 45.

165 Reed, Fourth Series, Vol. XII, 544.

166 *Annual Report of the Pennsylvania Commission of Soldiers' Orphans Schools for the year ending May 31, 1902*, 8, PSA, MG–181.

167 *Annual Report of the Pennsylvania Commission of Soldiers' Orphans Schools*, 10, PSA, MG–181.

168 Quarterly Report, March 31, 1899, PSA, MG–181, Soldiers' & Sailors' Home Post returns.

169 Stone & Stone Letterhead, PSA, MG–171, Executive Correspondence.

[170] Samuel Whitaker Pennypacker, *The Autobiography of a Pennsylvanian* (Philadelphia: The John C. Winston Company, 1918), 83.

[171] Ibid.

[172] Pennypacker, 90.

[173] Samuel Whitaker Pennypacker, *26th Pennsylvania Emergency Infantry Address by Hon. Samuel W. Pennypacker, LL.D. Private Co. "F" at the Dedication, Sept. 1 1892, of the Monument to commemorate the Services of the Regiment on the battlefield of Gettysburg* (Philadelphia, 1892), 6–7.

[174] Samuel Whitaker Pennypacker, "Six Weeks in Uniform" (Unpublished manuscript, November 22, 1863, Pennypacker Mills Collection), 2.

[175] Pennypacker, "Six Weeks in Uniform," 3.

[176] Pennypacker, "Six Weeks in Uniform," 5.

[177] Pennypacker, "Six Weeks in Uniform," 6.

[178] Pennypacker, "Six Weeks in Uniform," 7.

[179] Pennypacker, "Six Weeks in Uniform," 9.

[180] Pennypacker, "Six Weeks in Uniform," 11.

[181] Pennypacker, "Six Weeks in Uniform," 13.

[182] Pennypacker, *26th Pennsylvania Emergency Infantry Address*, 8.

[183] Pennypacker, "Six Weeks in Uniform," 15.

[184] Pennypacker, "Six Weeks in Uniform," 24.

[185] Pennypacker, *26th Pennsylvania Emergency Infantry Address*, 4–5.

[186] Pennypacker, "Six Weeks in Uniform," 27.

[187] Pennypacker, "Six Weeks in Uniform," 29–30.

[188] Pennypacker, "Six Weeks in Uniform," 30–31.

[189] Pennypacker, *The Autobiography of a Pennsylvanian*, 95.

[190] Pennypacker, *The Autobiography of a Pennsylvanian*, 96.

[191] Pennypacker, "Six Weeks in Uniform," 32.

[192] Pennypacker, "Six Weeks in Uniform," 33.

[193] Pennypacker, "Six Weeks in Uniform," 39.

[194] Pennypacker, "Six Weeks in Uniform," 41.

[195] Pennypacker, *26th Pennsylvania Emergency Infantry Address*, 12.

[196] Pennypacker, "Six Weeks in Uniform," 56.

[197] Pennypacker, "Six Weeks in Uniform," 57–58.

[198] Pennypacker, "Six Weeks in Uniform," 62–63.

[199] Pennypacker, "Six Weeks in Uniform," 64–65.

[200] Pennypacker, "Six Weeks in Uniform," 67.

[201] Pennypacker, "Six Weeks in Uniform," 72.

[202] Pennypacker, *The Autobiography of a Pennsylvanian*, 97.

[203] Pennypacker, *26th Pennsylvania Emergency Infantry Address*, 26.

[204] Letters from John P. Nicholson to Samuel W. Pennypacker May 5,1910; May 16,1910; June 28,1911; August 4, 1911; PSA, MG–171, General Correspondence.

[205] Pennypacker, *The Autobiography of a Pennsylvanian*, 97.

[206] Pennypacker, *The Autobiography of a Pennsylvanian*, 100–101.

[207] Notary public appointment certificate for Samuel Pennypacker, 1869, PSA, MG–171.

[208] Samuel Pennypacker Memorial Day speech, May 30, 1898, PSA, MG–171.

[209] Samuel Pennypacker campaign speech, 1902, PSA, MG–171.

[210] Pennypacker, *The Autobiography of a Pennsylvanian*, 263.

[211] Philadelphia Brigade Association's Republican State Convention Nomination, 1902, PSA, MG–171.

[212] Letter from W. R. Andrews to Samuel Pennypacker, August, 19, 1902, PSA, MG–171.

[213] Letter from James F. Dampman to Samuel Pennypacker, January 24, 1903, PSA, MG–171.

[214] Samuel Pennypacker's Antietam monument dedication speech, PSA, MG–171.

[215] Pennypacker , *The Autobiography of a Pennsylvanian*, 418.

[216] Telegram about Gov. Samuel Pennypacker commanding a division of troops at Theodore Roosevelt's inaugural parade, February 25, 1905, PSA, MG–171.

[217] Letter from Samuel Pennypacker to daughter Josephine, April 11, 1905, PSA, MG–171.

[218] Letter from Boies Penrose to Samuel Pennypacker, December 15, 1909, PSA, MG–171.

[219] Daniel Hastings campaign speech for Benjamin Harrison, 1892, PSA, MG–145.

[220] James M. Perry, *Touched With Fire* (New York: Public Affairs, 2003), 280.

[221] Philip S. Klein, and Ari Hoogenboom, *A History of Pennsylvania*, (University Park: The Pennsylvania State University Press,1980), 360.

[222] Klein and Hoogenboom, 361.

BIBLIOGRAPHY

Armor, William C. *Lives of the Governors of Pennsylvania, with the Incidental History of the State, From 1609 to 1873.* Norwich, Conn.: T. H. Davis & Co., 1874.

Ayers, Edward L., "The Valley of the Shadow," Virginia Center for Digital History, http://valley.vcdh.virginia.edu/.

Bates, Samuel P. *History of Pennsylvania Volunteers, 1861–1865.* Harrisburg: B. Singerly, State Printer, 1869.

_____. *Martial Deeds of Pennsylvania.* Philadelphia: T. H. Davis & Co., 1876.

Bazelon, Bruce S. "The Military Collections of the William Penn Memorial Museum." *North South Trader,* Sept.–Oct. 1980, 15–21.

Blair, William A. and Bell I. Wiley. *A Politician Goes to War: The Civil War Letters of John White Geary.* University Park: The Pennsylvania State University Press, 1995.

Bradley, Erwin Stanley. *The Triumph of Militant Republicanism: A Study of Pennsylvania and Presidential Politics, 1860–1872.* Philadelphia: University of Pennsylvania Press, 1964.

Burr, Frank A. *Life and Achievements of James Addams Beaver: Early Life, Military Services and Public Career.* Philadelphia: Ferguson Brothers and Company, 1882.

Dyer, Frederick H. *Compendium of the War of the Rebellion.* New York: Thomas Yoseloff, 1959.

Donehoo, George P., ed. *Pennsylvania: A History.* Volume III. New York: Lewis Historical Publishing Company, Inc., 1926.

Gallagher, Gary T., and Alan T. Nolan, eds. *The Myth of the Lost Cause and Civil War History.* Bloomington: Indiana University Press, 2000.

Gambone, A. M. *Major-General John Frederick Hartranft: Citizen Soldier and Pennsylvania Statesman.* Baltimore: Butternut and Blue, 1995.

Geary, John W. *Message of His Excellency, John W. Geary, to the General Assembly of Pennsylvania, January 6, 1869.* Harrisburg: B. Singerly, State Printer, 1869.

Greene, LeRoy. *Shelter for His Excellency.* Harrisburg: Stackpole Books, 1951.

Hartranft, John F. *Message of His Excellency, John F. Hartranft, to the General Assembly of Pennsylvania, January 6, 1875.* Harrisburg: B. F. Meyers, State Printer, 1875.

Hastings, Daniel H. *The American Soldier—An Address by Gen. Daniel H. Hastings.* Philadelphia: The Pennsylvania Club, 1890.

Historical Society of Pennsylvania, Geary Family Papers, Collection 2062.

Kehl, James A. *Boss Rule in the Gilded Age: Matt Quay of Pennsylvania.* Pittsburgh: University of Pittsburgh Press, 1981.

Klein, Philip S., and Ari Hoogenboom. *A History of Pennsylvania.* University Park: The Pennsylvania State University Press, 1980.

Ladd, David L., and Audrey J. Ladd, eds. *The Bachelder Papers: Gettysburg in Their Own Words.* Volume I. Dayton, Ohio: Morningside House Inc., 1994.

McCain, George Nox. *Through the Great Campaign with Hastings and his Spellbinders.* Philadelphia: Historical Publishing Company, 1895.

McPherson, James M. *Battle Cry of Freedom: The Civil War Era.* New York: Ballantine Books, 1989.

_____. *The Negro's Civil War*. New York: Pantheon Books, 1965.

Miller, William J. *Civil War City: Harrisburg, Pennsylvania, 1861–1865: The Training of an Army*. Shippensburg, Pa.: White Mane Publishing Company, 1990.

Montgomery, Thomas Lynch, ed. *Pennsylvania Archives*. Sixth Series, Volume X. Harrisburg: Harrisburg Publishing Company, 1907.

NARA (National Archives and Records Administration) Military Pension Files, Civil War and Later Complete File.

NARA Military Service Records, Volunteers, 1775–1902.

Pennypacker, Samuel Whitaker. *The Autobiography of a Pennsylvanian*. Philadelphia: The John C. Winston Company, 1918.

_____. "Six Weeks in Uniform." November 22, 1863, unpublished manuscript, Pennypacker Mills Collection, Schwenksville, Pa.

_____. *26ᵗʰ Pennsylvania Emergency Infantry Address by Hon. Samuel W. Pennypacker, LL.D. Private Co. "F" at the Dedication, Sept. 1 1892, of the Monument to Commemorate the Services of the Regiment on the battlefield of Gettysburg*. Philadelphia: [s.n.], 1892).

Perry, James M. *Touched With Fire*. New York: Public Affairs, 2003.

Record of Hiester Clymer; and Historical Parallel Between Him and Major-General John W. Geary. Philadelphia: T. K. Collins, 1866.

Reed, George Edward, ed. *Pennsylvania Archives*, Fourth Series, Volumes VIII–XII. Harrisburg: Wm. Stanley Ray, State Printer, 1902.

Sauers, Richard A. *Advance the Colors! Pennsylvania's Civil War Battle Flags*. Volumes I–II. Harrisburg: Pennsylvania Capitol Preservation Committee, 1987 and 1991.

Steers, Edward, Jr., and Harold Holzer, eds. *The Lincoln Assassination Conspirators: Their Confinement and Execution, as Recorded in the Letterbook of John Frederick Hartranft*. Baton Rouge: Louisana State University Press, 2009.

Stone, William A. *The Tale of a Plain Man*. Self Published, 1917.

Sutton, Robert K., ed. *Rally on the High Ground: The National Park Service Symposium on the Civil War*. Fort Washington, Pa: Eastern National, 2001.

Swetnam, George. *The Governors of Pennsylvania, 1790–1990*. Greensburg, Pa.: McDonald/Sward Publishing Co., 1990.

Tinkcom, Harry Marlin. *John White Geary: Soldier-Statesman, 1819–1873*. Philadelphia: University of Pennsylvania Press, 1940.

United States War Department. *The War of the Rebellion: a Compilation of the Official Records of the Union and Confederate Armies*. Washington, D.C.: Government Printing Office, 1880–1901.

U.S. Congress. House of Representatives. "Trial of Henry Wirz: Letter from the Secretary of War Ad Interim, in Answer to a Resolution of the House of April 16, 1866." 40ᵗʰ Cong., 2ᵈ Session, Vol. 8. Washington, D.C.: Government Printing Office, 1868.

Walker, James D., ed. *Pennsylvania at Andersonville, Georgia: Ceremonies at the Dedication of the Memorial Erected by the Commonwealth of Pennsylvania in the National Cemetery at Andersonville, Georgia*. Harrisburg: C. E. Aughinbaugh, 1909.

Warren, Robert Penn. *The Legacy of the Civil War: Meditations on the Centennial*. New York: Random House, 1961.

Westmoreland County Historical Society, Coulter Collection, Greensburg, Pa.

Governor
John White Geary
(1819–1873)
in office from 1867 to 1873

Governor
John Frederick Hartranft
(1830–1889)
in office from 1873 to 1879

Governor
Henry Martyn Hoyt
(1830–1892)
in office from 1879 to 1883

Governor
James Addams Beaver
(1837–1914)
in office from 1887 to 1891

Governor
William Alexis Stone
(1846–1920)
in office from 1899 to 1903

Governor
Samuel Whitaker Pennypacker
(1843–1916)
in office from 1903 to 1907